Living with Gandhi

Experiments in Utopia

LIVING WITH GANDHI

EXPERIMENTS IN UTOPIA

Karline McLain

ASIA SHORTS

Published by the Association for Asian Studies
Asia Shorts, Number 23
www.asianstudies.org

Visit the Living with Gandhi Archive at

www.livingwithgandhi.org

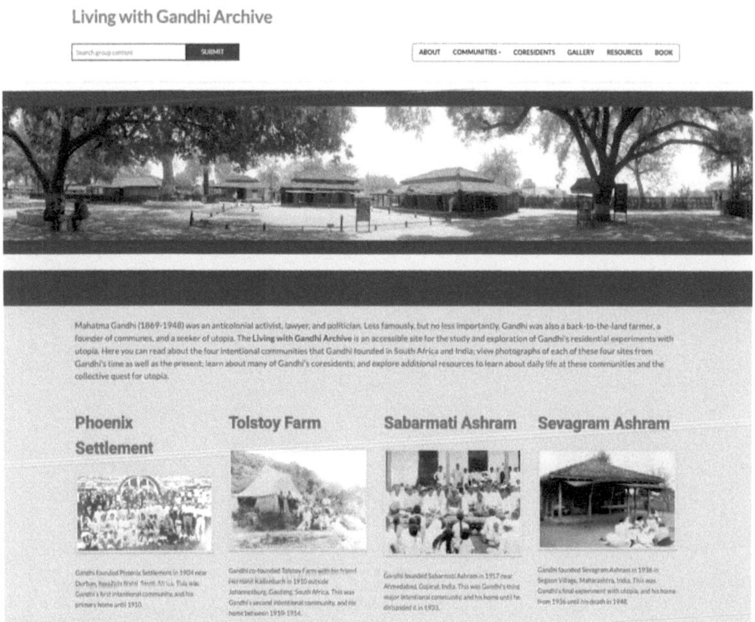

The Association for Asian Studies (AAS)

Formed in 1941, the Association for Asian Studies (AAS)—the largest society of its kind, with over 6,000 members worldwide—is a scholarly, non-political, non-profit professional association open to all persons interested in Asia. For further information, please visit www.asianstudies.org.

Cover Photo: Gandhi and Kasturba speaking with coresidents at Sevagram Ashram, circa 1940. Public domain.

Library of Congress Cataloging-in-Publication Data available from the Library of Congress

ASIA SHORTS

Series Editor: David Kenley
Dakota State University

ASIA SHORTS offers concise, engagingly written titles by highly qualified authors on topics of significance in Asian Studies. Topics are intended to be substantive, generate discussion and debate within the field, and attract interest beyond it.

The Asia Shorts series complements and leverages the success of the pedagogically-oriented AAS book series, Key Issues in Asian Studies, and is designed to engage broad audiences with up-to-date scholarship on important topics in Asian Studies. Rigorously peer-reviewed, Asia Shorts books provide cutting-edge scholarship and provocative analyses. They are jargon free, accessible, and speak to contemporary issues or larger themes. In so doing, Asia Shorts volumes make an impact on students, fellow scholars, and informed readers beyond academia.

For further information, visit the AAS website: www.asianstudies.org.

About the Author

Karline McLain is a Professor of Religious Studies at Bucknell University, where she teaches courses on the religion, history, and culture of South Asia. She is the editor and primary investigator of the companion online site for this book, the *Living With Gandhi Archive* (www.livingwithgandhi.org). Dr. McLain is also the author of *India's Immortal Comic Books: Gods, Kings, and Other Heroes* (Indiana University Press) and *The Afterlife of Shirdi Sai Baba: Competing Visions of a Global Saint* (University of Washington Press). She received her PhD in Asian Cultures & Languages from The University of Texas at Austin and her BA in Religious Studies from The University of Iowa.

Contents

Acknowledgments

There is always a community behind any solo-authored book, and I want to express my gratitude to the extensive community that supported this book.

Bringing a multisited research project to fruition requires significant time and resources. This book took ten years to research and write, and it entailed multiple visits to field sites and archives in India and South Africa, as well as travel to additional domestic and international libraries and archives. Grants and fellowships from multiple institutions have been crucial to supporting this knowledge-production process. Bucknell University has generously supported my research through a high-impact research grant and a summer residency writing grant from the Bucknell Humanities Center; an international research travel grant from the College of Arts & Sciences; a Presidential Professorship that provided multiyear research funding; an institutional sabbatical that provided release from my teaching obligations to enable essential research and writing time; and a publication subvention award. A multiyear grant from the Enhancing Life Project, in collaboration with the University of Chicago and the John Templeton Foundation, not only provided the funding for my first research trips to India and South Africa for this project but also introduced me to an amazing cohort of interdisciplinary scholars. A fellowship from the National Endowment for the Humanities provided important financial support during a sabbatical year for research and writing.

I want to thank the staff at Phoenix Settlement, Tolstoy Farm, Sabarmati Ashram, and Sevagram Ashram, as well as Gujarat Vidyapith, for patiently showing me around these historic sites, allowing me access to archives, and answering my questions. I am also grateful to all of the staff at the additional libraries and archives I visited in India, South Africa, and the United States, who helped me locate resources. Several members of the extended Gandhi family took time to personally show me around Phoenix Settlement and Sabarmati Ashram on my first visits to these sites, and for this generosity, I am particularly appreciative of Ela Gandhi (in South Africa) and of Arun Gandhi and Tushar Gandhi (in India).

Earlier versions of some chapters were presented at professional conferences and workshops, including the American Academy of Religion, the Conference on the Study of Religions of India, and the Enhancing Life Project conferences, as well as by invited lecture at the Bucknell Humanities Center and at the Pennsylvania State University. I thank everyone who made time to attend these presentations and respond with questions and constructive criticism. I also thank the many scholars who read earlier drafts of one or more chapters and who offered insightful comments along the way. I particularly want to thank Maria Antonaccio, Dennis Dalton, Richard H. Davis, Erica Delsandro, Brantley Gasaway, A. Gardner Harris, Ali Karjoo-Ravary, Janice Leoshko, Philip Lutgendorf, Patrick Olivelle, Caitlyn Olson, John Penniman, Martha Ann Selby, Rachel Trusty, Rivka Ulmer, Jarrod Whitaker, Carol Wayne White, and Stuart Young. In addition, Diane Jakacki has dedicated many hours to helping me build the Living with Gandhi Archive (www.livingwithgandhi.org) as an online companion site for this book. My thoughts in this book have also benefited from conversations with the undergraduate students who have enrolled in my Gandhi seminars over the past decade.

At the Association for Asian Studies, I am grateful to the Asia Shorts series editor, David Kenley, for his enthusiasm for this work; to Jon Wilson for seeing this book through all phases of production and for his thoughtfulness; to Mike Jauchen for his meticulous attention to detail as a copy editor; and to the anonymous reviewers for their considerate and detailed response to the book manuscript.

I thank my whole extended family for their support, and I want to express my heartfelt thanks to three special individuals. My mother, Nancy, visited three of Gandhi's communities with me, providing companionship and essential childcare when my son was young. My son, Curran, has visited all of Gandhi's communities with me, some more than once. I am ever grateful for his intellectual curiosity; he also served as my photographic assistant on one trip to Phoenix Settlement and Tolstoy Farm. My husband, Chad, has visited two of Gandhi's communities with me, and I am especially thankful for his adventurous spirit as he joined me on a quest throughout the farmland outside of Johannesburg, South Africa, when I sought to locate the former site of the Tolstoy Farm community. Finally, this book is dedicated to those who live with me; I am a far better person for your love and presence in my life.

Timeline of Gandhi's Communities

1904 Gandhi founds Phoenix Settlement (outside Durban, KwaZulu-Natal, South Africa), his first intentional community, and relocates the *Indian Opinion* printing press to this settlement.

1906 Gandhi and coresidents from Phoenix Settlement begin engaging in nonviolent protest of the Asiatic Registration Act (also known as the "Black Act"), advocating for greater equality for Indians living in South Africa.

1910 Gandhi and Hermann Kallenbach cofound Tolstoy Farm (outside Johannesburg, Gauteng, South Africa), Gandhi's second intentional community.

1913 Gandhi and coresidents from Tolstoy Farm lead the Great March, a nonviolent protest against racial injustice on behalf of Indians living in South Africa.

1914 Gandhi and Kallenbach close Tolstoy Farm; Gandhi departs South Africa to return to India, along with his immediate family and approximately two dozen coresidents from Phoenix Settlement and Tolstoy Farm. The Tolstoy Farm land is eventually sold, and its buildings razed. Phoenix Settlement remains a living community into the 1970s before becoming a heritage site.

1915 Gandhi founds Satyagraha Ashram at Kochrab Village (Ahmedabad, Gujarat, India).

1917 Gandhi founds Sabarmati Ashram (outside Ahmedabad, Gujarat, India), moving the Satyagraha Ashram community to Sabarmati Ashram, which becomes Gandhi's third major intentional community.

1917 Manilal Gandhi, Gandhi's second-eldest son, returns from India to South Africa to lead Phoenix Settlement, which he does until his death in 1956, at which time, Manilal's wife, Sushila Gandhi, assumes leadership of Phoenix Settlement until it disbands in the 1970s.

1921 Gandhi establishes a small satellite of Sabarmati Ashram, called Paunar Ashram, in Wardha (Maharashtra, India) and sends Vinoba Bhave from Sabarmati Ashram to manage it.

1930 Gandhi and seventy-eight coresidents leave from Sabarmati Ashram to begin the Salt March and to lead the larger Salt Satyagraha nonviolent anti-colonial campaign.

1933 Gandhi disbands and closes Sabarmati Ashram. Today, it is preserved as a heritage site.

1936 Gandhi moves to Segaon Village, which becomes Sevagram Ashram (near Wardha, Maharashtra, India), Gandhi's final intentional community and his home until his death. To this day, Sevagram Ashram remains a living community for a small group of residents and is also preserved as a heritage site.

1942 Gandhi launches the Quit India campaign from Sevagram Ashram, a nationwide anti-colonial campaign for India's independence.

1947 India attains independence.

1948 Gandhi is assassinated by Nathuram Godse.

A Day in the Life at Gandhi's Communities

4:00 a.m.

Wake-up time. Residents awoke with the morning bell before sunrise and had fifteen minutes to quickly brush their teeth and rinse their faces.

4:15–4:45 a.m.

Morning prayer. The morning prayer was held on the designated communal prayer ground, a simple square plot of land demarcated for this use. Gandhi or another coresident would lead the morning and evening prayer services, and the expectation was that all residents would attend. Prayer was ecumenical, incorporating scripture readings and devotional songs from Hindu, Muslim, Christian, and other traditions.

5:00–7:00 a.m.

Breakfast and free time. After prayer, it was time for a simple vegetarian communal breakfast. Responsibility for preparing the communal meals and cleaning up after them rotated among all residents. In the free time after breakfast, one could exercise, bathe, socialize, read, or engage in correspondence.

7:00–10:30 a.m.

Manual labor. This included the varieties of work necessary for the self-sufficiency of the intentional community: farming (growing vegetables and fruits, milking cows, grinding grain, etc.), sanitation, and meal preparation. All adult residents were expected to take turns in each of these areas of labor. For minors, the time designated for manual labor was the time for their classes, and teachers were expected to educate the children in the above areas of manual labor as well as the study of history, geography, mathematics, writing, and Indian languages.

10:45 a.m.–12:00 p.m.

Lunch and rest. A simple vegetarian communal lunch was served, followed by time to rest.

12:00–4:30 p.m.

Manual labor. This included the same varieties of work as the morning manual labor session. At different intentional communities, Gandhi and his coresidents experimented with additional types of labor for self-sufficiency: at Phoenix Settlement, this included operating the printing press to publish the newspaper *Indian Opinion*; at Phoenix Settlement and Tolstoy Farm, the residents learned to make sandals out of rope and to carve bowls and spoons out of wood; at Sabarmati Ashram and Sevagram Ashram, spinning was added as an expected form of daily manual labor.

4:30–5:30 p.m.

Recreation time. Residents could again exercise, socialize, read, or engage in correspondence.

5:30–7:00 p.m.

Dinner and free time. A simple vegetarian communal dinner was served, followed by time to clean up and relax.

7:00–7:30 p.m.

Evening prayer. In addition to ecumenical scripture readings, lessons, and hymns, Gandhi often used the communal prayer times to give short speeches on current issues and events to the community members.

7:30–9:00 p.m.

Recreation time.

9:00 p.m.

Bedtime. When the evening bell rang, all residents were expected to retire for the night.

GLOSSARY

Ahimsa	Nonviolence
Ashram	A forest hermitage or place of religious retreat
Brahmacharya	Celibacy
Charkha	A spinning wheel used to make handspun cloth (*khadi*)
Dalit	Literally "broken down." A term for "untouchables," those at the bottom of the caste hierarchy, that was used by Ambedkar
Harijan	Literally "children of God." A term for "untouchables," those at the bottom of the caste hierarchy, that was used by Gandhi
Khadi	Handspun cloth, or clothing made from handspun cloth
Moksha	Spiritual liberation
Sarvodaya	Literally "the uplift of all." Translated throughout this book as "universal well-being"; Gandhi sometimes translated it as "universal welfare"
Satya	Truth
Satyagraha	Literally "grasping on to truth." Gandhi's term for nonviolent civil resistance, which he sometimes translated as "truth force" or "soul force"
Satyagrahi	A person engaged in nonviolent civil resistance
Seva	Selfless service

Swadeshi	Economic independence
Swaraj	Literally "self-rule." Often used to refer to political independence or Indian home rule (alternate spelling: *swarajya*)
Tapas	Austere meditation practices, acts of spiritual penance that entail physical and/or mental suffering. Used by Gandhi to refer to suffering more broadly (alternate spelling: *tapascharya)*
Varna	Caste
Varna-ashrama-dharma	One's duty as determined by their caste and stage of life
Yajna	Ritual sacrifice. Used by Gandhi to refer to sacrifice more broadly

List of Illustrations

Introduction

Living with Gandhi

Life will not be a pyramid with the apex sustained by the bottom. But it will be an oceanic circle whose center will be the individual always ready to perish for the village, the latter ready to perish for the circle of villages, till at last the whole becomes one life composed of individuals, never aggressive in their arrogance but ever humble, sharing the majesty of the oceanic circle of which they are integral units.

— Gandhi, discussing his vision for independent India in an interview published in *Harijan* magazine in 1946[1]

In 1933, when Gandhi was released from one of his many stints in prison for leading nonviolent anti-colonial campaigns, he decided to step away from politics and settle down in rural central India. Gandhi wrote to a dear friend, "I am trying to become a villager. The place where I am writing this has a population of about 600—no roads, no post-office, no shop."[2] Here in this remote village, Gandhi wanted to spend his days working shoulder to shoulder with his fellow villagers to build earthen latrines, compost manure, grow vegetables, and spin cotton. This work, Gandhi deemed, was far more constructive than spending his days in the capital engaged in political haggling over India's future—better to just pick up a shovel and get dirty, working to enact the India he envisioned one village at a time.

Mohandas Karamchand Gandhi (1869–1948), commonly known by the epithet "Mahatma" ("Great Soul"), attained global recognition for his method of nonviolent civil disobedience known as *satyagraha*. Gandhi was many things in his lifetime, including an anti-colonial activist, a lawyer, and a politician. Less famously, but no less importantly, Gandhi was also a back-to-the-land farmer, a founder of communes, and a seeker of utopia. Throughout his adult life, Gandhi experimented with intentional living arrangements, founding multiple residential communities where he and those who chose to join him experimented together with the ideals and methods for enhancing the collective good.

What was it like to live with Gandhi? That is the central question that this book seeks to answer by investigating everyday life at the four primary intentional communities Gandhi established: Phoenix Settlement, Tolstoy Farm, Sabarmati Ashram, and Sevagram Ashram. These communities attracted a diverse group of residents who came from multiple religious, racial, and national backgrounds, and who were drawn to both Gandhi and the collective effort to forge their own "oceanic circle," their own community of equals that could challenge the inequalities and inequities of the colonial and capitalist status quo. Gandhi acknowledged that one might critique his vision of the oceanic circle as "all Utopian and, therefore, not worth a single thought," but he asked us to try to imagine this utopia nonetheless, for we must "have a proper picture of what we want, before we can have something approaching it."[3] For over four decades—from the founding of his first intentional community in South Africa in 1904 until his death in India in 1948—Gandhi not only tried to imagine utopia; he also tried to enact it, hoping, with the establishment of each successive community, to approach ever closer to his imagined ideal.

At these residential communities, Gandhi first began to articulate, and then continually sought to refine and implement, the utopian philosophy that he called *sarvodaya*, meaning "universal well-being." Scholarship in the field of Gandhian studies has focused predominantly on Gandhi's biography and his political philosophy, paying substantial attention to his method of nonviolent civil disobedience (*satyagraha*).[4] However, over the past two decades, a handful of scholars have begun to point out various lacunae in Gandhian studies, demonstrating what can be gained by approaching the field of Gandhian studies with methods that extend beyond the disciplinary approaches of political science and historical biography.[5] This book draws upon my expertise in religious studies and colonial South Asian studies to investigate one substantial omission in Gandhian studies: everyday life at Gandhi's intentional communities and the significance of these spaces to Gandhi's utopic quest for universal well-being (*sarvodaya*).[6]

With its focus on everyday life and residential community, this book tells a very different story of Gandhi than is currently available, and it makes two primary arguments. First, this book argues that these intentional communities were not formed in response to Gandhi's political vision, but, on the contrary, the collective quest for utopic life at these communities was foundational to Gandhi's developing political vision and nonviolent method of activism. This book demonstrates how the community members and their shared communal values were central to the political actions that Gandhi became famous for, such as the protest of the

Asiatic Registration Act in South Africa, and the Salt March in India. Second, this book argues that Gandhi increasingly amplified the rhetoric and expectation of self-sacrifice and voluntary suffering for the collective good at these intentional communities. This book demonstrates how residents were asked to sacrifice more and more over time in their shared pursuit of universal well-being, from offering up their labor and their individual possessions at Gandhi's early communities to offering up their very lives in the pursuit of political self-rule and universal well-being at Gandhi's final community.

Focusing on Gandhi's intentional communities allows us to not only understand Gandhi better but also to open up space to consider our own choices about where, with whom, and how we live, as well as the impact that these choices have upon us as individuals and upon our families and our larger communities. Gandhi constantly experimented with the residential facets of daily life, engaging with his coresidents in communal trials with multifaith and multiracial community building, pluralistic cohousing, subsistence farming, cooperative labor, and alternative education, to name just some of the experiments undertaken at these communities in the shared pursuit of universal well-being. Examining Gandhi's residential experiments in this way helps us to think more deeply and intentionally about what it means to live well in community with one another.

Scholarship in the field of utopian studies has predominantly focused on the Global North—and particularly on Europe and North America—in its examination of utopian literature and theory on the one hand, and the formation of particular intentional communities on the other.[7] Yet people around the globe and throughout time have engaged in the heuristic pursuit of envisioning and enacting a better world. Gandhi's communities are arguably among the most important utopian experiments in Asia and Africa and studying them contributes to recent efforts to broaden and decolonize utopian studies. Relatedly, the fields of utopian studies and religious studies have not often engaged in dialogue with one another beyond the Judeo-Christian worldview. This book contributes to recent efforts to foster further dialogue between these two fields of study by illuminating the ambiguity of the concept of utopia through an examination of Gandhi's philosophy of *sarvodaya*, with attention to the intersection of multifaith religious and political ideals as well as attention to the nexus of ideal vision and lived praxis at Gandhi's communities.[8]

Gandhi first began to experiment with his living conditions as a young man when he left his home in India to attend law school in London, England. In his autobiography, Gandhi records how, during these years, he initially rented a room from an Anglo-Indian family and tried to become a proper Victorian English gentleman by buying an evening suit on Bond Street and a gold chain for his pocket watch, and by taking lessons in French, dancing, elocution, and violin. But after repeatedly having to ask his elder brother back home in India for additional funds, Gandhi decided to simplify his life by moving into a small studio apartment in a less desirable location, learning to cook meals at home, canceling his private lessons (in violin, French, etc.), and, in other ways, simplifying and economizing his daily life. Gandhi wrote of this decision, "Let not the reader think that this living made my life by any means a dreary affair. On the contrary the change harmonized my inward and outward life. It was also more in keeping with the means of my family. My life was certainly more truthful and my soul knew no bounds of joy."[9] It was in London that Gandhi began to think about the virtue of living a simple life in economic terms, but it was not until he moved to South Africa that he began to connect his impetus for simple living to a larger utopian philosophy.

Gandhi moved to Durban, South Africa, in 1893 as a novice lawyer who had been hired under a twelve-month contract to serve as legal counsel to a wealthy Indian merchant. Gandhi had no idea when he arrived that he would ultimately spend twenty-one years living and working in South Africa. Gandhi initially tried to live and act in a manner befitting a lawyer in South Africa: renting a fine house, dressing in expensive suits, and traveling first class on trains. But Gandhi was repeatedly shocked by the prejudicial treatment he experienced as a person of color during his first year in South Africa: he was called a "coolie barrister"; he was told to remove his turban in court; he was kicked off the train at Pietermaritzburg Station for riding in the first-class cabin in spite of being a ticketed passenger; and he was shoved off the footpath while walking in Pretoria. By the time he left South Africa in 1914 to return to India, Gandhi had radically rethought what it meant to live a good life, orienting his daily life around his developing philosophy of universal well-being (*sarvodaya*).

Gandhi founded his first intentional community, Phoenix Settlement, on farmland outside of Durban (KwaZulu-Natal, South Africa) in 1904. Here, Gandhi became a farmer and operated a printing press as he began to connect his nascent interest in living a simple and self-sufficient life with the value of physical as well as intellectual labor, and with the commitment to providing equal wages and living conditions for all residents regardless of race, religion, or gender. Gandhi and his fellow coresidents endeavored to establish a just society, one that would advance the economic well-being of all residents—Indians and Europeans in South Africa—through shared labor, while simultaneously advancing their equity with and affection for one another. Gandhi viewed this as a microlevel residential experiment for the ideal he hoped to help bring about in the world beyond Phoenix Settlement, an ideal that would challenge the colonialist and capitalist status quo, where those at the apex were sustained by the labor of those at the bottom.

It was at Phoenix Settlement that Gandhi coined the term "*sarvodaya*" in 1904. Created by joining two Sanskrit conjuncts, *sarva* ("all") and *udaya* ("uplift"), *sarvodaya* means the "uplift of all" or—as Gandhi translated the term into English in some of his essays—"universal welfare." Throughout this book, I have chosen to use the translation "universal well-being" for *sarvodaya*, a translation that is very close to Gandhi's own but replaces "welfare" with "well-being" because the word "welfare" often carries a negative connotation for English-language speakers today that Gandhi did not intend to call to mind with this concept. At Phoenix Settlement, Gandhi began to think deeply about how one's everyday lifestyle could either benefit or harm the common good, and he began to engage in a series of residential experiments intended to determine how to enhance universal well-being. These residential experiments did not arise out of Gandhi's political commitments; rather, his utopian philosophy of universal well-being (*sarvodaya*) informed his growing sociopolitical consciousness and the development of his nonviolent method of civil resistance. It was only after Gandhi had lived at Phoenix Settlement for two years, engaging in further residential experiments intended to enhance universal well-being, that he came up with the term for his method of nonviolent civil disobedience, calling that method "*satyagraha*" in 1906. Similarly, it was at Phoenix Settlement that Gandhi began to formulate the ideas for his most famous political treatise, *Indian Home Rule* (*Hind Swaraj*, 1909), wherein he first articulated his vision for an independent India.

After Phoenix Settlement, Gandhi went on to found three other primary intentional communities. In South Africa, he lived at Tolstoy Farm (Johannesburg, Gauteng) from 1910 to 1914, locating this intentional community in the countryside outside of Johannesburg, as his legal work and civic activism took him increasingly to this city. After returning to India, Gandhi lived at Sabarmati Ashram (outside Ahmedabad, Gujarat) from 1917 to 1933, and he made Sevagram Ashram (near Wardha, Maharashtra) his final home until his death in 1948. At each of these communities, Gandhi tried out additional experiments as he continually sought to refine and enact his philosophy of universal well-being. Some of these experiments included ecumenical religious study and interfaith community building, vows of celibacy, cohousing arrangements, communal kitchens and vegetarian cooking, naturopathy and holistic medicine, alternative education, and developing village and cottage industries in addition to the labor of farming. These experiments and more were undertaken with the goal of promoting self-sufficiency, discipline, equality, and affection among the residents of these communities.

As Gandhi tried to imagine and enact utopia at these intentional communities, he also increasingly emphasized service, sacrifice, and suffering for the collective good. Gandhi's sentiment that at the center of his ideal communal village was "the individual always ready to perish for the village" was not empty rhetoric. His developing philosophy of universal well-being required progressively more self-sacrifice from his coresidents. In South Africa, Gandhi's coresidents not only learned to work for the collective good by taking up farming and other manual labor in the interest of economic self-sufficiency; they also learned to live like prisoners by sleeping on the floor on bedrolls, dressing in prisoners' uniforms, and eating porridge. Gandhi emphasized that by living this way, his coresidents could learn to thrive even in prison, writing, "The secret of the struggle lies in going to jail cheerfully, and being happy while there."[10] Some of Gandhi's coresidents flourished under these conditions, such as his dear friend Hermann Kallenbach, with whom Gandhi cofounded his second intentional community, Tolstoy Farm. Other coresidents, however, found the emphasis on self-discipline and voluntary suffering to be too much, such as Gandhi's eldest son, Harilal, who eventually rejected his father's lifestyle and left Tolstoy Farm.

In India, Gandhi praised select coresidents for their ability to suffer in silence and to embrace the ideal of selfless service. Residents were encouraged to direct their service toward the villagers of rural India by building latrines and teaching spinning; toward the nation at large through participation in anti-colonial civil disobedience campaigns; and, for a subset of residents who were young and female, toward Gandhi himself in his controversial experiments with celibate sexuality at Sevagram Ashram. Gandhi gradually encouraged more sacrifice from his coresidents, ultimately expecting them to be willing to put their lives on the line for the collective good, whether by risking death by disease while laboring in rural India, death while being incarcerated, or death while engaging in anti-colonial protest. At his final intentional community, Gandhi took up the motto "do or die," emphasizing nonviolent self-sacrifice for universal well-being and describing his ideal coresident in this way: "He and his village are able to defy the might of a world. For the law governing every villager is that he will suffer death in the defense of his and his village's honor."[11] In India, as in South Africa, some of Gandhi's coresidents flourished at his intentional communities, such as Madeleine Slade (who came to be known as Mirabehn), who lived with Gandhi at both Sabarmati Ashram and Sevagram Ashram. Others, however, ultimately left, finding life at these communities far from idyllic, such as Gandhi's "adopted" Dalit (or so-called "untouchable") daughter, Lakshmi Dafda Sharma.

To examine what it was like to live at Gandhi's communities, this book relies on the analysis of the rich corpus of Gandhi's published writings and archived correspondence as well as multiple field research trips to all of the historic sites of these intentional communities in South Africa and India. Gandhi was a prodigious writer who wrote editorials in newspapers, published political pamphlets, authored books, and corresponded regularly through letters. As a lawyer, he learned at a young age the importance of preserving a paper trail, hiring his first secretary in South Africa and then regularly using a personal secretary after his return to India to keep copies of his speeches and correspondence. I have read through this voluminous historical archive carefully to draw out Gandhi's thoughts about his intentional communities.

I have also worked hard to include the voices and experiences of other key figures who chose to live with Gandhi at these communities, at least for a time. Some of these figures have written about their experiences, though these are predominantly white European figures such as Millie Graham Polak, Madeleine Slade (Mirabehn), and Albert West. To include other voices, I have striven to read the historical archive—and its gaps—carefully. For instance, sometimes we can glean from Gandhi's correspondence the sorts of questions or concerns that were being raised by members of his communities, even if the correspondence is one-sided, preserving only Gandhi's letters to others but not the letters written to him. This strategy is particularly useful in chapter 4, when I discuss Gandhi's controversial experiments with celibate sexuality and the concerns that were raised by other members in the Sevagram Ashram community. At times, I have pieced together fragments of the lives of residents at these communities, extrapolating about the experiences of figures who were in residence but whose voices are minimized or even silenced in the archive. This strategy is particularly useful in chapter 3, when I write about the Dalit ("untouchable") family that joined Sabarmati Ashram. My goal in drawing forward the voices and experiences of Gandhi's coresidents is not only to enable a fuller, more humanistic understanding of Gandhi and his place in history but also to bring to light the contributions made by Gandhi's coresidents (Indian and European, female and male, low caste and high caste, Hindu and non-Hindu) toward envisioning and enacting utopia on the small scale, and an alternative India on the national scale.

This book is organized to tell two stories of Gandhi's intentional communities. First, the four primary chapters are grounded in my analysis of historical archival materials and tell in chronological order the story of each of these communities during the years that Gandhi lived at them. These chapters explore who chose to live at each community with Gandhi, what daily life was like, and what their shared goals were. Together, these primary chapters draw out the group experiments with cohousing, shared labor, self-discipline, social equality, and political and spiritual liberation in the collective pursuit of utopia. Second, the short interludes following each of the four primary chapters are grounded in my field research at each of these historic sites and tell the story of these communities since Gandhi's time there. These interludes explore which communities have closed as residences but have been preserved as heritage sites and museums; which have endeavored to live on as residential communities; and which have been razed and largely forgotten. Together, these interludes highlight the multiple and, at times, contested legacy of Gandhi as he is remembered in South Africa and India today.

As early as 1909, when Gandhi published his political treatise *Indian Home Rule* (*Hind Swaraj*), he decried both British colonization and modern industrial civilization, and he described his ideal village for the future of India. This utopic village would have no machinery save hand-built ploughs and spinning wheels. It would have no rich and poor, no haves and have-nots, for everyone would work and equally share the fruits of their communal labor. For the next four decades, this vision was repeatedly challenged by prominent Indian politicians and activists (including B. R. Ambedkar, Muhammad Ali Jinnah, Jawaharlal Nehru, and Rabindranath Tagore) who decried Gandhi's traditionalism—even as many of them embraced his political tactics—for they viewed villages as backward, both intellectually and culturally. But near the end of Gandhi's life, he reiterated in a letter to his friend and political protégé Jawaharlal Nehru (who eventually became the first prime minister of independent India) that he stood by the vision he had earlier set forth in *Indian Home Rule*, writing in 1945, "I am convinced that if India is to attain true freedom and through India the world also, then sooner or later the fact must be recognized that people will have to live in villages, not in towns, in huts, not in palaces. . . . We can realize truth and nonviolence only in the simplicity of village life."[12] In our world today, the need to simplify life and focus on the greater good is no less urgent than it was in Gandhi's time. Reading about Gandhi's intentional communities allows us to think with Gandhi about a range of topics that can help each of us formulate our own conception of living the good life, including how we as individuals should spend our finite time together on this earth; how the boundaries of inclusion and exclusion operate in our daily lives; how we would each define utopia and what differentiates a utopic community from a dystopic one; and whether or to what extent self-sacrifice is necessary in the pursuit of universal well-being.

1

Phoenix Settlement

Gandhi arrived in South Africa in 1893. He was just twenty-three years old, fresh out of law school, and had been hired by a merchant named Dada Abdulla to serve as legal counsel to his firm, Dada Abdulla & Company. Gandhi left his wife, Kasturba, and their children behind with family in India, intending to return at the end of one year. Little did Gandhi know, he would spend the next twenty-one years in South Africa. He would establish two intentional communities there that would radically transform his life and also transform the political landscape for Indians in South Africa. In his first year living and working in South Africa, Gandhi felt a call to action against racial and economic injustices. He was repeatedly shocked by the prejudicial treatment he experienced as a person of color in South Africa: he was called a "coolie barrister"; he was told to remove his turban in court; he was kicked off the train at Pietermaritzburg Station for riding in the first-class cabin, in spite of being a ticketed passenger; he was shoved off the footpath while walking in Pretoria. Gandhi began paying attention to how the whites in South Africa treated Indians, and to how the law was used to legitimate discriminatory treatment. In his autobiography, he writes that he quickly came to realize that "South Africa was no country for a self-respecting Indian, and my mind became more and more occupied with the question as to how this state of things might be improved."[1]

Gandhi resolved to endeavor to improve the situation for Indians in South Africa while working for Dada Abdulla. At the end of the year-long contract, he was persuaded of the need to remain in South Africa for a month longer to fight for civil rights for the Indian community. That month stretched into two decades, during which time Gandhi transformed from a novice lawyer into a full-fledged legal and political activist. In his first year in Durban, South Africa, Gandhi realized the crucial need for community organization. He therefore founded the Natal Indian Congress in 1894 and served as its first secretary. He also encouraged a friend, Viyavaharik Madanjit, to establish a printing press, arguing that such a press would enable the printing of news in multiple Indian languages to help the Indian community stay informed, and provide training in the art of printing to young Indian men. At that time, Durban was home to fourteen presses, all white-owned. With new legal restrictions being proposed in South Africa that would increasingly segregate the Indian community, Madanjit agreed to the need for a community-focused press, and in 1898, the International Printing Press held its opening ceremony in Durban. The International Printing Press began with two hand-operated presses and type in English, Gujarati, Hindi, and Tamil languages. It undertook general-job printing for the Indian community and also published short-lived newspapers. Most significantly, beginning in June 1903, it began printing a weekly newspaper called *Indian Opinion*.[2]

Gandhi was the driving force behind *Indian Opinion*, serving as its primary financial backer and its lead author, though he never served as editor of this weekly newspaper. In founding *Indian Opinion*, Gandhi felt that the sole aim of journalism should be service, and he describes writing for the newspaper as a "training in self-restraint," for he poured out his soul in its columns, setting down each word with thought and deliberation.[3] In her detailed study of Gandhi's printing press, Isabel Hofmeyr describes *Indian Opinion* not as a weekly newspaper in the strict sense of the genre but instead as a weekly periodical that included cuttings and summaries from global exchange papers, Gandhi's ethical opinion pieces, and extracts of a wide variety of philosophical, ethical, and religious texts selected primarily by Gandhi. She writes, "Through summary and abridgment of texts from across the world, he instituted new kinds of ethical 'exchanges,' helping readers see themselves as part of a vast reading commonwealth while making the ethical extracts and the 'news' clippings among which they were placed equivalent to each other."[4]

The story of Phoenix Settlement, Gandhi's first intentional community, is intimately woven together with the story of *Indian Opinion*. Phoenix Settlement—a rural community located on farmland outside Durban—would become the permanent site for the publication of the newspaper, with the communal settlers serving as its labor force. Both the newspaper and settlement shared in common the ideals of service, self-restraint, and communal labor for the betterment of the Indian community in South Africa. When *Indian Opinion* first began, Gandhi had moved from the city of Durban to Johannesburg for his legal career. While in Johannesburg, Gandhi stayed in close contact with the newspaper's first editor, M. H. Nazar, submitting regular essays and providing advice on general operations.[5] Gandhi was aware that *Indian Opinion* was running at a substantial loss. Gandhi supplemented the newspaper's operations with his own income but knew this was unsustainable, and he turned to Albert West for help. West was a printer from Lincolnshire, England, who ran a printing operation in Johannesburg. West and Gandhi had met at a vegetarian restaurant in Johannesburg and formed a friendship. Gandhi asked West if he would be willing to move to Durban and take over the press operations. West agreed and went to Durban to look into the financial state of the press in detail.

In the fall of 1904, Gandhi received a letter from Albert West alerting him that *Indian Opinion* was running at an even greater loss than they had estimated. Gandhi decided to travel from Johannesburg to Durban to meet West and together try to sort out the newspaper's financial situation. Gandhi's friend Henry Polak came to see him off at the train station and loaned him a copy of John Ruskin's essay *Unto This Last*. Gandhi read it on the overnight train and was so influenced by the essay that he decided to immediately put its ideals into practice. These ideals Gandhi summed up in three points:

> The good of the individual is contained in the good of all.
>
> 1. A lawyer's work has the same value as the barber's inasmuch as all have the same right of earning their livelihood from their work.
> 2. A life of labour, i.e. the life of the tiller of the soil and the handicraftsman is the life worth living.[6]

Reaching Durban, Gandhi described to West the impact of Ruskin's essay upon him and proposed that they move the printing press to a remote location outside Durban, where Gandhi, West, the press workers, and a cohort of like-minded friends could live and work together. Recollecting this conversation in his autobiography, Gandhi writes:

> I talked over the whole thing with Mr. West, described to him the effect *Unto This Last* had produced on my mind, and proposed that *Indian Opinion* should be removed to a farm, on which everyone should labour, drawing the same living wage, and attending to the press work in spare time. Mr. West approved of the proposal, and £3 was laid down as the monthly allowance per head, irrespective of colour or nationality.[7]

Albert West readily agreed to this proposal, and he recalled being drawn as much to the utopic idea of living and working on a collective farm as he was to Gandhi himself:

> This scheme was idealistic, if not very practical. The idea appealed to me because I was accustomed to a country life. I loved to be on the farms when I was a lad, although I did not become a farm worker myself. So I did not have to wake up to the importance and value of manual work or come to realise that a lawyer's work was only as valuable as the barber's. I was convinced already of this truth. The scheme was attractive because, if it proved successful, we should be able to gain our subsistence from the soil and have no need to expect much from the newspaper. It would

> be spare-time work. A monthly allowance per head of £3 was laid down. In this way it was hoped to run the paper without loss. To say that I approved of the proposal suggests a certain amount of wishful thinking. I was certainly in love with the idea, and my love for Gandhi was sufficient to make me want to succeed in this venture. Had we stopped to consider such matters as trade-union rules, minimum wages and so forth, we might never have started the scheme.[8]

Such was the birth of Gandhi's first intentional community, Phoenix Settlement—a utopic scheme founded on the ideas of shared manual labor (farming and printing press work), equality across racial and ethnic lines, and living and working together for the common good. On the one hand, Phoenix Settlement was remarkable for bringing Indians and Europeans from Hindu, Muslim, Christian, and Jewish faiths together as equals in race-conscious colonial South Africa. On the other hand, Phoenix Settlement's scope was simultaneously limited by its exclusion of Black South Africans. Phoenix Settlement was the communal site where Gandhi first began to experiment with enacting his philosophy of universal well-being, *sarvodaya*, and where he first developed his method of nonviolent civil disobedience, *satyagraha*.

The Move to Phoenix Settlement

Albert West was an enthusiastic partner in this "scheme" (those who joined Phoenix Settlement often called themselves "schemers" for participating in the communal scheme to work the land and the newspaper for £3 per month per person), but not all of the press workers met the idea with equal enthusiasm. Gandhi encouraged those who were hesitant to think it over, while he sprang into action. Gandhi learned of some land for sale fourteen miles northwest of Durban, and he and West inspected it together. The land consisted of one hundred acres with orange trees and date palms, a creek, and a dilapidated cottage. Gandhi and West found this land ideal for their purposes, so Gandhi purchased it for a thousand pounds.[9] The land was previously owned by a sugarcane farmer named Thomas Watkins, whose first crop was destroyed by fire. Watkins then called the farm "Phoenix" because he had replanted the crop in the ashes; the nearest railway station located a couple of miles from the farm was then called Phoenix Station.[10] The name stuck; Gandhi decided to call his intentional community Phoenix Settlement. The symbolism of the phoenix in Greek mythology appealed to Gandhi, who reportedly appreciated the qualities of purity, sacrifice, and immortality associated with the mythical bird.[11]

After purchasing farmland, the next step was to build a shelter for the printing press. Gandhi received patronage from the wealthy, Durban-based Indian merchant Parsee Rustomjee, who donated corrugated iron sheets and other second-hand building materials. Working with Indian carpenters and bricklayers whom Gandhi had served alongside in the ambulance corps during the Second Boer War, Gandhi and West constructed a shed for the press. Gandhi notes that West and the laborers camped on the land "at great personal risk" during the construction phase, for in addition to the lovely orange trees and date palms on the land, it was also infested with snakes.[12] Once the press building was constructed, they had to move the printing press from downtown Durban to Phoenix Settlement. They dismantled the press and then carried the printing machinery and type in four large wagons, each pulled by sixteen bullocks across the countryside. West recollected that the team worked long hours to reassemble the machines at Phoenix Settlement within a week. West also purchased a petrol engine from a farmer, as there was no electricity at the settlement. Although Gandhi wanted to operate the press solely by hand, West insisted on the necessity of the petrol engine:

> This engine was necessary because we had no electric motor. With Gandhi's new-found gospel of handicrafts and manual labour he would have much preferred working the machines by hand, but, with my experience of machinery, I knew we must have power to drive heavy machines. I agreed, however, that we should have some means of working them by hand in case the engine failed. So I designed a hand machine with a driving wheel mounted on a stout wooden frame. Attached to the axle was a handle on either side, so that four persons could turn the wheel and drive the printing machine by means of a long belt. Gandhi was immensely pleased with this contraption. We very soon had to put this hand machine, which we called "The Wheel," to good use.[13]

"The Wheel" was used to print the first edition of *Indian Opinion* from its new location at Phoenix Settlement. When the petrol engine would not start, Gandhi, West, the other press workers, and the remaining carpenters all took turns at the wheel (which required relays of four people at a time), working through the night to meet their weekly deadline. At last, the press workers "rang with peals of joy" as all of the necessary copies were printed and then dispatched to the nearest train station for distribution.[14]

This first issue of *Indian Opinion* printed at Phoenix Settlement was dated December 24, 1904, and it included an essay by Gandhi titled "Ourselves" that announced to readers the move to the farm.[15] After acknowledging the financial challenges faced by the paper, Gandhi describes this move as a "novel and revolutionary project" that is meant to fulfill the mission of *Indian Opinion*, which was to "bring the European and the Indian subjects of King Edward closer together. It was to educate public opinion, to remove causes for misunderstanding; to put before the Indians their own blemishes; and to show them the path of duty while they insisted on securing their rights."[16] Gandhi describes in this essay the scheme in detail, including the provision that workers would receive a set monthly stipend and a plot of land to live upon, while the paper's profits (if any) would be divided evenly amongst them each year. In his words:

> Living under such conditions and amid the beautiful surroundings which have given Natal the name of the Garden Colony, the workers could live a more simple and natural life, and the ideas of Ruskin and Tolstoy [could be] combined with strict business principles. . . . There would be a closer brotherly combination between the European and the Indian workers. There was a possibility that the daily working hours could be reduced. Each could become his own agriculturist. . . . The incentive would be threefold to all: an ideal to work for in the shape of *Indian Opinion*; perfectly healthy surroundings to live in, and an immediate prospect of owning a piece of land on the most advantageous terms; and a direct tangible interest and participation in the scheme.[17]

Gandhi proudly states that this plan has now been translated into action, and there are already Englishmen and Indians living and working together. He appeals to "both the great communities residing in South Africa"—presumably, Europeans and Indians—to support this undertaking, and concludes by noting, "It is a bold experiment and fraught with momentous consequences. We know of no non-religious organization that is or has been managed on the principles above laid down. If it succeeds, we cannot but think that it would be worthy of imitation."[18]

Phoenix Settlement thus began in 1904 as a residential experiment in self-sufficiency, simplicity, and equality. The residents were Indians and Europeans who lived and labored together, seeking to forge an ideal community united together as co-citizens of the British Empire and sharing not only equal rights and responsibilities but also affection for one another. Central to their collective life was the goal of promoting equality between Indians and Europeans living in South Africa. The newspaper was the primary means for such promotion, and as such, it was central to daily life at the settlement. In her detailed study of Gandhi's printing press, Isabel Hofmeyr notes that not only did *Indian Opinion* come to be important to the success of Gandhi's later political campaigns in South Africa, but the press itself was central to Phoenix Settlement "and operated as an embodiment of its utopian ideals. Virtually all residents—men, women, and children—were involved in at least some aspect of the printing process."[19] Literate members of the settlement worked on typesetting; men took turns manually operating the press; and children helped with folding the newspapers, wrapping them up, and pasting on the mailing addresses. Implementing Ruskin's ideals (as Gandhi interpreted them) on the farmland at Phoenix Settlement entailed a life of labor at the printing press as well as tilling the soil.

The First Phoenix Settlers

As soon as the printing press was operational at Phoenix Settlement, settlers were eager to build houses so that they could stop sleeping in tents or on the press floor. Each settler was allotted three acres of land upon which they could build a small house and plant a garden. They wanted to build earthen structures for houses but instead used the remaining corrugated iron that had been donated to them, as Gandhi recalled:

> To enable everyone to make a living by manual labor, we parceled out the land round the press in pieces of three acres each. One of these fell to my lot. On all these plots we, much against our wish, built houses with corrugated iron. Our desire had been to have mud huts thatched with straw or small brick houses such as would become ordinary peasants, but it could not be. They would have been more expensive and would have meant more time, and everyone was eager to settle down as soon as possible.[20]

The corrugated iron hut Gandhi built for himself he named Sarvodaya House.

The first settlers to join Gandhi and Albert West at Phoenix Settlement were two press workers who moved from Durban: Chhaganlal Gandhi and Sam Govindswamy. Chhaganlal was one of Gandhi's nephews, and he had been responsible for the Gujarati section of *Indian Opinion* in Durban.[21] At Phoenix Settlement, Chhaganlal continued to oversee the Gujarati-language work, and he also became comanager of the press alongside Albert West. Gandhi proposed to Chhaganlal the idea of moving the press to Phoenix at the same time as he pitched the idea to West, and he reported that Chhaganlal had "full faith" in Gandhi and agreed to the scheme without hesitation.[22] Sam Govindswamy was the press machinist who oversaw the disassembly and reassembly of the printing press during the move from Durban to Phoenix; it was also his job to ensure that the machinery stayed operational.[23]

Unlike Albert West, Chhaganlal Gandhi, and Sam Govindswamy, the other press workers decided not to move to Phoenix Settlement. The original proprietor of the International Printing Press, Viyavaharik Madanjit, predicted that if the press moved to a rural farm, then, in short order, the workers would bolt, *Indian Opinion* would come to a stop, and the press would have to close down.[24] He agreed to cede the press to Gandhi in order to settle the debts he had accrued in South Africa and then returned to India.[25] M. H. Nazar, the first editor of *Indian Opinion*, also declined to move to Phoenix, as he preferred to remain in Durban for professional reasons.[26] The other handful of press workers also decided not to join the scheme as settlers, although some did continue to work on the press as day laborers who commuted from Durban during its first months of operation at

Phoenix Settlement.[27] Gandhi reached out to friends and family, inviting them to join Phoenix Settlement. One of the first relatives to join was Maganlal Gandhi, the younger brother of Chhaganlal, who left his small store in Tongaat behind to cast his lot with Gandhi.[28] Maganlal turned out to be an especially skilled compositor, quick in speed and accurate in typesetting in spite of his lack of printing press experience.[29] Other relatives who joined Phoenix at this time included Anandlal Gandhi and Abhaychand Gandhi.[30]

In addition to press workers and Gandhi's relatives, several white settlers were also among the early joiners of Phoenix Settlement. Among the first, following Albert West, was Henry Polak. Polak first came to South Africa from London in 1903 as a young man of twenty-two years. He met Gandhi at a vegetarian society gathering in Johannesburg in March of 1904. Polak was then working on the editorial staff of the *Transvaal Critic* newspaper, and as a journalist, he was familiar with *Indian Opinion*. Polak recalled being drawn to *Indian Opinion* because it helped him understand the Indian point of view on current events and because, as a Jew, he felt that his own people had suffered from racial and religious discrimination, much as the Indians were being discriminated against in South Africa.[31] Shortly after meeting Gandhi, Polak told his editor that he would no longer attach his name to anti-Asian paragraphs in the *Transvaal Critic*, and he also began to freelance for *Indian Opinion*. Six months later, when Gandhi took the train from Johannesburg to Durban to check into the financial situation of *Indian Opinion*, it was Polak who loaned Gandhi the copy of John Ruskin's *Unto This Last*. Polak recalls that he did not know what impact this book would have on Gandhi but simply felt he would enjoy reading it, given their common interest in alternative socioeconomic systems:

> Full of my social and economic enthusiasms, in which he [Gandhi] had been much interested but with which he had not always agreed, I handed him a book that I had just finished, and which I felt sure he would much enjoy. Little did I realise how far-reaching would be the consequences! The book was John Ruskin's *Unto This Last*. Gandhiji always regarded the perusal of this book as one of the great turning points of his life. He describes how he was so fascinated by the book that he could not put it down all night until he had finished it, and he declares that, upon his arrival at Durban, it had changed his outlook for ever. He determined immediately to adopt and to advocate the "simple life," with all its attendant consequences.[32]

When Polak learned that Gandhi had decided to found Phoenix Settlement, he immediately asked to join the community. Gandhi was eager to have him, and so Polak resigned from the *Transvaal Critic* and moved to Phoenix. Gandhi described Polak as taking to the simple life "like a duck to water," noting that he won the hearts of all residents and quickly became a member of their extended family.[33] For the idealistic Polak, his time at Phoenix Settlement and his work on *Indian Opinion* brought him "great happiness in being able thereby to make a useful contribution to the improvement of racial relations and to the better understanding in South Africa of India's part in world culture."[34]

Other white settlers who joined Phoenix Settlement in its early years included A. J. Bean, John Cordes, Rev. Joseph Doke, Herbert Kitchin, and W. J. MacIntyre. These men were all drawn to the idea of living in a moral community that was jointly inhabited by Europeans and Indians. Bean and MacIntyre were professional acquaintances of Gandhi in South Africa: Bean was a lawyer, and MacIntyre was an articled clerk in Gandhi's law office.[35] Cordes was a German who had previously lived in Rhodesia. He shared in common with Gandhi an interest in nature cure, and for the years he was in residence at Phoenix, he administered naturopathic treatment to the settlers and also served as one of the teachers to the children in residence.[36] On school holidays, Cordes's son Willie joined him at Phoenix; Willie lived for the remainder of the time with his mother in Rhodesia. Doke was a Christian missionary from New Zealand who resided only part-time at Phoenix Settlement but was impacted deeply by the experience; he also wrote the first biography of Gandhi.[37] Kitchin was an electrical contractor who met Gandhi while serving in the ambulance corps during the Second Boer War. Kitchin briefly served as editor of *Indian Opinion*, until Polak assumed editorship in February 1906 and served in this role for ten years.[38]

Many of these white residents of Phoenix Settlement were friends that Gandhi had made through the Theosophical Society or the Esoteric Christian Union. Gandhi had joined the Theosophical Society during his time in London, and he sought members of this group out when he arrived in South Africa. The Theosophical Society was founded in 1875 in New York, and it called for the establishment of a universal, multireligious "brotherhood" of humanity and advocated for the comparative study of world religions. It became popular among certain educated classes in Europe, North America, and colonial India, and its members often advocated an anti-colonial politics. The Esoteric Christian Union was founded in 1891 in South Africa by a theosophist, and it advocated for an esoteric interpretation of Christianity, as well as for vegetarianism. Gandhi's participation in these theosophic and esoteric communities impacted his belief that all religions refer to the same truth (a basic tenet of theosophy), as well as his desire to live in a multifaith community of equals.[39]

In June of 1906, Gandhi moved his wife, Kasturba, and their three youngest sons—Manilal, Ramdas, and Devdas (the eldest son, Harilal, was then in India but joined the settlement upon his return to South Africa)—from their Johannesburg home to Phoenix Settlement. Gandhi had been commuting between Johannesburg and Phoenix Settlement since 1904 and had been considering moving his family to Phoenix for some time. The outbreak of the Bambatha (Zulu) Rebellion in Natal Colony in early 1906 provided the impetus for the move. The Zulu people are the largest indigenous ethnic group in South Africa. When the Zulus rose up in protest against British taxation, Gandhi felt that, as a citizen of the British Empire who was seeking equal rights for the Indian community under British law, it was his duty to aid the British, albeit in a nonviolent way. He volunteered to form an Indian Ambulance Corps and recruited other volunteers to join it. Reflecting on this in his autobiography, Gandhi recalled:

> I bore no grudge against the Zulus, they had harmed no Indian. I had doubts about the "rebellion" itself. But I then believed that the British Empire existed for the welfare of the world. A genuine sense of loyalty prevented me from even wishing ill to the Empire. The rightness or otherwise of the "rebellion" was therefore not likely to affect my decision. . . . At any rate my heart was with the Zulus, and I was delighted, on reaching headquarters, to hear that our main work was to be the nursing of the wounded Zulus.[40]

Phoenix Settlement was located next to Zulu territory in Natal Colony. Thus, Gandhi now relocated to Phoenix as his full-time home base, bringing the volunteers he recruited and his family with him.

When Gandhi moved his family to Phoenix in 1906, Henry Polak's wife also moved there.[41] Henry had married Millie Graham Polak (née Downs) in 1905. They first met at the London Ethical Society prior to Henry's move to South Africa, and Gandhi encouraged Henry to propose to her. Millie accepted the proposal and moved from London to Johannesburg to join Henry, where they were married (with Gandhi acting as their best man), and then resided at Gandhi's Johannesburg household. Like Gandhi, Henry also traveled back and forth regularly between Phoenix Settlement and Johannesburg, while Millie initially remained in Johannesburg and became the teacher to Gandhi and Kasturba's children. Millie provides a vivid description of Phoenix Settlement at the time of her arrival, emphasizing that "the colony was to be as much as possible self-supporting, and life's material requirements were to be reduced to a minimum."[42] The simple way of life was seen in the architecture of the homes, and Millie notes that eight small bungalow-style houses had then been constructed out of corrugated iron. She describes Gandhi's house in detail:

> Mr. Gandhi's bungalow was no different from the others, except that it was a little larger. It consisted of a large room, which was living- and dining-room, two small bedrooms, another small room as kitchen and a lean-to structure for bathroom. The fittings of the bathroom were primitive but ingenious; a good-sized hole was made in the iron roof, an ordinary

> garden watering-can was balanced on a piece of wood, and to the can was attached a piece of cord. After the can was filled with water and fixed in its place one could get a good imitation shower-bath by standing under the hole and pulling the cord.[43]

Millie describes the settlement as quite remote from the urban environment that she was accustomed to. She notes that one could see acre upon acre of sugar estate land from the settlement, but no buildings could be seen beyond a few small Zulu farm huts, and apart from one "miserable nondescript little general store" near the Phoenix railway station, there was no shopping convenience.[44]

Now that the first houses had been built, Gandhi encouraged the other married settlers to bring their wives and children to Phoenix as well. Chhaganlal brought his wife, Kashi, and their sons, Prabhudas and Krishnadas; and Maganlal brought his wife, Santok, who soon gave birth to several children at Phoenix—Keshavlal, Radha, and Rukhi.[45] Gandhi also encouraged the settlers who were bachelors to get married and start families, including Albert West: "When, in due course, West made a pilgrimage to Louth [Lincolnshire] to see his parents, I advised him to return married if possible. Phoenix was the common home, and as we were all supposed to have become farmers, we were not afraid of marriage and its usual consequences."[46] Albert's marriage to Ada West (née Pywell) was celebrated at Phoenix Settlement in 1908. Gandhi described Ada as a hardworking woman with true moral beauty.[47] Albert also brought his elder sister, also named Ada (who came to be known as Devibehn), from England to join the community, and his mother-in-law, Mrs. Pywell (who came to be known as Granny). Albert and Ada's children, Hilda and Harry, were born at Phoenix. Gandhi envisaged this growing community as a family, "an essentially heterogeneous family, where people of all kinds and temperaments were freely admitted."[48]

These Phoenix settlers were Indians and Europeans who lived and labored together on the farm as equals and likened themselves to an extended family. In the context of colonialism broadly speaking, and in race-conscious South Africa in particular, this project was noteworthy. The community mixed residents not only across race lines but also across religious and class lines. And yet, the community's scope was also limited. While the residents of Phoenix could see Zulu farming huts on the horizon, and while they occasionally employed members of the nearby Zulu community as day laborers, no Zulus or other Black South Africans were invited to live at Phoenix Settlement. Part of the reasoning behind this had to do with the settlement's goal of creating a model society wherein Indians and Europeans could live together as equal citizens of the British Empire. This goal was selective in its focus on the Indian and European communities living in South Africa within the colonial context, and it kept Black South Africans at an arm's-length distance. Another part of the reasoning also had to do with the competition that then existed between African and Indian tenant farmers in Natal Colony, a competition that pitted these communities against one another as economic rivals within the colonial context.[49]

An example of the arm's-length distance between the Phoenix settlers and Black South Africans can be seen in the relationship with a community that was located just a couple miles down the road from Phoenix Settlement. The Ohlange Institute was a coeducational all-African school founded in 1901 by John Langalibalele Dube, who would later become the first president of the African National Congress. Both Gandhi and Dube created their neighboring alternative communities in the effort to improve the rights of their own communities (Indians and Black South Africans, respectively). There were noticeable parallels between Phoenix and Ohlange: both were intentional communities that emphasized civil rights and education, and they both operated printing presses. Yet, as Heather Hughes has noted, their political differences made close association between these communities "at best difficult and at worst impossible."[50] Whereas Dube's newspaper, *Ilanga*, contained articles about the "Indian invasion" and its adverse economic impact upon Black South Africans, Gandhi's newspaper, *Indian Opinion*, contained articles emphasizing the advancement of Indians over Black South Africans due to their different standards for hard work and levels of civilizational achievement. As Hughes has pointed out in her study of Dube, the colonial condition in which Gandhi and Dube operated "produced a situation in which claims for greater rights by one subaltern group seemed to imply an equivalent loss of justice for another," and while relations between Ohlange and Phoenix would improve markedly in later decades, in the first decade of existence of these neighboring communities, there was little cooperation between them in their struggles against colonial and racial injustices.[51]

Daily Life at Phoenix Settlement

Building their own utopia at Phoenix Settlement was hard work. Daily life entailed long hours spent laboring to construct houses and other communal structures, striving to eke out sufficient food from garden plots, and running the printing press. The corrugated iron houses were built near one another on a hilltop, each house with a courtyard and garden plot, and interconnected to one another by narrow walking paths. The houses were simple bungalows: small rectangular structures with interior walls to divide the living area from the bedroom, a couple of glass windows inset into the exterior walls, raised wooden floors to aid in water drainage and help keep out the snakes and mice, and flat roofs to enable residents to sleep on top of them in the summer heat.[52] Some residents made alterations to their houses to improve and personalize them, such as adding water tanks, sealing walls, and building small additions.[53] John Cordes's house stood out, for he built a rondoval with a conical thatched roof in the indigenous style he admired.[54]

As the Phoenix settlers grew their first garden crops, they began to realize some of the challenges of farming. All available building material was being used to construct houses, and none remained to fence in the garden plots. Free-roaming donkeys and mules owned by neighboring farmers began to feast upon the gardens. Venomous snakes proved another obstacle, and settlers had to keep an eye out for green mambas in fruit trees and other snakes coiled up in garden sheds. Rainwater was captured and stored in large tanks during the rainy season, but the long dry season meant that obtaining sufficient water for drinking, let alone obtaining water for crops, could be challenging.[55] Phoenix Settlement never became a completely self-sufficient farm, but the settlers were committed to the hard work of farming as both a matter of principle and of practicality. In principle, the schemers committed to living on a working farm where everyone took part in the labor of growing produce. In practice, the schemers only had the monthly allowance of £3 to live on, so the more that could be grown in the garden plots, the farther this amount could stretch.

Some settlers took to the transition from city life to country life more naturally than others. Albert West and his family settled smoothly into life at Phoenix, where Albert enjoyed working on the press and on the land. Similarly, Prabhudas Gandhi recalls in his memoir how easily his uncle, Maganlal Gandhi, transitioned to life at Phoenix, writing that he enjoyed learning carpentry and gardening work, and thus, in just a couple of years, Maganlal's garden plot was one of the best on the settlement.[56] For others, however, the transition to life at Phoenix proved more challenging than anticipated. Millie Graham Polak wrote candidly about her difficulties living at the settlement. Her initial impression of Phoenix after she and Kasturba arrived there from Johannesburg was not positive. She wrote in her diary:

> My first view of Phoenix disappointed and depressed me. Mrs. Gandhi, too, did not feel happy at being transplanted from the town, with its domestic and human amenities, to the more primitive conditions which prevailed at the settlement. She and I shared a little room the first night we arrived, and lay awake talking and grumbling for hours. We were probably overtired, both nervously and physically; for we had had two days and a night in a train, and at the end of that a long two-mile tramp along a badly constructed road across difficult country, our path lighted only by a flickering lamp, and the fear of snakes constantly in our minds. The youngest boy also had become tired and commenced to cry miserably.[57]

Millie reports that early the next morning, Gandhi spoke with them, expressing concern about their dissatisfaction. "Eventually, Mr. Gandhi begged us to be patient and see what we could do with the things around us, promising to get any other really necessary things that we required. The essence of the last sentence lay in the word 'necessary,' however, for so many things we desired we could not prove to be necessary, and so life was lived at Phoenix in a very simple way."[58]

Millie tried to make herself at home with Henry in their two-room bungalow in the settlement but ultimately decided she could not stay:

> Here I tried to make a little home, the first of my married life. But the impossibility of getting suitable food, the knowledge and fear of the snakes, spiders and other poisonous or unpleasant creatures, the disappointment to me, a town-bred girl, of the whole place, and, lastly, the [Bambatha] rebellion, proved too much. I could not sleep, and would lie awake nearly all night, watching for insects and crawling creatures and listening in imagination to the reports of guns and the shrieks of people dying.[59]

Thus, after two months living at Phoenix, Millie moved back to Gandhi's house in Johannesburg, from where she continued to support Gandhi's work in South Africa and occasionally returned to Phoenix for visits. Henry continued in his role as editor of *Indian Opinion*, splitting his time between Johannesburg and Phoenix Settlement, working both on the newspaper while at Phoenix and also in his new legal capacity out of Gandhi's Johannesburg office (Gandhi persuaded Polak to study law, and Polak was articled to Gandhi as a lawyer-in-training from 1905 to 1908).

Living at Phoenix Settlement meant transitioning to a new way of life that embraced manual labor and limited resources and also brought the challenge of illness. Archived correspondence shows that a number of residents fell sick in the settlement's first years. Gandhi and other residents who were interested in nature cure began honing their techniques with hydrotherapy, advocating for Kuhne's sitz baths along with a vegetarian diet to eliminate toxins.[60] At one point, Albert West wrote to Gandhi, who was then traveling, asking for advice on the practical question of whether schemers should receive their monthly £3 allotment if they had fallen sick with an illness lasting more than a month and were unable to contribute their share of labor. Gandhi's reply sums up the ideals that the community was trying to cultivate: "My answer is that we are a family and that we are bound to support them and even find what medical help as poor people we are capable of finding. I am quite willing that my guarantee should stand for such cases. . . . It is in such matters that in my opinion we best realize our ideals. We are trying to live a life of perpetual self-sacrifice and find joy in it."[61] Gandhi's emphasis here on finding joy through perpetual self-sacrifice for the good of the community is significant, and it was something that he gave considerable thought to as he traveled between his simple home at Phoenix Settlement and his legal career in Johannesburg during these years. The goal in living and laboring together was to forge an egalitarian community that was joined together by bonds of affection, a community that would serve as a counterworld to the colonialist and capitalist status quo.

Gandhi and the other founding settlers agreed that the residents at Phoenix should live and work together, mixing as equals across lines of race and ethnicity in ways that confronted colonial norms, and living alongside members from multiple religious communities in ways that confronted religious orthodoxy. Prabhudas Gandhi recalls the challenge this posed for his parents, Chhaganlal and Kashi Gandhi, in their initial transition to life at Phoenix. Coming from orthodox Hindu Vaishnava families, Chhaganlal and Kashi had learned that it was taboo to dine with people of different castes and faiths, and that any household dishes used by a person from a lower caste or a different religion would become polluted. Prabhudas writes, "My parents were orthodox followers of the Vaishnava creed. I cannot forget how my mother and aunt would purify brass utensils used by Muslim friends of Gandhiji by putting them in the fire. It was also a problem for my father to eat with Muslims. But since he had surrendered himself to Gandhiji he did his best to follow Gandhi's ideas without protest."[62] In his diary, Chhaganlal notes that initially, when interdining occurred, he took his meals separately, as he did on one occasion in 1906 when Gandhi invited him to lunch along with several Muslim, Christian, and Jewish people.[63] In time, Chhaganlal grew comfortable dining and socializing with people from other religions, castes, and races. Ultimately, when Gandhi opened the Phoenix school to student boarders from the Indian community in 1908 and 1909, Chhaganlal agreed to allow three non-Hindu boys to live with his family; two of them were Muslims and one was Parsi.[64]

During the six weeks when Gandhi served in the Indian Ambulance Corps during the Bambatha Rebellion, he gave further thought to what it meant to conceive of the Phoenix community as an extended family. Gandhi decided to undertake a formal vow of celibacy, called *brahmacharya*, in 1906. He writes, "the idea flashed upon me that if I wanted to devote myself to the service of the community, I must relinquish the desire for children and wealth and live the life of a *vanaprastha* [forest hermit]."[65] Gandhi remained married to his wife, Kasturba, until her death in 1944 but committed to his vow of celibacy from 1906 until his own death in 1948.[66] In taking this vow, Gandhi had two interrelated goals. The first was the pursuit of communal equality at Phoenix Settlement. Through this vow, Gandhi sought to treat every coresident as an equal, without privileging his own wife or sons. The second involved the pursuit of spiritual liberation (*moksha*). Celibacy is a traditional means used by Hindu renouncers to lessen attachments to householder life as they strive toward spiritual liberation. It was at this time that Gandhi began to think of this intentional community not only as an experiment in equality and egalitarian economics but also as an ashram. In classical Hinduism, an ashram was a forest hermitage, a place on the outskirts of civilization to which a renouncer could retreat in search of spiritual advancement.

There, having abandoned householder life, renouncers could practice physical and mental discipline to pursue an experiential knowledge of ultimate reality that would ideally lead to freedom from the bondage of transmigration. Gandhi later reflected upon his shifting conception of this intentional community, writing, "I purchased 100 acres of land and founded Phoenix Settlement, which neither we nor anyone else [then] called an ashram. It had a religious basis, but the visible object was purity of body and mind as well as economic equality. I did not then consider *brahmacharya* (chastity) to be essential; [rather] it was expected that co-workers would live as family men and have children."[67]

Shortly after making his vow of celibacy at Phoenix Settlement, Gandhi began to conceive of his method of nonviolent civil disobedience, which he would eventually call *satyagraha*. The communal context of living with his Phoenix coresidents and thinking about their collective well-being was central to the emergence of *satyagraha*. In his autobiography, Gandhi writes that just a month after taking his vow of celibacy, "the foundation of *satyagraha* was laid. As though unknown to me the *brahmacharya* vow had been preparing me for it. *Satyagraha* . . . came on spontaneously, without my having willed it. But I could see that all my previous steps led up to that goal."[68] Gandhi was concerned not only with how to treat all members of Phoenix Settlement equally but also with how to resolve the inevitable conflicts that arose between members. He attributed his development of *satyagraha* to the domestic resistance that his wife, Kasturba, offered him on occasions when she disagreed with him. Reflecting upon this, Gandhi later said:

> I learnt the lesson of non-violence from my wife, when I tried to bend her to my will. Her determined resistance to my will on the one hand, and her quiet submission to the suffering my stupidity involved on the other, ultimately made me ashamed of myself and cured me of my stupidity in thinking that I was born to rule over her, and in the end she became my teacher in non-violence. And what I did in South Africa was but an extension of the rule of satyagraha which she unwillingly practised in her own person.[69]

Gandhi understood *satyagraha* not merely as nonviolent resistance against injustice but as a form of resistance that entailed the pursuit of truth (*satya*) on all sides of the conflict, with the goal of finding a resolution that improved the situation for all parties.[70] Gandhi began to think further about nonviolent resistance and conflict resolution as a strategy to employ beyond domestic squabbles at Phoenix Settlement when the Asiatic Registration Act arose.

On August 22, 1906, the draft Asiatic Registration Act, often known among Indians as the "Black Act," was introduced into Legislative Council in Transvaal Colony. Gandhi was in Johannesburg working at his legal practice that day and read the announcement of the draft act in the paper. He recalls shuddering as he read it, for he "saw nothing in it except hatred of Indians."[71] That evening, he translated the draft act into Gujarati so that he could publish it in both English and Gujarati in *Indian Opinion* to alert the Indian community.[72] Gandhi viewed this proposed act as discriminatory and humiliating, for it would require all Asians (Indians and Chinese) living in Transvaal Colony, South Africa, to register with the government, including fingerprinting and body stripping to identify birthmarks. At a meeting of the British Indian Association in Johannesburg, Gandhi asked each of the approximately three thousand individuals present to pledge to resist the act. He explained that when the government has taken leave of all sense of decency, then it is the citizen's duty to bravely refuse to endure unethical laws. He also warned that resistance could entail serious hardship:

> We might have to go to jail, where we might be insulted. We might have to go hungry and suffer extreme heat or cold. Hard labour might be imposed upon us. We might be flogged by rude warders. We might be fined heavily and our property might be attached and held up to auction if there are only a few resisters left. Opulent today, we might be reduced to abject poverty tomorrow. We might be deported. Suffering from starvation and similar hardships in jail, some of us might fall ill and even die. In short, therefore, it is not at all impossible that we might have to endure every hardship that we can imagine, and wisdom lies in pledging ourselves on the understanding that we shall have to suffer all that and worse.[73]

Gandhi closed his speech by asking each person to pledge to resist the act, even at the cost of their life: "Everyone should fully realize his responsibility, then only pledge himself independently of others and understand that he himself must be true to his pledge even unto death, no matter what others do."[74]

Several resolutions were formally passed at this meeting. One resolution entailed submitting a formal request to the governor of the Transvaal that the Asiatic Registration Act be withdrawn. A second resolution appointed a delegation of Indians to travel to London to formally present their complaint to the imperial authorities. And a third resolved that the Indians present at the meeting would submit to imprisonment rather than comply with the act.[75] In the weeks that followed, more and more Indians made pledges of resistance. As this *satyagraha* campaign mounted, life at Phoenix Settlement transformed significantly as Gandhi looked to his coresidents to help him lead the campaign. Founded as a back-to-the-land community grounded in the ideas of Ruskin and Tolstoy, the emphasis on laboring for equality at Phoenix Settlement now shifted from its initial focus on agriculture, construction, and press work to an increased focus on press work in combination with community organizing. All of the Phoenix settlers were expected to contribute their labor to publishing *Indian Opinion*, and this newspaper played a key role in the resistance campaign. Gandhi described *Indian Opinion* as a "most useful and potent weapon" in the struggle against the Asiatic Registration Act:

> Through the medium of this paper we could very well disseminate the news of the week among the community. The English section kept those Indians informed about the movement who did not know Gujarati, and for Englishmen in India, England and South Africa, *Indian Opinion* served the purpose of a weekly newsletter. I believe that a struggle which chiefly relies upon internal strength can be carried on without a newspaper, but it is also my experience that we could not perhaps have educated the local Indian community, nor kept Indians all over the world in touch with the course of events in South Africa in any other way, with the same ease and success as through *Indian Opinion*, which therefore was certainly a most useful and potent weapon in our struggle.[76]

In addition to printing the newspaper, Gandhi also looked to his coresidents to join him on the front lines in the resistance campaign.

Printing Labor, Prison Labor

The Asiatic Registration Act was passed by the Transvaal Parliament on March 21, 1907, and Asians were informed that they must register by July 31. Gandhi and the other Phoenix settlers made this act a central topic of discussion in *Indian Opinion*. The newspaper was printed at Phoenix Settlement in both English and Gujarati, and it had multiple audiences, a fact that Gandhi was aware of and used strategically. Isabel Hofmeyr has shown how Gandhi's Gujarati readers were not only given information about the Asiatic Registration Act but were also instructed to actively resist it and to encourage other Indians to join the resistance by recruiting new subscribers, propagandizing, and acting as postal agents on its behalf. The ideal reader of the Gujarati *Indian Opinion* was one who would read the paper and then act upon the knowledge gained therefrom by becoming a *satyagrahi* (a person engaged in nonviolent civil resistance).[77] For example, included in the Gujarati-language edition of *Indian Opinion* on August 8, 1907, was a "Suggestion to Readers" that explicitly encouraged active reading and proselytizing among its Gujarati readers living in South Africa and also in India:

> In our opinion, the Gujarati section of *Indian Opinion* is at present rendering invaluable service. This claim will probably appear exaggerated. However, the statement is justified. The Transvaal Indians are at present carrying on a heroic struggle and this paper is engaged in furthering that struggle in every possible manner. We therefore deem it to be the duty of every Indian to read every line of it pertaining to the struggle. Whatever is read is afterwards to be acted upon, and the issue, after being read, is to

> be preserved and not thrown away. We recommend that certain articles and translations should be read and re-read. Moreover, our cause needs to be discussed in every home in India. Our readers can do much to bring this about. They can send the required number of copies of *Indian Opinion* to their friends and, advising them to read them, seek all possible help from them.[78]

The English-language edition of *Indian Opinion* targeted two different audiences. The first included Indians living in South Africa and elsewhere who were not native Gujarati speakers but were fluent in English. These readers were occasionally addressed directly and encouraged to read the paper aloud to those Indians who were illiterate (translating it from English into their native language as needed), and also to share the English-language paper with whites living in South Africa.[79] The second group included white readers in South Africa, and Gandhi was aware that some were—and some were not—sympathetic to the Indian struggle for civil rights. Some of the English essays written by Gandhi and Henry Polak were intended to explain the rationale for the resistance movement in an effort to convince white readers to support the struggle against the Asiatic Registration Act. For example, included in the English edition of *Indian Opinion* on September 7, 1907, was an essay titled "On the Duty of Civil Disobedience," which was written by Gandhi and drew upon Henry David Thoreau's essay of the same title to explain why Indians in South Africa are obligated to resist registering under the Asiatic Registration Act: "In the Asiatic Registration Act, British Indians have not only a law which has some evil in it, that is to say, using Thoreau's words, a machine with friction in it, but it is evil legalized, or it represents friction with machinery provided for it. Resistance to such an evil is a divine duty which no human being can with impunity disregard."[80] Other English essays were intended as direct communication to colonial officers of the Asiatic Department, and Gandhi noted that these officers did become "diligent readers" of *Indian Opinion*.[81] Gandhi insisted that their resistance movement should be transparent, and he used the newspaper to inform the colonial officers of each step of their resistance and the rationale behind it.

Gandhi struggled with the question of terminology for this resistance effort. While he used terms such as "civil disobedience" and "passive resistance," he was not satisfied by these English phrases. He wrote in a letter to the editor that was published in the *Rand Daily Mail* on July 1, 1907, "I call the passive resistance to be offered by the Indian community 'so-called' because, in my opinion, it is really not resistance but a policy of communal suffering."[82] As we have seen, Gandhi was aware that defying this new law would entail consequences, and he asked his fellow resisters to be prepared to suffer those consequences as they waged their nonviolent battle against this unjust law. Seeking a better term for their movement, one that encapsulated the idea of active (not passive) self-sacrifice for the greater good, Gandhi announced a competition in *Indian Opinion*, promising a small prize to the reader who invented the best term:

> Maganlal Gandhi was one of the competitors and he suggested the word "Sadagraha," meaning "firmness in a good cause." I liked the word, but it did not fully represent the whole idea I wished it to connote. I therefore corrected it to "Satyagraha." Truth (*Satya*) implies love, and firmness (*agraha*) engenders and therefore serves as a synonym for force. I thus began to call the Indian movement "Satyagraha," that is to say, the Force which is born of Truth and Love or non-violence, and gave up the use of the phrase "passive resistance."[83]

The struggle against the Asiatic Registration Act therefore came to be known as the Black Act Satyagraha, and it was the first of many *satyagraha* campaigns that Gandhi would lead in his lifetime. Importantly, these campaigns had a close connection to Gandhi's intentional communities, with Gandhi's coresidents becoming essential organizers and activists.

On December 28, 1907, Gandhi was informed that he had to leave Transvaal Colony within forty-eight hours for failing to submit his registration. He refused, and on January 10, 1908, he was arrested and sentenced to two months in prison—the first of many prison sentences that Gandhi would serve in his lifetime for civil disobedience.[84] Before entering prison, Gandhi published an essay titled "Last Message to South African Indians" in the Gujarati edition of *Indian Opinion*, calling upon Indians to remain firm in their pledge to undergo hardship and not be tempted to submit to the Asiatic Registration Act out of fear of the threat of fines, deportation, or imprisonment: "If only they will prepare themselves in their own minds, they will find that jail is not something to be frightened of."[85]

From his jail cell, Gandhi began to negotiate with General Jan Smuts over a compromise settlement that would entail the repeal of the Asiatic Registration Act in favor of the voluntary registration of Asians. According to Gandhi, the compromise would remove the "sting of compulsion" and treat Asians with "honour and responsibility."[86] This settlement was finalized on January 30, 1908, and Gandhi was set free. Gandhi now encouraged the Indian community to register voluntarily. Gandhi proclaimed this as a victory in *Indian Opinion*, but not everyone in the Indian community was happy with the compromise.[87] As Gandhi realized just how contested voluntary registration was, he published "A Dialogue on the Compromise" in the Gujarati edition of *Indian Opinion*. In this lengthy essay that took the form of a conversation between a reader and the editor, the editor attempts to convince the reader that the compromise settlement is a good thing and concludes that even if the reader disagrees, "Nothing can detract from the perfect success of our satyagraha campaign."[88]

Gandhi returned to Phoenix Settlement and immediately began training the settlers for further civil resistance campaigns. Central to this training was preparation for imprisonment, so Gandhi began to give daily lessons instructing the settlers about what to expect in prison. Gandhi also published a four-part essay on his experience in jail in weekly installments in *Indian Opinion* beginning on March 7, 1908. He began his first essay by stating that he wanted to share details of his experience in prison because he believed that the *satyagraha* campaign was a success, and that there were many other rights that the Indian community could yet win by courting imprisonment, and it was "therefore necessary for everyone to have an idea of the hardships of jail life."[89] The first hardship Gandhi emphasizes is that Asians are classified as Blacks, not whites, in the biracial segregated prison system. They are given prison garments stamped with "N" for "natives" and housed with the Black South African prisoners. Gandhi interpreted this as further proof that Indians were not respected by the colonial officials. "Kaffirs are as a rule uncivilized—the convicts even more so" he writes, using the pejorative term for Black South Africans.[90] Other hardships entail the limitations placed upon the Asian prisoners in terms of space, sleeping and bathing arrangements, and their daily routines and regulations. Gandhi describes the limited diet consisting mainly of mealie pap, a corn porridge that was a breakfast staple for many Black South Africans, and the petition he filed to request a diet more suitable for Indians.[91] Additional hardships include the very limited access of visitors (just one per month) and the lack of religious instruction for Hindus and Muslims (as opposed to Christian and Jewish inmates). He encourages prisoners not sentenced to hard labor to take advantage of the library and to develop an exercise routine to help pass the time usefully, for "those who can control their minds can find happiness even amidst hardships and enjoy being in jail."[92]

The residents at Phoenix Settlement were expected not only to labor at the printing press to publish *Indian Opinion* but also to be willing to engage in prison labor as needed. As Isabel Hofmeyr notes, Gandhi now came to see a connection between printing labor and prison labor:

> Gandhi saw Phoenix as a training ground for satyagrahis, and for prison. There was hence a rigorous labor regime of which the press formed a part. Working a hand-operated iron press is noisy, and it involves long hours. It is physically demanding, and those who did it on a full-time basis often developed back and kidney problems from the constant strain of pulling the bar of the press. Typesetters also developed aching fingers and felons (painful, pus-producing infections at the ends of their fingers). While the settlers at Phoenix appear to have avoided these ailments, they were nonetheless subject to the labor disciplines of the print shop, which increasingly became part of the project of training for satyagraha.[93]

Gandhi expected that the Phoenix settlers would train themselves daily to live a simple life of labor for the common good, and thereby, they could become leaders in future *satyagraha* struggles, able to persevere through the trials and tribulations of prison when necessary.

Universal Well-being

During Gandhi's time in prison, he reread Ruskin's *Unto This Last* and began translating it into Gujarati. After his release, he continued to work on this translation, sharing it with the Phoenix settlers and then publishing it in a series of nine essays in *Indian Opinion* in 1908. Significantly, Gandhi titled this work "Sarvodaya." Gandhi explained that his translation was not literal but was instead a paraphrase that sought to capture the essence of Ruskin's ideas:

> If we translated it, the common reader might be unable to follow some of the Biblical allusions, etc. We present therefore only the substance of Ruskin's work. We do not even explain what the title of the book means, for it can be understood only by a person who has read the Bible in English. But since the object which the book works towards is the welfare of all—that is, the advancement of all and not merely of the greatest number—we have entitled these articles "Sarvodaya."[94]

Gandhi explicitly contrasted this concept of universal well-being, *sarvodaya*, with the utilitarian emphasis on the majority. In the first essay in the series, Gandhi articulated his primary critique of Jeremy Bentham's utilitarian concept of justice:

> People in the West generally hold that it is man's duty to promote the happiness—prosperity, that is—of the greatest number. Happiness is taken to mean material happiness exclusively, that is, economic prosperity. If, in the pursuit of this happiness, moral laws are violated, it does not matter much. Again, as the object is the happiness of the greatest number, people in the West do not believe it to be wrong if it is secured at the cost of the minority.[95]

Gandhi insisted that true justice was to be found in the advancement of all, not merely the majority. Writing in the context of colonialism and capitalist industrialization, Gandhi paraphrased Ruskin to argue that utilitarian economics had advanced some people at the expense of others, and then presented his argument about how labor and economics should properly be understood.

Gandhi begins his "Sarvodaya" essays by arguing that the major fault of colonialist and capitalist economics is that in the focus on the law of supply and demand, humans are regarded simply as moneymaking machines. This overlooks the human bond of social affection. Using the example of a master-servant relationship, Gandhi states that a colonialist-capitalist theory of economics holds that it is profitable for the master to exact the maximum amount of work from the servant for the minimum wage. This theory holds that in the long run, this will benefit not only the master but the entire society and, through it, even the servant. The flaw with this theory, Gandhi argues, is that it assumes that the human servant is a mere machine, and it does not consider the importance of human affection: "in this case the motive power of the servant is his soul, and soul-force contradicts and falsifies all the calculations of the economists. The machine that is man cannot be driven by the money-fuel to do the maximum amount of work. Man will give of his best only when his affections are brought into play. The master-servant nexus must not be a pecuniary one, but one of love."[96]

Delving further into this theme of affection, Gandhi points out that a general who shares the joys and the hardships with his troops will be able to exact the most arduous work from them, even at the expense of their life in battle—for the general too is willing to give his life in battle. A factory supervisor, on the other hand, who simply demands the most work for the least pay from his factory workers develops a bond of disaffection and antagonism with them. The result is that these workers may go on strike or take different jobs.[97] But, Gandhi ponders, what if we asked the factory supervisor or the merchant to behave like a general or a ship's captain or a doctor—for all of these develop affection for the people they serve and are willing to sacrifice their lives in pursuit of their professional duties. Gandhi asks, "What, then, is the proper occasion for the merchant to lay down his life? This is a question which all, the merchant included, must ask themselves. The man who does not know when to die does not know how to live."[98] Gandhi proposes that the merchant should focus not only on profit but on his duty of producing or procuring high-quality commodities and distributing them at an affordable price, while ensuring the safety and well-being of his employees. "At every step, therefore, the merchant or the master must ask himself this question, 'Do I deal with my servants as I do with my sons?'. . . This is the true meaning of economics."[99]

Building upon this argument that the true meaning of economics entails a bond of affection between employer and employees, Gandhi asserts that political economics should concern itself not just with profits but with laborers. He writes, "The farmer who reaps his harvest at the right time, the builder who lays bricks properly, the carpenter who attends to woodwork with care, the woman who runs her kitchen efficiently are all true political economists. All of them add to the national income."[100] The goal of true economics should not be for a nation to accumulate as much wealth as possible at any cost. Rather, one must consider the moral question of how wealth is acquired: "the true law of economics is that men must be maintained in the best possible health, both of body and mind, and in the highest state of honour."[101] A person or a nation should not grow rich by cheating others or reducing them to beggars. Under a colonialist-capitalist theory of economics, the rich become richer and the poor become poorer. This, Gandhi argues, is "a kind of moral perversity that presages doom. To teach the people to get rich at any cost is to teach them an evil lesson."[102] Instead, true economics is the economics of justice, and true labor is that which is conducted by healthy workers in an honest and just system to produce useful products that enhance human life.[103]

In concluding his paraphrase of Ruskin's *Unto This Last*, Gandhi encourages his *Indian Opinion* readers to study this collection of "Sarvodaya" essays and to act on the ideas presented therein. He states that Ruskin's writings are a thousand times more applicable to Indians now than when they were written for his British countrymen, for many Indians are demanding political self-rule and want to follow in the economic footsteps of the West. This is not the future that Gandhi desires for Indians and India. He agrees that it is wrong in principle for any nation to rule over another, and he criticizes colonialism for its racist economics: "All nations look upon the black races as their legitimate prey. This is inevitable when money is the only thing that matters. Wherever they find any territory, they swoop down on it like crows upon carrion."[104] But real self-rule (*swaraj*) cannot be achieved by killing the British or setting up factories: "Real swaraj consists in restraint. He alone is capable of this who leads a moral life, does not cheat anyone, does not forsake truth and does his duty to his parents, his wife, his children, his servant and his neighbor. Such a man will enjoy swaraj wherever he may happen to live. A nation that has many such men always enjoys swaraj."[105]

At Phoenix Settlement, then, Gandhi sought to enact Ruskin's ideals by cultivating this self-rule within himself and encouraging his coresidents to cultivate it as well. Together, the Phoenix settlers led a disciplined life, waking early in the morning to farm their plots, build their houses, educate their children, and print the newspaper. Here, Indians and white South Africans agreed to live together in community as economic and political equals, seeking to create a utopic society that embodied Gandhi's vision of true economics as the path toward universal well-being. Here, Indians and white South Africans also united together in the campaign against the Asiatic Registration Act, printing *Indian Opinion* and training for the hardships of imprisonment as they began to wage a nonviolent battle for civil rights for the Indian minority in South Africa.

Self-Rule

Despite the compromise settlement that was reached between General Smuts and Gandhi, wherein the Asiatic Registration Act was to be repealed and replaced with the voluntary registration of Asians, by May of 1908, the act still had not been repealed. Gandhi announced in *Indian Opinion* that General Smuts was not upholding the settlement, and he explained the need to resume *satyagraha* to again fight for the repeal of the Asiatic Registration Act.[106] Gandhi began to advocate that the nine thousand Indians who had voluntarily registered should burn their registration cards. Gandhi and his coresidents at Phoenix Settlement also began to plan their protest, and Gandhi selected his eldest son, nineteen-year-old Harilal Gandhi, to lead it.

When the government began to arrest Indian street hawkers in Transvaal for trading without a license, Gandhi instructed Harilal to leave Phoenix Settlement and join the street hawkers. Harilal did so and was arrested on July 27, 1908, for selling fruit without the proper permit. Gandhi served as his lawyer in court and requested that Harilal receive the maximum sentence. Harilal was imprisoned for seven days with hard labor. Gandhi wrote in *Indian Opinion* that going to jail was an important part of Harilal's education, and he encouraged others to follow in Harilal's footsteps and flood the jails: "I want every Indian to do what Harilal has done. Harilal is only a child. He may have merely deferred to his father's wishes in acting in this manner. It is essential that every Indian should act on his own as Harilal did (at my insistence) and I wish everyone would do so. Satyagraha can be claimed to have been perfectly successful only if we do so."[107] Gandhi expected that Harilal and the other members of Phoenix Settlement would be leaders in the ongoing struggle against the Asiatic Registration Act, having learned while living in community together how to lead a disciplined life and undergo hardships in pursuit of universal well-being.

In the weeks after Harilal's arrest, the *satyagraha* struggle escalated. On August 16 and 23, Asians assembled in large gatherings to burn their voluntary registration certificates. Gandhi emphasized the value of suffering for the greater good over submitting to indignity in his speech to the crowd on August 16, stating, "if the burning of the certificates will impose untold suffering on you, the keeping of these certificates and submission to the Asiatic Act . . . will impose on my countrymen untold indignity, and I say with the greatest emphasis at my command that I would far rather that my countrymen suffered all they have to suffer than that they imposed on themselves indignity."[108] Harilal was arrested again on August 18 and sentenced to a month in prison with hard labor. Phoenix settlers began to refer to him as "Little Gandhi" in reference to his willingness to endure prison just like his father.[109]

The next stage of the struggle continued for another year and entailed the arrest of Indians who crossed the border into Transvaal Colony without possessing registration certificates. Gandhi was arrested for crossing from Natal Colony (where Phoenix Settlement was located) into Transvaal without the requisite registration certificate (which he had burned) on October 14, 1908, and sentenced to two months in prison with hard labor. Gandhi was again arrested on February 25, 1909, and sentenced to three months in prison with hard labor; Harilal was also arrested and sentenced to six months in prison. Other Phoenix settlers received sentences ranging from one to six months. After each release, Gandhi again described prison for readers of *Indian Opinion*, writing about what hard labor entailed for him, Harilal, and the other imprisoned settlers, and repeating his message that it was every reader's duty to find happiness in going to jail "for the sake of his motherland or his religion, in submitting himself to the suffering involved in it, or bearing hardships in other ways."[110] By June 1909, the number of Indians imprisoned had risen to 2,500.

Gandhi sailed to England on June 23, 1909, to seek a settlement with the imperial authorities, while Henry Polak sailed to India on a mission to raise funding and awareness in support of the *satyagraha* struggle in South Africa. Polak was successful in his mission, but Gandhi was not, although Gandhi did succeed in raising significant popular support. After four months of negotiations, Gandhi notified Lord Ampthill, chairman of the South Africa British Indian Committee, that he would "leave definitely on the 13th November for South Africa, and challenge arrest on the Transvaal border."[111] While in England, Gandhi continued to write for *Indian Opinion*, mailing essays back to Phoenix Settlement for publication and encouraging the settlers to be fearless: "A satyagrahi must be afraid neither of imprisonment nor of deportation. He must neither mind even being reduced to poverty, nor be frightened, if it comes to that, of being mashed into pulp with a mortar and pestle. A satyagrahi will shine the brighter and grow the more courageous the more he is crushed."[112]

Gandhi exchanged frequent letters with Henry Polak while in England, encouraging Polak to remind the leaders he met with in India that they should support the Indian cause in South Africa, for "in fighting the battle, we are presenting the Indian Motherland with a disciplined army of the future; an army that will be able to give a good account of itself against any amount of brute force that may be matched against it."[113] In their private correspondence, Gandhi revealed to Polak that he had reached some "definite conclusions" during his trip, and he lists them in sixteen points in a letter dated October 14, 1909. In these points, Gandhi begins to articulate his criticism of modern civilization, which he dismisses as "purely material," and expresses his concern that if British rule was replaced with Indian rule based on modern methods, India would be no better morally, albeit perhaps it would retain more of its wealth. Gandhi asserts, "India's salvation lies in unlearning what she has learnt during the past fifty years. The railways, telegraphs, hospitals, lawyers, doctors, and such like have all to go, and the so-called upper classes have to learn to live conscientiously and religiously and deliberately the simple peasant life, knowing it to be a life giving true happiness."[114]

Gandhi departed England on November 13, 1909. On his return voyage to South Africa aboard the SS *Kildonan Castle* from November 13 to November 30,

Gandhi wrote his most famous political treatise, *Indian Home Rule* (*Hind Swaraj*), building upon the conclusions he had set forth in his letter to Henry Polak. In this treatise, Gandhi articulates his vision for independent India. He decries not only British colonization but also modern industrial civilization, which he labels a "disease." Instead, his ideal India is village-based. In Gandhi's ideal India, there are no cities, no railways, and no machinery save hand-built plows and spinning wheels. There are no rich and poor, no haves and have-nots; everyone works and equally shares the fruits of their communal labor. At this time, many nationalist Indians were advocating for *swaraj*, a term that translates as "self-rule" and was then commonly used to refer to the political goal of Indian home rule as opposed to British colonial rule; and some nationalists advocated the use of violent methods to obtain home rule. But in *Indian Home Rule*, Gandhi built upon the argument presented in his "Sarvodaya" paraphrase of Ruskin's *Unto This Last* and emphasized the need to understand *swaraj* as self-rule on an individual level, writing, "If we become free, India is free. And in this thought you have a definition of Swaraj. It is Swaraj when we learn to rule ourselves. It is, therefore, in the palm of our hands. . . . But such Swaraj has to be experienced, by each one for himself."[115] Furthermore, Gandhi argues, such *swaraj*, as he defines it, does not necessarily entail the expulsion of the English from India, for "if the English become Indianised, we can accommodate them. If they wish to remain in India along with their civilization, there is no room for them. It lies with us to bring about such a state of things."[116]

Although *Indian Home Rule* has normally been interpreted as a political treatise advocating a nonviolent approach to Indian independence, it is far more than this—in this concise argument, Gandhi sets forth in writing the ideals that he and his coresidents had begun trying to live by at his first intentional community, Phoenix Settlement. For Gandhi, the essence of freedom was not political liberty; it was self-rule in the sense of self-mastery and restraint. He argued that such self-rule was central, first and foremost, at the individual level, as part of everyday communal life, for it was only when each individual practiced self-rule that the community as a whole could flourish, leading the way to universal well-being. It is worth highlighting that in order to learn such individual restraint, one had to be a resident in a community. For Gandhi, individual self-control was fundamentally social, for it was focused both on self-discipline and on appropriate affection for other members of one's community. Written in Gujarati in the form of a dialogue between a reader and an editor, Gandhi first published *Indian Home Rule* in two installments on December 11 and 18, 1909. In January 1910, it was published from the Phoenix printing press in booklet form, first in Gujarati and then in English for wider distribution as well as transparency after the British colonial government of India proscribed it as seditious.[117]

Phoenix Settlement was Gandhi's first experiment in communal living, and his years living in this community were foundational for both his personal and political development. As it became apparent that the *satyagraha* struggle in South Africa would continue for the foreseeable future, Gandhi sought support for those families whose primary breadwinners had been imprisoned or deported for civil disobedience. Gandhi's friend Hermann Kallenbach offered to Gandhi and the *satyagrahis* the use of a farm, located twenty-one miles outside of Johannesburg, rent free for the duration of the struggle. Gandhi then established his second intentional community in June of 1910, named Tolstoy Farm.

Interlude 1

Phoenix Settlement after Gandhi

Figure 1. Sarvodaya House at Phoenix Settlement. Photo by Curran Lyons.

Standing in front of Sarvodaya House, Gandhi's home at Phoenix Settlement, I took in its simple design—a small bungalow, with its four walls and roof made from corrugated metal, and a row of windows at the front. The house is positioned on a hilltop, and from inside, one can take in the view of the Inanda Valley and the surrounding hills. Looking out at this view from what was once Gandhi's porch, gazing past the plateau where Gandhi would have tended his garden plot, I took in the vast number of small homes dotting every space on the hillside along the horizon. Phoenix Settlement is now a suburb of the city of Durban due to urban sprawl. In Gandhi's day, by contrast, this was rural farmland, and Gandhi's view from his home would have been of sugarcane fields dotted with a small scattering of round Zulu huts. Ela Gandhi, Gandhi's granddaughter, had graciously agreed to meet me at Phoenix Settlement on my first visit there (in 2015) to give me a personal tour and answer my questions about its history. Walking around Sarvodaya House with her, I was awestruck not only by Gandhi's choice to forego the everyday conveniences afforded by his profession as a lawyer working in the city of Durban, in order to try to build a more equitable communal life on this rural farmland, but also by the multigenerational impact this decision had upon one branch of the Gandhi family lineage.

Here at Phoenix Settlement, Gandhi lived in a small home that he built by hand; he slept on raised wooden floors that were added to keep out snakes and mice and to help with water drainage during the rainy season; he showered using a garden watering can for lack of indoor plumbing; and he learned to grow vegetables and collect rainwater while also running the printing press. It was in this rustic structure, which Gandhi named Sarvodaya House (House of Universal Well-being), that he began his experiments with utopia in 1904, taking the first step in what would become his lifelong journey to live a communal life dedicated to the pursuit of universal well-being (*sarvodaya*).

When Gandhi eventually left South Africa in 1914 to return to India, he gave the residents of Phoenix Settlement the option of joining him in India, where they would build a new community together, or remaining at Phoenix Settlement to carry on its mission. Prior to departing South Africa, Gandhi set up a board of trustees (composed of members of both Indian and European heritage) and filed a legal trust, the Phoenix Trust Deed (1912), to ensure the continued collective management of the community in accordance with its mission. This document enumerated eight specific components of its mission that were to be upheld by the settlers and the trustees:

1. So far as possible to order their lives so as to be able ultimately to earn their living by handicraft or agriculture carried on without the aid so far as possible of machinery;
2. To work publicly so as to promote a better understanding between the Europeans and British Indians established in South Africa, and to voice and work to remove the grievances of the latter;
3. To follow and promote the ideals set forth by Tolstoy and Ruskin in their lives and works;

Figure 2. Printing press building at Phoenix Settlement. Photo by Karline McLain.

4. To promote purity of private life in individuals by living pure lives themselves;
5. To establish a school for the education principally of Indian children mainly through their own vernaculars;
6. To establish a sanatorium and hygienic institute, with a view to the prevention of disease by methods generally known as "nature treatment";
7. To train themselves generally for the service of humanity;
8. To conduct the said *Indian Opinion* for the advancement of the ideals mentioned in the foregoing paragraphs.[1]

Gandhi's wife and three younger children returned to India with him (Gandhi's eldest son, Harilal, had already returned to India), and a couple dozen members of the extended Phoenix "family" also decided to go to India. Many other residents chose to remain in South Africa, including Albert West, who continued to live at Phoenix Settlement with his family, and who now served as editor of *Indian Opinion.*

In 1917, Gandhi's second-eldest son, Manilal—then twenty-five years old—returned to South Africa to help run Phoenix Settlement. In 1920, Manilal took

Figure 3. Kasturba Bhavan at Phoenix Settlement. Photo by Karline McLain.

over as the editor of *Indian Opinion* and made South Africa his permanent home. Manilal married his wife, Sushila, in 1927, and together, they raised their children—Sita, Arun, and Ela—at Phoenix Settlement.[2]

Manilal and Sushila lived in Sarvodaya House until 1944, when they built a larger house of their own at Phoenix Settlement for their growing family. This house, called "Kasturba Bhavan" (named after Manilal's mother and Gandhi's wife, Kasturba), was one story and made of brick rather than corrugated metal. It incorporated a small garage as well as a rooftop deck, from where I took in stunning 360-degree views of the Inanda Valley region.

Manilal served as the manager of Phoenix Settlement and the editor of *Indian Opinion* from 1920 until his death in 1956. Sushila shared in this labor alongside Manilal, taking on increasing responsibilities over time. Sushila had begun working with the press, learning to set Gujarati type in the first months after her marriage to Manilal. In the ensuing years, she became the manager of the paper's Gujarati-language section and took up managing the publication of the paper entirely, as well as the affairs of the community, whenever Manilal was traveling beyond the settlement. After Manilal's death, Sushila did not initially want to manage Phoenix Settlement and the *Indian Opinion* newspaper without her husband at her side, writing in a letter, "I wish to free myself from the responsibilities of the newspaper and the 100 acres land," and noting that she wanted to pass this role on to someone else who would uphold Gandhi's principles.[3] Nonetheless, Sushila rose to the occasion, working to manage both the settlement and the press. As Uma Dhupelia Mesthrie notes, this was a difficult time for Sushila, not only because it was a period of mourning but also because she faced financial difficulties. Sushila received only £5 per month from the Phoenix Settlement trust in 1956 for her work at the press, whereas Manilal had received £100 per month. In her letters, she wrote about her struggle to have the trustees transfer her husband's monthly stipend into her name for doing his work, asking, "Is it not my right to ask for six months salary?" and complaining, "If I stay here I cannot live on grass and water."[4]

The 1950s through the 1970s were a time of rapid change for the Phoenix Settlement community. In 1961, Sushila's youngest child, Ela Gandhi (also known as Ela Ramgobin), moved back to Phoenix Settlement. Ela was then twenty-one years old, and she and her husband, Mewa Ramgobin, moved in to help Sushila run the settlement and to raise their own children there. Ela's five children were the fourth generation of the Gandhi family to live at Phoenix Settlement. Sushila decided to shut down the printing press, publishing the last edition of *Indian Opinion* in August 1961. She turned her energy instead to a new medical clinic, named the Mahatma Gandhi Clinic, which she opened two months later in the press building with a mission of providing needed health care to the residents of the Inanda Valley. Doctors came twice a week to treat local patients, predominantly Black South Africans, and Sushila felt that the clinic met a community need and also reenergized the settlement, writing, "this way more life has been injected into the settlement."[5] Sushila, Ela, and other trustees worked on fundraising and added new buildings to the settlement to meet additional community needs. These included a larger building for the Kasturba Gandhi School that was added in 1954 (originally, students were taught in the small Sarvodaya House, but the new building allowed for 270 students to enroll); a new building for the Mahatma Gandhi Clinic in 1969 and 1970; and the addition of a new building to serve as the community museum and library in 1969 and 1970.

These decades also saw a new round of nonviolent activism at Phoenix Settlement in response to increasing apartheid laws being enacted in South Africa after 1948. In 1950, the Population Registration Act classified all South Africans into one of four racial groups (White, Black, Colored, and Indian), and the government began to strictly segregate neighborhoods under the Group Areas Act and to limit non-white access to public spaces. Before his death, Manilal actively defied these apartheid rules by entering places demarcated "Whites Only" and by participating in boycotts and other nonviolent acts of the Disobedience Campaign (1952) led by the African National Congress. Manilal was arrested and imprisoned numerous times for this activism. Sushila also took part in some of the nonviolent protests. Anti-apartheid activism continued at Phoenix Settlement in the years after Manilal's death. For instance, the community hosted a five-day-long fast in 1960 to protest against the police firing upon nonviolent protestors in the Sharpeville Massacre and the placement of anti-apartheid activists under house arrest. Ela Gandhi grew increasingly active in the anti-apartheid protest movement, joining the Natal Indian Congress and the United Democratic Front. In the 1970s, however, the government banned Ela Gandhi from political activism, and she was subjected to house arrest for a total of nine years for her opposition to apartheid.[6]

During the late 1970s and early 1980s, there were rising tensions in the Inanda Valley area and the area surrounding Phoenix Settlement in particular. As a result of the Group Areas Act, an increasing number of displaced Indians were being relocated to Phoenix Township, an apartheid housing scheme located to the east of Phoenix Settlement, while an increasing number of displaced Black South Africans were settling into a new informal settlement they called Bhambayi near the Mahatma Gandhi Clinic. Ela Gandhi and her husband decided to move their family from Phoenix Settlement into a new house of their own in Verulam, a town north of Durban that had been proclaimed a group area for Indians by the government. Sushila, then sixty-nine years old, remained at Phoenix Settlement for a short time but soon realized that her health necessitated greater support from family, and she too moved away from Phoenix Settlement.[7] While Sushila and Ela remained active as trustees, they no longer lived on the land. Tensions continued to rise as more and more displaced families moved into the Inanda Valley. The situation came to a head during the Inanda Riots of 1985, when urban incendiarism caused much damage to both Indian and Black South African homes and businesses. At Phoenix Settlement, Gandhi's former home, Sarvodaya House, was burned down, as were most of the other houses, along with the primary school. Kasturba Bhavan and the printing press building survived the arson but were looted. In addition to this damage, the land was encroached overnight, with thousands of rudimentary dwellings quickly erected all over the Phoenix Settlement territory by Black South Africans seeking claim to the land.[8]

Phoenix Settlement has now been officially recognized as a national heritage site in South Africa (since 2020). Following the end of apartheid in 1994, significant efforts have been undertaken to preserve what remains of the historic legacy of Phoenix Settlement, with funds raised by members of the Phoenix Settlement Trust and the broader Indian community in South Africa. Trustees have also worked over the past two decades to promote tourism to Phoenix Settlement as part of the burgeoning Inanda Heritage Route.[9] The settlement currently has a much smaller footprint than it did in Gandhi's time: the medical clinic is now part of the township and officially outside of the heritage site, and there is no longer a working farm or most of the houses of the once residential community. Kasturba Bhavan and the printing press building still stand. Gandhi's home, Sarvodaya House, was rebuilt by the architect Rodney Harber to resemble the original corrugated iron house, and it was inaugurated in 2000 by President Thabo Mbeki. Sarvodaya House now serves as a small museum.

Inside the rebuilt Sarvodaya House, the museum tells the story of Gandhi's emergent leadership in the struggle for the Indian community's civil rights in South Africa under the colonial regime. It equally seeks to position Gandhi as an important figure in modern South African history and as an ally of Black South Africans in the fight for equality. A statement placed at the beginning of the museum pathway sets forth this agenda. Titled "South Africa: The Nursery for Gandhi's Experiments with Truth," it reads:

> Gandhi lived in South Africa for 21 years. Although he never directly interfered in the local politics of the black versus the racist regime and confined his activities within the Indian community, the import of his leadership did not go unnoticed by the native black oppressed populace of South Africa, particularly the unity that he could wrought amongst the Indians belonging to different castes, region[s] and communities. Gandhi suffered prison terms in South Africa, he led the great march against the unethical laws of the land against the indentured labourers. His non-violent satyagraha was observed and studied, albeit from a distance by the black leadership. The unshackling of the majestic personality of black power in South Africa is the culmination of this same fight.[10]

The small exhibit in Sarvodaya House is complemented by a larger exhibit in another building on the Phoenix Settlement grounds, the Mahatma Gandhi Interpretation Centre. This building serves as a community space and contains an exhibit that grounds Gandhi in the larger context of the Inanda Valley region and the South African struggle against apartheid. A highlighted map of Inanda shows that John Dube, Mahatma Gandhi, Isaiah Shembe, and the Inanda Seminary were all neighbors, and states that they "shared a deep spirituality, a lively social conscience, a commitment to hard work, a hunger for education, and an intense concern for the weakest and poorest in society."[11] Displays on each of these figures and their intentional communities provide further background about their various reform efforts. Collectively, we are told, they were committed to social justice: "Dube, Gandhiji and Shembe shared a burning desire to right the wrongs of society. In South Africa in the early twentieth century these wrongs were glaringly obvious: the oppression of the majority of people by a small white minority, and, as a result, the social, economic, and political dispossession of black, Indian, and coloured South Africans."[12]

Beyond these two indoor exhibits, numbered plaques located throughout Phoenix Settlement highlight important places (such as the printing press and the clinic) or events (such as the founding of the settlement). One plaque reminds visitors of the long history of activism at Phoenix, linking Gandhi's efforts on behalf of the Indian community to the anti-apartheid activism that later took place at the settlement in the 1960s and 70s:

> Gandhiji believed that places like Phoenix were ideal training grounds for the struggle against social injustice. In the 1960s and 1970s Phoenix attracted people from all over the political spectrum. Steve Biko, Rick Turner, Beyers Naude, Mewa Ramgobin, Barney Pityana and Pravin Gordhan, among others, all participated in political education and training programmes at Phoenix. . . . Volunteerism took root at Phoenix as a way to reconstruct the damages caused by apartheid.[13]

In the past decade, several scholars have commented on Gandhi's anti-Blackness during his twenty-one years in South Africa, citing not only his usage of the pejorative term "Kaffir" in his public writings but also his efforts to better the status of the Indian community in South Africa to the exclusion of the native African communities. For instance, Ashwin Desai and Goolam Vahed critique those who wrap Gandhi "in the halo of an anti-racist, anti-colonial fighter on African soil" and argue, "instead of helping break down colonial racial boundaries, let alone other boundaries that divided Empire's subjects such as gender, class, and sexuality, Gandhi's strategic approach to fend off discriminatory legislation and incrementally improve the lot of Indians resulted in his maintaining strict segregation from Africans and, on occasion, supporting the British in their quest to subjugate them."[14]

Other scholars, however, have drawn attention to the gradual evolution in Gandhi's attitude toward Black South Africans. Ajay Skaria, for instance, writes that the short answer to the question of whether Gandhi was racist is, "before 1906, emphatically yes; from 1906 to 1913, qualifiedly yes; after 1913 or so, increasingly no."[15] These scholars attribute Gandhi's progressive attitude toward race to his increasing awareness of the adverse impacts of colonialism on multiple subaltern communities, including Black South Africans, during his years of political activism in South Africa. I would add that it was not only Gandhi's political activism and his evolution as a spiritual person but also his residential experiences—living as neighbors at Phoenix Settlement next to Dube's Ohlange Institute, as well as temporarily co-residing with Black South Africans during his numerous prison terms in South Africa—that contributed significantly to the transformation of his attitude toward race during his many years in South Africa. Recognizing the contested conversation about Gandhi and race, the museum exhibits at Phoenix Settlement are intended to remember both the settlement itself as a site of inclusive activism and to preserve a place for Gandhi specifically among the leaders of South Africa's struggle for equality and democracy.

2

Tolstoy Farm

Gandhi founded Tolstoy Farm, his second intentional community, in 1910 as a satellite of his first community, Phoenix Settlement. The need for a second site came about as a result of the ongoing protest against the discriminatory Asiatic Registration Act (deemed the "Black Act" by many Indians in South Africa). Gandhi and his coresidents at Phoenix Settlement had begun protesting this act when it became law in 1906 through nonviolent civil disobedience, which Gandhi called *satyagraha*. As discussed in chapter 1, this legislation required all Asians in the Transvaal Colony of South Africa to register with the government, including fingerprinting and body stripping to identify birthmarks. Gandhi viewed this law as discriminatory and humiliating and began organizing a protest. Gandhi was first arrested on January 10, 1908, for refusing to submit to this law, and he was sentenced to two months in prison. Following Gandhi's arrest, a wave of *satyagrahis* (nonviolent civil resisters) was also arrested, with over one hundred Indians arriving during Gandhi's first week in prison in Johannesburg. By June 1909, the number of political prisoners had risen to 2,500. By 1910, as the number of political prisoners continued to rise, and as discharged prisoners were being rearrested and resentenced for continuing their refusal to submit to the law, several things became clear to Gandhi. First, the struggle would need to persist for the foreseeable future. Second, a support system was needed for the families whose primary breadwinners were being imprisoned or deported for civil disobedience. Third, conducting the struggle from Phoenix Settlement in Durban was not sustainable, and Gandhi needed a home base closer to Johannesburg that would be within a day's commute of the court and the prison.

Gandhi called upon his fellow Indians for support, writing in his weekly newspaper, *Indian Opinion*, in May of 1910 that while the civil resisters have a duty to continue their civil disobedience campaign until the unjust law is rectified, so too does the Indian community in South Africa have a reciprocal duty to open up their homes in support of such civil resisters and their families:

> Whatever happens, as passive resisters they have only one course left open, and that is to abide by their obligation not to submit to the Law until the grievance for which they have been suffering has been redressed, irrespective of the results that may follow such a course. The Indians of Durban, too, have a duty to perform. It will be expected of them that they receive these passive resisters and make them as comfortable as possible, and give them such an ovation as would enable them to know that their self-sacrificing work is being appreciated by their countrymen throughout South Africa, and to enable the South African Government to understand that the whole of the Indian community in South Africa is at the back of the movement.[1]

Such calls resulted in temporary aid for the civil resisters and their families, in the form of short-term housing and financial donations. Gandhi had been maintaining the families of imprisoned civil resisters on a monthly allowance provided through such donations, but this was expensive, and Gandhi realized that it would not permit the movement to be conducted for the length of time that might be needed to effect change.[2] He looked for a more long-term solution and decided, "There was only one solution for this difficulty, namely, that all the families should be kept at one place and should become members of a sort of co-operative commonwealth. . . . Public funds would largely be saved and the families of Satyagrahis would be trained to live a new and simple life in harmony with one another. Indians belonging to various provinces and professing diverse faiths would have an opportunity of living together."[3] As he had previously done in Durban, here too, in Johannesburg, Gandhi determined it was important to get away from the city—city life was too costly, it would be too hard to find shelter for a significant number of people, and it held too many distractions. Gandhi considered relocating the families to Phoenix Settlement but ultimately decided that at a distance of three hundred miles from Johannesburg, it was too far away from the current center of the protest movement, and the families would not want to be so far from their loved ones in prison. The place, then, should ideally be in a rural area in the Transvaal Colony and near the city of Johannesburg.[4]

At this time, Gandhi's friend Hermann Kallenbach offered to purchase a sizeable tract of farmland. Unlike Natal Colony—where free Indians were permitted to own land and, thus, Gandhi could purchase the farmland for Phoenix Settlement himself—in Transvaal Colony, Indians were barred from legally owning land. Thus, in order to establish a home base near Johannesburg from which he could lead the civil disobedience campaign and shelter the civil resisters and their families, Gandhi needed the support of a white ally. Hermann Kallenbach spoke with Gandhi and offered to purchase farmland outside of Johannesburg, to which Gandhi agreed. The terms of the agreement were spelled out formally in a letter dated May 30, 1910, wherein Kallenbach noted, "In accordance with our conversation, I offer to you the use of my farm near Lawley for passive resisters and their indigent families; the families and passive resisters to live on the farm free of any rent or charge, as long as the struggle with the Transvaal Government lasts. They may also use, free of charge, all the buildings not at present used by me."[5] In addition to providing the use of the farm free of charge, Kallenbach also specified that on the termination of occupation, he would pay for any structural alterations, additions, or improvements made by the settlers, as well as all agricultural improvements. In Gandhi's return letter, he expressed his gratitude to Kallenbach and formally accepted the offer.[6]

Gandhi published these letters in *Indian Opinion* on June 11, 1910, along with separate essays in the English and Gujarati editions of the newspaper. The English edition of this publication catered to Indians in South Africa who were not Gujarati speakers, as well as white readers who may—or may not—have been sympathetic to the Indian struggle for civil rights in South Africa. In the English essay, Gandhi implicitly addressed his white readers when he praised Kallenbach and highlighted how such tangible acts of generosity by white allies were instrumental to fostering greater mutuality between whites and non-whites: "The terms of Mr. Kallenbach's letter are one-sided. He has given all he legitimately could and has expected no return. He does not want to develop his estate through the labour of those passive resisters who could put in their labour without paying them for it. Acts such as Mr. Kallenbach's are calculated to bring East and West nearer in real fellowship than any amount of rhetorical writing or speaking."[7] The Gujarati edition of this publication, on the other hand, targeted free Indians who were supportive of—and ideally active participants in—the Indian struggle for civil rights. In the Gujarati essay on June 11, Gandhi addresses these Indian readers and urges the families of civil resisters to take advantage of Kallenbach's generous offer and relocate to the farm:

> We place a very high value on Mr. Kallenbach's offer of his farm for the benefit of satyagrahis. If the families of the latter use it well, we shall have no occasion for anxiety, however long the struggle lasts. There will be much saving in expenditure, and those who settle on the farm will learn to be happy. They will have, on the farm, a noble life in place of the unclean and monotonous way of town-life. Moreover, what they will learn on the farm will prove useful for a life-time. Indeed, we have said in the past that the Indian community would be well rewarded if it were to take to agriculture and would be saved the anxieties incidental to business. We have to pay a heavy price for not recognizing the value of this best of

> occupations. We hope the leaders [of the Indian community] will address letters of thanks to Mr. Kallenbach. His gift will be appreciated at its proper worth only when Indians settle there in large numbers.[8]

By making public the terms of Kallenbach's offer of his farm to the civil resisters in *Indian Opinion*, Gandhi not only highlighted some of the injustices faced by Indians in South Africa (Indians could not own land in the Transvaal; Indians were often taken advantage of as indentured laborers on white-owned farms in South Africa; Indians were being penalized for fighting for their civil rights) but also proposed a path forward—the "experiment" of Tolstoy Farm. Indian readers and white allies should consider joining Tolstoy Farm, where they would live together with Gandhi and Kallenbach and the civil resisters. On this farm, they would learn to work the land and live a simple life in community together while continuing the struggle for civil rights. Furthermore, Gandhi appeals to those members of the Indian and white communities in South Africa who are not willing or able to join them on the farm, emphasizing that they can still support the civil disobedience movement through monetary support of Tolstoy Farm.

Gandhi lived at Tolstoy Farm for four years only, from 1910 to 1914. Despite the short duration of this intentional community, it was a crucial site for the ongoing evolution in Gandhi's thinking about his philosophy of universal well-being, *sarvodaya*. Life at Tolstoy Farm entailed continuities with the rules and routines set at Phoenix Settlement, but it also included important additional experiments as Gandhi and his coresidents continually sought to refine and implement this utopian philosophy. At Tolstoy Farm, Gandhi placed an increasing emphasis on self-discipline and voluntary suffering in all aspects of everyday life, from diet to dress to mode of sleep. Eventually, Gandhi encouraged residents to elect to live the life of prisoners on the farm as preparation for their participation in civil disobedience campaigns.

The Move to Tolstoy Farm

Gandhi first met Hermann Kallenbach (1871–1945) in South Africa in 1903 through a mutual friend. Gandhi's recollection of his first impression of Kallenbach focuses on two of his character traits, which Gandhi perceived as contradictory: his otherworldly spiritualism and his this-worldly materialism. Gandhi writes in his autobiography that in their first meeting, Kallenbach asked Gandhi "searching questions concerning matters of religion," and they spoke of the historical Buddha's renunciation; Gandhi also writes that in this meeting, he was startled by Kallenbach's "love of luxury and extravagance."[9] This meeting set the stage for many more conversations in the years to come, conversations that would lead to important experiments in communal living in each of their lives and transform both of them. It is important to note, however, that what we know of the relationship between Gandhi and Kallenbach comes primarily from Gandhi's perspective, as his letters to Kallenbach have been archived among his collected works, and he wrote about his relationship with Kallenbach in his autobiography and other books. Unfortunately, the majority of Kallenbach's letters to Gandhi are no longer extant.[10] However, some of Kallenbach's correspondence with his siblings has been preserved, and I have read these letters carefully to draw Kallenbach's voice into this chapter as the cofounder of Tolstoy Farm.

Hermann Kallenbach was born into a large Lithuanian Jewish family in 1871. He was educated in German schools and became an apprentice carpenter in Konigsberg in 1890, and then an apprentice mason in Stuttgart. He studied at the Royal School for Architects in Stuttgart, graduating in 1896 with qualifications as a carpenter, mason, and architect. After graduating and completing a year of military service, Kallenbach moved to Johannesburg, South Africa, where he joined two of his uncles and began practicing as an architect, eventually becoming a senior partner in the firm Kallenbach & Reynolds.[11] In the early years of Kallenbach's acquaintance with Gandhi, they met over meals at vegetarian restaurants when Gandhi was working in Johannesburg, and Gandhi persuaded Kallenbach to join him in implementing daily habits of self-discipline, including giving up meat, alcohol, and tobacco, and reducing his expenditures.

When Gandhi was released from prison in 1908, he decided it was no longer feasible to continue waging the civil disobedience campaign from Phoenix Settlement. Leaving his wife and his four sons at Phoenix for the time being, and giving up his Johannesburg lease as a cost-saving measure, Gandhi began to live with Kallenbach at his home in Johannesburg. Writing about this time, Gandhi describes Kallenbach as "a man of strong feelings, wide sympathies and childlike simplicity. He is an architect by profession, but there is no work, however lowly, which he would consider to be beneath his dignity. When I broke up my Johannesburg establishment, I lived with him, but he would be hurt if I offered to pay him my share of the household expenses, and would plead that I was responsible for considerable savings in his domestic economy."[12] Gandhi notes in his autobiography that when he first met Kallenbach, he helped him reduce his monthly expenses by 90 percent.[13]

Gandhi and Kallenbach became very close friends during this time. Gandhi describes Kallenbach as his chief companion in making dietary experiments.[14] At Gandhi's prodding, Kallenbach gave up eating red meat first, then fish, and then began to simplify his diet even further following Gandhi's lead. Under Gandhi's tutelage, Kallenbach also grew more aware of—and then outspoken about—race relations in South Africa. When Gandhi was on trial or imprisoned, Kallenbach would visit and bring him meals, and he began to show his support for other civil resisters from Phoenix Settlement by visiting many of them in prison as well.[15]

Kallenbach wrote letters to *The Star* newspaper in Johannesburg and to *The Times* in London, criticizing the Asiatic Registration Act and supporting the Indians' struggle for civil rights. In a letter to *The Times*, which was signed by Kallenbach and twenty-six other white South Africans, he notes that the "Asiatics' complaints are, on the whole, justified," and then praises their nonviolent resistance, describes the suffering they undergo in and out of prison, and calls for a settlement that concedes to the Asiatic demands.[16] As Thomas Weber notes, such opinion pieces would have been a risky public statement, with the potential for other whites in South Africa to see Kallenbach, a successful businessman, branded a race traitor.[17]

In 1908, Kallenbach was clearly influenced by Gandhi, but he was not willing to fully embrace Gandhi's lifestyle by moving to Phoenix Settlement. In a letter to his brother Simon dated June 10, 1908, Kallenbach praised the merits of Phoenix Settlement, noting that Gandhi had founded it as part of his mission to lead the Indians in South Africa toward greater political equality, while simultaneously reassuring his brother that he did not intend to uproot his professional lifestyle in Johannesburg and move to join the Phoenix community:

> For this purpose he [Gandhi] has founded a colony named "Phoenix" about 14 miles from Durban on which approximately 60 persons have made their homes, helping in agricultural aspects of country life. There is a school and a prayer room, and the machinery for a printing press. The system of the colony is to educate and show them a way of life in which they can live as an example to their fellow Indians, a tremendously modest and yet a lovable way of life. I do *not* intend to join the community of this colony.[18]

By 1910, however, Kallenbach was ready to fully participate in the communal life. And so it was that in May of 1910, Hermann Kallenbach purchased 1,100 acres of farmland in a rural setting twenty-two miles southwest of Johannesburg. Though in a rural setting, the land was just a twenty-minute walk from the Lawley train station, where one could catch the train to Johannesburg and arrive in the city an hour and a half later. The farmland had two wells and a small spring, and it was fertile, with a thousand fruit and nut trees—peaches, apricots, figs, almonds, and walnuts.[19] A dilapidated four-room farmhouse came with the land, and though it was in dire need of repair, Gandhi and Kallenbach agreed that it was suitable for their immediate habitation while they planned their additions to the property in preparation for the arrival of the civil resisters and their families.

Gandhi and Kallenbach decided to name the place Tolstoy Farm in honor of Count Leo Tolstoy. Gandhi first read Tolstoy's *The Kingdom of God Is Within You* in the 1890s, and he described the book as leaving an "abiding impression" on him throughout his lifetime.[20] Kallenbach was also familiar with Tolstoy's writings and was particularly touched by *A Confession*.[21] Gandhi appreciated Tolstoy's ethical interpretation of religion, and he was drawn to Tolstoy's advocacy of a simple and nonviolent life. He agreed with Tolstoy's rejection of industrial civilization, and he appreciated that Tolstoy not only advocated nonviolent resistance but also enacted it. Gandhi praised Tolstoy in public speeches, in letters to friends and colleagues, and to residents at Phoenix Settlement as the "best and brightest" exponent of the doctrine of nonviolence.[22] After being released from prison in May 1909, Gandhi traveled briefly to London in an attempt to educate and influence British authorities about the Indian cause in South Africa. While in London, Gandhi wrote his first letter to Tolstoy, describing the civil disobedience struggle in South Africa and also asking for permission to translate and print Tolstoy's "Letter to a Hindoo [Hindu]."[23] Between 1909 and 1910, Gandhi and Tolstoy exchanged a series of letters, and Gandhi sent him an English translation of his political treatise, *Indian Home Rule* (*Hind Swaraj*). During this same trip to London, Gandhi was inspired to visit Whiteway in the Cotswolds, a former Tolstoyan colony. He briefly describes this visit in a letter to Henry Polak (a coresident at Phoenix Settlement), stating it was a delightful walk in charming country but noting his disappointment that the "settlers have not been able to live up to the ideal" and singling out only one resident who has been able to maintain his house and land using simple tools and no modern machinery.[24]

Kallenbach now determined to leave behind his former life of material abundance and embrace these Tolstoyan ideals alongside Gandhi. In a letter to his brother Simon in August 1910, he wrote that he considered the purchase of Tolstoy Farm

> neither as an extreme return to natural life, nor as an abrupt transition from civilization to nature. Already as a schoolboy, I loved God's free nature, but only now circumstances have allowed me to realize this love of nature by purchasing a farm. The presence of the Indians on the farm is of mutual advantage. . . . What Tolstoy wants and what I want too, am striving for, is to recognize the right . . . to live accordingly without disturbing my fellow beings as far as possible.[25]

On June 4, 1910, Gandhi and Kallenbach, along with Gandhi's two eldest sons, Harilal and Manilal, moved to the farm to begin preparing it for additional residents.

Daily Life at Tolstoy Farm

At Tolstoy Farm, the residents built upon many of the values and practices from Phoenix Settlement, but they also undertook additional experiments in cohousing, celibacy, farming, dietary restriction, economic self-sufficiency, alternative medicine, homeschooling, and multifaith community building as their collective understanding of universal well-being continued to evolve. The first pressing need on Tolstoy Farm was to construct shelter for the civil resisters and their families. When the farm was purchased, Gandhi was providing monetary support for approximately fifty families.[26] He anticipated that some of these families would relocate to the farm and that he would need additional space for a number of younger, unmarried men who would be housed there in between their successive prison terms. Rather than follow the model at Phoenix, wherein separate plots were allotted to each settler or family unit for the construction of their own house and the cultivation of their own garden, Gandhi and Kallenbach decided to use a dormitory-style arrangement, with one building for male settlers and another for female settlers and young children: "As regards accommodation for families, we resolved from the first that the men and women should be housed separately. The houses therefore were to be built in two separate blocks, each at some distance from the other. For the time it was considered sufficient to provide accommodation for ten women and sixty men."[27]

As discussed in chapter 1, Gandhi had taken a vow of celibacy (*brahmacharya*) in 1906. He viewed this vow as central to his pursuit of spiritual liberation (*moksha*, in keeping with the traditional Indian religious emphasis on renunciation) and also to his pursuit of communal equality at Phoenix Settlement (as he wanted to treat all coresidents equally without privileging his wife and children). He also increasingly linked this vow with nonviolent civil disobedience (*satyagraha*), arguing that celibacy was crucial to the cultivation of the self-discipline required to enact civil disobedience using nonviolent means. While living with Kallenbach in Johannesburg, Gandhi encouraged his friend to practice celibacy as well, urging him to cultivate self-restraint as an experiment and see what benefits would come of it. Together, they also began to minimize the consumption of foods, such as milk, that they believed were antithetical to the practice of celibacy.[28] Writing to his brother Simon, Kallenbach described these experiments and the personal benefits he perceived to gain from them:

> We are leading a most unusual life which helps a person to develop more independently, and the person becomes better. Mr. Gandhi is a vegetarian according to his religious conviction as a Hindu. For the last two years I have given up meat-eating; for the last year I also did not touch fish any more; and for the last 18 months I have given up my sex life. I believe that I have gained in character—strength—and mental vitality and physical development; my bodily well-being has become better and bigger. I have never been "eccentric" and I believe I am not so now! I have changed my daily life in order to simplify it and I found out that, in every direction, this change has helped me; and I hope that I shall be able to continue my life accordingly.[29]

Thus, in designing the housing at Tolstoy Farm, Gandhi and Kallenbach determined to house even married couples separately, in order to encourage the practice of celibacy, even if only for the duration of the married couples' residency on the farm.[30]

In the June 18, 2010, Gujarati edition of *Indian Opinion*, an update on Tolstoy Farm was provided. This update noted that Gandhi, Kallenbach, and two of Gandhi's sons were living on the farm and making arrangements for the arrival of new residents. Some Indian visitors had already come to look around and decided to stay, and others had promised to send construction materials from their shops. The update shares news that some of the new buildings will be ready by the end of the month, and it ends by using an agricultural metaphor to call upon potential settlers to join the farm: "This is a very important venture. Its roots go deep; it is up to the satyagrahis who settle there to make it bear sweet fruit by the way they live."[31] Here, Gandhi invites civil resisters and their families to come to Tolstoy Farm, holding out the promise that living on the farm will be gratifying for those able to embrace a simple and moral mode of life.

Throughout July and August of 2010, supporters came on Sundays on day trips from Johannesburg to bring materials and help with the construction, and the new residents who had already arrived camped in tents during this construction phase. The women's dormitory was completed first, followed by the men's dormitory. Gandhi notes that the settlers who arrived at this time were from a variety of Indian states, spoke a variety of Indian languages, and practiced a variety of religions: "The settlers hailed from Gujarat, Tamilnad, Andhradesh and North India, and there were Hindus, Musalmans, Parsis and Christians among them. About forty of them were young men, two or three old men, five women and twenty to thirty children of whom four or five were girls."[32] Gandhi's wife, Kasturba, relocated to Tolstoy Farm from Phoenix Settlement along with their two younger sons, Ramdas and Devdas, in October of 1910. Phoenix Settlement was not shut down at this time; rather, a small group remained there to continue printing *Indian Opinion*. Gandhi sought to establish a sense of community among this diverse group, wherein the residents would engage in mutual care for one another as an extended family, help provide for those impacted by the imprisonment of civil resisters, and promote the values of self-sufficiency, simplicity, equality, and affection. Gandhi wrote, "Here we insisted that we should not have any servants either for the household work or as far as might be even for the farming and building operations. Everything therefore from cooking to scavenging was done with our own hands."[33]

Rather than individual garden plots as at Phoenix Settlement, one large garden was maintained for the entire community at Tolstoy Farm. Kallenbach had studied governmental model gardens in Potchefstroom, South Africa, and he designed the communal garden at Tolstoy Farm to include a large vegetable plot as well as an orchard with orange, apricot, and plum trees. He constructed a windmill to pump water into a reservoir and laid irrigation pipes from the reservoir to the garden, as well as to several buildings.[34] In a letter to Maganlal Gandhi, who remained at Phoenix Settlement, Gandhi discusses favorably this difference between Tolstoy Farm and Phoenix Settlement. Gandhi now identifies as a farmer and advises Maganlal and the extended Phoenix community to become more genuine farmers:

> I for one am a farmer and I wish you all to become farmers, or to continue as such if you have already become farmers. My way of life has completely changed here. The whole day is spent digging the land and other manual labor instead of in writing and explaining things to people. I prefer this work and consider this alone to be my duty. . . . In pampering this corpulent body that has been given to us and pretending that we earn by our intellect, we become sinners and are tempted to fall into a thousand and one evil ways. . . . I am constantly trying to keep away the shortcomings of Phoenix from this Farm [Tolstoy Farm]. That is why a different standard of living has been laid down. If instead of each cultivating his own plot separately all cultivate the entire land together, we can produce a larger crop more quickly. I do not think this is possible there [Phoenix Settlement] for the present. But I did make the suggestion that it would be good if those who could cooperate cultivated their plots together.[35]

This emphasis on communal labor also influenced other aspects of the design of Tolstoy Farm. Rather than individual kitchens in separate houses, as at Phoenix Settlement, one large communal kitchen was built to feed all residents at Tolstoy Farm. In another letter to Maganlal Gandhi a few months later, Gandhi advised that the Phoenix settlers should create a common kitchen, writing, "It has great merit. It looks very selfish to take one's food all by oneself. Eating in company, one has perforce to control one's palate."[36] At Tolstoy Farm, Gandhi was implementing changes that he saw as improvements upon his first intentional community, changes that emphasized the communal experience along with self-discipline.

At Tolstoy Farm, everyone was to spend time gardening, cooking, and cleaning to ensure equity in the labor arrangements, to foster the self-sufficiency of the farm, and, ideally, to generate surplus produce that could be sold to raise funds for the civil disobedience campaign. In a letter to his friend Dr. Pranjivan Mehta in June 1910, Gandhi described his role in such daily work, taking pride in the unleavened flatbread and "caramel coffee" he had learned to make:

> I prepare the bread that is required on the farm. The general opinion about it is that it is well made. Manilal and a few others have learnt how to prepare it. We put in no yeast and no baking powder. We grind our own wheat. We have just prepared some marmalade from the oranges grown

> on the farm. I have also learnt how to prepare caramel coffee. It can be given as a beverage even to babies. The passive resisters on the farm have given up the use of tea and coffee, and taken to caramel coffee prepared on the farm. It is made from wheat which is first baked a certain way and then ground. We intend to sell our surplus production of the above articles to the public later on. Just at present, we are working as labourers on the construction work that is going on, on the farm, and have not time to produce more of the articles above mentioned than we need for ourselves.[37]

One challenge that came with setting up a single communal kitchen was the question of whether meat-eating diets should be accommodated. Gandhi was a committed vegetarian, and Kallenbach had now also embraced a vegetarian lifestyle. Indeed, during these years together at Tolstoy Farm, Gandhi and Kallenbach experimented with restricting their diets further and embracing a "purely fruitarian" diet, eschewing meat, dairy, and cooked food.[38] And yet Gandhi did not want to exclude meat-eating families from the farm. Gandhi reports that he spoke with the families on the farm, sharing his convictions about the health and financial benefits of a vegetarian diet, and he persuaded everyone to consent to a vegetarian diet while living on the farm. This decided, the kitchen rules were finalized: "The time as well as the number of meals was fixed. There was to be one single kitchen, and all were to dine in a single row. Everyone was to see to the cleaning of his own dish and other things. The common pots were to be cleaned by different parties in turn. I must state that Satyagrahis lived on Tolstoy Farm for a long time, but neither the women nor the men ever asked for meat."[39] In the first year, the simple meals were Indian-style, featuring fruit, vegetables, nuts, and wheat grown on the farm. Rice, butter, and other grocery items not grown on the farm were donated by supporters. Gandhi used *Indian Opinion* to provide regular updates on Tolstoy Farm and to request supplies and monetary donations; for instance, in the July 2, 1910, Gujarati edition, Gandhi published a list of needed items, including fruits, vegetables, and grains of any kind, and also requested cooking utensils, cloth, sewing needles, gardening implements, blankets, and wooden planks for construction.[40]

Gandhi emphasized the connection between self-sufficiency on Tolstoy Farm and the civil disobedience struggle: "The work before us was to make the Farm a busy hive of industry, thus to save money and in the end to make the families self-supporting. If we achieved this goal, we could battle with the Transvaal Government for an indefinite period."[41] One example of this emphasis on self-sufficiency is seen in Kallenbach and Gandhi's decision to learn to make sandals so as to avoid spending money on shoes for the settlers. Kallenbach visited the Mariannhill Monastery near Pinetown, outside of Durban, to learn the art of making sandals. After returning to Tolstoy Farm, Kallenbach taught this skill to Gandhi and several other settlers.[42] From that point forward, homemade sandals became part of the uniform that all settlers wore on the farm. Similarly, they worked out their own waste and sanitation arrangements on the farm so as not to rely on any outside service providers.[43] Additional experiments in self-sufficiency on the farm took place in the areas of health and education.

Gandhi was an avid believer in nature therapy at this stage of his life. At Phoenix Settlement, he had begun to practice nature cure to treat a variety of ailments, and his interest in such health experiments continued at Tolstoy Farm. Although the farm was located in a remote area, Gandhi noted that they did not keep in stock "even the commonest appliances against the possible attacks of illness," for he was confident that their lifestyle would limit diseases and that he would be able to deal with any sickness that did arise without recourse to doctors or pharmaceutical drugs but instead through "earth and water treatment, fasting or changes in diet."[44] Gandhi describes curing an elderly indentured laborer named Lutavan on the farm, who suffered from chronic asthma and cough, as well as a young child who had been diagnosed with typhoid.[45] While Gandhi was fully confident of this method at the time, he did later strike a note of caution in his book *Satyagraha in South Africa*, telling readers that while these treatments were successful on Tolstoy Farm, he "would not venture to employ the same treatment today," noting that it may not work in a different climate.[46]

Gandhi's approach to education at Tolstoy Farm emphasized physical labor, secular learning, and ecumenical religious instruction. Gandhi and Kallenbach both served as teachers for the children at the farm in its early days, and additional settlers (both male and female) rotated in as teachers as the community grew. Writing to Chhaganlal Gandhi in 1911, who remained at Phoenix Settlement, Gandhi stated that his "only interest at present is in the school" and that all other matters have fallen to second place, concluding that his "teaching work is in the nature of an experiment. It is to be seen what results it brings."[47] Gandhi described his schedule at this time as entailing physical labor on the farm from the time he woke up until 10:00 a.m., teaching classes in the school from 1:00 to 4:30 p.m., and then taking care of correspondence in the evenings after dinner; he went to Johannesburg to take care of any necessary legal business on Mondays.[48] In terms of manual labor, children were to spend several hours each morning contributing to routine farmwork: gardening, cleaning, cooking, sewing, making sandals, etc. For secular learning, which took place several afternoons each week, Gandhi emphasized the subjects of history, geography, mathematics, and writing. Gandhi taught these subjects primarily in English, given the multilinguistic nature of the group of settlers, but encouraged each child to read materials in their own vernacular language (Hindi, Gujarati, Tamil, Urdu).[49] For the religious edification of the children—and the whole community—Gandhi wanted to ensure that everyone had a basic level of familiarity with the religions of all members living at the farm, which included Hinduism, Islam, Christianity, Judaism, and Zoroastrianism. He conducted class sessions during some afternoons in which passages were read from the primary religious scriptures of each of these traditions. Beyond school hours, the major religious holidays of each tradition were celebrated collectively at the farm, and the daily morning and evening prayer sessions held on the communal prayer ground for all residents of Tolstoy Farm included singing hymns from multiple religions. Through this, Gandhi wrote, "the children were saved from the infection of intolerance, and learnt to view one another's religions and customs with a large-hearted charity. They learnt how to live together like blood-brothers. They imbibed the lessons of mutual service, courtesy and industry."[50] The biggest change at Tolstoy Farm from Phoenix Settlement, however, entailed the growing emphasis on educating for time in prison.

Preparing for Prison

At Tolstoy Farm, Gandhi began to give the older children an added layer of educational instruction: preparation for their first experience in prison. Soon, this educational focus expanded to become a priority for all residents. At the founding of Tolstoy Farm in 1910, Gandhi's eldest sons, Harilal and Manilal, were upheld as examples for the other children on the farm, for each of them had recently been released from serving stints in prison as civil resisters. Harilal had served a six-month sentence in prison (his third imprisonment for civil disobedience), while Manilal had served a three-month sentence with hard labor (his first imprisonment for civil disobedience). Harilal, at twenty-one years old, was now an adult, whereas Manilal was aged seventeen and still a minor. Gandhi shared his reasoning for involving young Manilal in the civil disobedience struggle publicly, writing in *Indian Opinion*:

> My second son (Manilal) lives with me. For some time past I had been thinking of asking him to join the struggle. He was insistent. It appeared to me, on deep reflection, that it would be right to bring him in. I believe that to go to jail or suffer similar hardships with a pure motive for the sake of the motherland is the truest kind of education. Since I look upon jail as a kind of palace, how can I deny the privilege of being there to those whom I hold dear? My son has attained the age (17) when he can think for himself. For my part, I should like to tell all Indian parents and all Indian youths that success will attend those who have joined the struggle. It is they that do the fighting, who profit most from it. To those who are in jail now I make this request, that they should make up their minds to return to jail the moment they are released, without so much as pausing for breath.[51]

Both Harilal and Manilal were released from prison in May of 1910, and upon their release, the boys joined their father at Kallenbach's home in Johannesburg and thereafter helped to undertake the founding of Tolstoy Farm.

Gandhi taught the youth at Tolstoy Farm that, just as he and his sons had done, so too could they survive time in jail, and ideally even learn to thrive there: "The secret of the struggle lies in going to jail cheerfully, and being happy while there. . . . For realizing the self, the first essential thing is to cultivate a strong moral sense. Morality means the acquisition of virtues such as fearlessness, truth, *brahmacharya* [celibacy] and so on. Service is automatically rendered to the country in this process of cultivating morality."[52] In the classes Gandhi taught the youth at Tolstoy Farm, he emphasized the need to cultivate self-discipline so that they would not be afraid when imprisoned but had both the mental and physical fortitude to endure their sentences. The memorization and study of passages from religious texts would help to fortify their virtues and provide material to reflect upon, even when imprisoned without access to books. The labor done in working the farm and building its infrastructure would give them the physical strength necessary to endure prison sentences that entailed mandatory hard labor.

Soon, Gandhi expanded this focus on preparing for prison beyond educating the youth. Describing life at Tolstoy Farm in its first year of existence, he wrote, "there was on the Farm an ebb and flow of Satyagrahis, some of whom would be expecting to go to prison while others had been released from it."[53] Gandhi began to increasingly orient daily life at Tolstoy Farm, in all of its facets, around the cultivation of the strong moral sense and the self-discipline that he believed would allow his coresidents to flourish, no matter whether they were on the farm or in prison. Residents began to listen to regular talks given by Gandhi, Harilal, and others who had been released from prison about what to expect while incarcerated. Residents began to sleep on skinny bedrolls on the floor rather than in soft beds or on raised cots. Residents began to dress in clothing modeled upon prisoners' uniforms as they went about their daily farm labor. Residents began to further simplify their vegetarian meals and eat them from a single dish that Gandhi described as "a kind of bowl such as is supplied to prisoners in jail," with wooden spoons that they carved themselves.[54] For dinner each day, residents began to eat "mealie pap," a maize porridge that Gandhi initially opposed as a diet that was "not at all suitable for the Asiatic constitution" when he was first served it in prison in 1908, but he now argued that he and his coresidents would find it "useful to accustom" themselves to this food that was served to prisoners of color (African and Asian) in South African jails.[55] Residents began to engage in outdoor physical labor no matter what the weather conditions were like—digging sanitation ditches, building housing and sheds, farming, etc.—in training for penal labor sentences that could entail agricultural, mining, or quarry work.

In all of these ways, to live at Tolstoy Farm was to live as if one was a prisoner. Some residents flourished under these conditions. Hermann Kallenbach did, embracing the occasion to live a "Tolstoyan" lifestyle on the farm and viewing the restrictions as opportunities to cultivate self-discipline, physical vigor, and spiritual fellowship. He took on a leading role in the carpentry work, he relished walking to and from Johannesburg with Gandhi and other residents on Mondays when they went into town (they occasionally competed to see who could cover the full twenty-two-mile distance the fastest on foot), and he embraced the ascetic practices they undertook such as celibacy, nonviolence, and a restrictive vegetarian diet. A pair of archival photographs of Kallenbach that were published in *Indian Opinion* in 1912 show him wearing his homemade sandals, prison-style trousers, and a backpack as he leaves Tolstoy Farm to walk to Johannesburg. The photographs are captioned "A Staunch Tolstoyan." In these photos, Kallenbach has left behind the professional, striped suit jacket and reading glasses that he was earlier photographed in, when a photo featuring him as a successful South African businessman was published in *Indian Opinion* in 1911, captioned "The Owner of Tolstoy Farm."[56] Kallenbach had proudly transformed from a businessman and patron of Tolstoy Farm into a full-fledged coresident and dedicated Tolstoyan.[57]

Other residents, however, struggled under these conditions. Gandhi's eldest son, Harilal, perhaps struggled the most. Between 1908 and 1911, he was imprisoned six times for civil disobedience. By 1911, he concluded that he did not want to live at Tolstoy Farm any longer, nor did he want to spend additional time in prison. Harilal had repeatedly asked his father to send him to England for professional education (an opportunity that Gandhi had pursued himself), but Gandhi repeatedly told Harilal that an education on the farm and in prison was sufficient for him and his younger brothers. In May of 1911, Harilal confronted his father, telling him that he was upset that, unlike other fathers who have the ability to help their children, Gandhi had done nothing special for him or his other sons but had instead put them last.[58] Kasturba also confronted her husband on Harilal's behalf, asking Gandhi about his intentions for their sons' formal education and careers: "What is it that you intend to do? Do you want to keep the sons illiterate? Do you want them to wear a loincloth? Do you want them to remain poor beggars?"[59] Gandhi listened to their concerns but remained firm in his belief that education on Tolstoy Farm was the best form of education for his sons.

Harilal decided to leave South Africa and sail home to India. After returning to India, Harilal enrolled in a school in Ahmedabad, determined to pass the matriculation examination in order to qualify for further formal study. Gandhi, writing to his friend Dr. Pranjivan Mehta after Harilal's departure from Tolstoy Farm, stated that he had tried hard to persuade Harilal that there was nothing to be gained from the matriculation examination but failed, and now he could only hope that Harilal would eventually "see the light," writing, "He refuses to come out of the state in which I once was, when I was infatuated with degrees. How can one blame him for it?"[60] Unfortunately, the relationship between Gandhi and his son Harilal never recovered.[61]

Civil Disobedience

The residents at Tolstoy Farm thus built upon the ideals of Phoenix Settlement—self-sufficiency, simplicity, and equality—adding at this second community intentional training for prison life as essential to their pursuit of universal well-being. Gandhi wrote that this training enabled them to continue the multiyear struggle for civil rights for the Indian community in South Africa: "Thus the Satyagrahis were pursuing the even tenor of their life on Tolstoy Farm, and preparing for whatever the future had in store for them. They did not know, nor did they care, when the struggle would end. They were only under one pledge, namely to refuse submission to the Black Act and to suffer whatever hardships were involved in such disobedience."[62] For Gandhi, communal living was the necessary condition for the cultivation of the self-control that was requisite for the pursuit of universal well-being through the broader civil disobedience campaign.

When the Union of South Africa was formed in May 1910, the Cape, Natal, Transvaal, and Orange Free State colonies were united as one self-governing dominion within the British Empire. Gandhi worried that the proposed consolidation of immigration laws would mean that Indians living in the Cape and Natal colonies would soon face the same harsher restrictions as Indians living in Transvaal that he and his coresidents had already been protesting.[63] In 1912, when a proposed Immigrants' Restriction Bill was introduced in the assembly of the Union of South Africa, Gandhi grew alarmed by its terms, writing in *Indian Opinion* that the bill left "many things from an Asiatic standpoint in an unsatisfactory condition"—in particular, the restriction on interstate immigration and the inability of lawful residents to own land in some colonies.[64] Gandhi worked to raise awareness of the problems with this proposed bill by organizing meetings of the Indian community, sending letters to politicians requesting amendments to the bill, petitioning the Senate and House of Assembly with objections to the bill, and publishing numerous essays in *Indian Opinion*.[65]

Gandhi turned to Gopal Krishna Gokhale, a leading politician in the Indian National Congress and Gandhi's political mentor in India, updating him on the situation in South Africa and requesting that he visit South Africa. Gokhale agreed and arrived in Cape Town on October 22, 1912. Gandhi accompanied Gokhale as he toured South Africa, meeting with white South Africans and Indians alike in Cape Town, Johannesburg, Pretoria, and other cities to assess the Indian situation. Gokhale also visited Tolstoy Farm, and Gandhi records that in spite of Gokhale's delicate health, he was good-natured about living like a prisoner during his stay, including eating their simple meals and sleeping on a floor mat.[66] Gokhale eventually met with Prime Minister Botha, leader of the recently formed Union of South Africa, and General Smuts. When Gokhale emerged from a two-hour-long negotiation session with Botha and Smuts, he informed Gandhi that everything had been settled: the Asiatic Registration Act would be repealed, the racial bar would be removed from the immigration law, the £3 tax would be abolished. In exchange, Gandhi must agree to return to India within a year. Gandhi responded to Gokhale that while he appreciated the latter's optimism, and while he was willing to return to India if all of this came to pass, he was quite doubtful that these reforms would happen within a year and without many more Indians going to jail.[67]

Gandhi's skepticism proved correct. In February of 1913, Gandhi wrote to Gokhale (who had returned to India), informing him that he was unlikely to be able to return to India within the year and explaining that the promised legislation was likely to be postponed. He noted, "The ministers are not carrying out their assurances. The Immigration Acts are being administered with an ever-growing severity. Wives of lawfully resident Indians are being put to great trouble and expense."[68] Gandhi was referring to several recent cases wherein immigration officers had refused to allow wives coming from India to join their husbands in South Africa. The most famous of these was the case of Bai Miriam, a woman who had married her husband according to Muslim rites in India and whose husband sought to bring her from India to join him in South Africa. The immigration officer refused Bai Miriam entry to Cape Colony on the grounds that her marriage could not be recognized as legal. The case made its way to the Cape Supreme Court and resulted in a ruling that marriages that had been conducted outside of South Africa were invalid unless they were celebrated according to Christian rites and registered by the registrar of marriages. Gandhi described the impact of this ruling in *Indian Opinion*, writing, "This decision means that as from today all Hindu or Muslim wives living in South Africa lose their right to live there. In other words, a Hindu, Muslim, or Parsi wife can live in this country only by the grace of the Government. It is quite on the cards that the Government will not permit any more wives to come in or that, if it does, it will be entirely as a matter of favour. We cannot conceive of a more degrading state of affairs."[69] This shocked the Indian community in South Africa; in addition to barring wives currently in India from joining their husbands who had established themselves in South Africa, and calling into question the legality of the residency of the wives who were already living in South Africa, Gandhi pointed out that it also legally nullified most marriages in the Indian community in South Africa and reduced the wives to the status of concubines. It also called into legal question the right of the children of such nullified marriages to inherit their parents' property.[70]

Another issue galvanizing the Indian community at this time was the £3 tax. Gandhi had previously lobbied for greater rights for indentured laborers in South Africa, and he eventually campaigned for the prohibition of indenture, helping to bring about the government of India's official prohibition of Indian indenture to South Africa in 1911.[71] Prior to 1911, the £3 tax was an annual tax that was imposed on all Indians who had completed their term of indenture and desired to stay in Natal Colony as free Indians. Gandhi had previously argued that this annual tax was discriminatory and placed an undue financial burden on ex-indentured immigrants; now that indenture was prohibited, Gandhi argued that the tax should be abolished in its entirety. Gandhi wrote letters to politicians and published editorials in South African newspapers reminding the public that during Gokhale's visit, an agreement had been made to end the £3 tax and that this had been announced publicly in joint speeches made by Gokhale and Senator Marshall Campbell.[72] When the government then proposed in early 1913 to remove the £3 tax from Indian women but not men, Gandhi argued that this was a betrayal of the terms of the negotiation with Gokhale and demonstrated beyond doubt the South African government's "consistently hostile attitude and bad faith towards the Indian community."[73]

By June of 1913, Gandhi wrote to Gokhale again, informing him that "passive resistance is a necessity."[74] Gandhi began to prepare the residents of Tolstoy Farm for an expanded civil disobedience campaign and now invited the women as well as the men to be active participants:

> We first invited the sisters who lived at Tolstoy Farm. I found that they were only too glad to enter the struggle. I gave them an idea of the risks incidental to such participation. I explained to them that they would have to put up with restraints in the matter of food, dress and personal movements. I warned them that they might be given hard work in jail, made to wash clothes and even subjected to insult by the warders. But these sisters were all brave and feared none of these things. One of them was pregnant while six of them had young babies in arms. But one and all were eager to join and I simply could not come in their way.[75]

Gandhi then went to Phoenix Settlement, where he shared his plans with the residents, and here too, he found many women eager to actively participate. Gandhi's wife, Kasturba, was one of these women. She had returned to Phoenix six months earlier, in January 1913. Gandhi records that he spoke with all of the women at Phoenix except Kasturba, and they expressed their interest in participating and their willingness to serve time in jail if needed. Gandhi intentionally did not approach Kasturba, as he felt that his wife might feel compelled to agree to any proposal he made. But Kasturba confronted Gandhi, insisting that she would participate, stating, "If you can endure hardships and so can my boys, why cannot I?"[76]

As Gandhi planned this civil disobedience campaign, he continued his efforts to negotiate in good faith with South African politicians throughout July and August of 1913.[77] On September 13, however, Gandhi declared in an essay titled "No Settlement" in *Indian Opinion* that negotiations had failed. He now called upon the Indian community to follow the lead of his coresidents at Tolstoy Farm and Phoenix Settlement, writing:

> The real object of our fight must be to kill the monster of racial prejudice in the heart of the Government and the local whites. We feel the presence of this monster in the Government's administration of the Gold Law in the Transvaal and the new immigrant law, in its insistence on the collection of the £3 tax from poor, miserable, helpless Indians, and in its attitude towards our women. . . . There is only one way to kill the monster and that is to offer ourselves as a sacrifice. . . . The only effective way of bringing about a change in his attitude is satyagraha. It is a divine law that even the most hard-hearted man will melt if he sees his enemy suffering in innocence. The satyagrahi volunteers to suffer in this way.[78]

Gandhi now asked the Indian community to join the civil disobedience struggle and to be willing to endure suffering as nonviolent protestors, following the lead of his coresidents from Tolstoy Farm and Phoenix Settlement. Gandhi further called upon those who volunteered as civil resisters to be willing to die for the cause, and called for those Indians who were unable to actively join the struggle to give whatever financial help they could to the movement.

The Great March

To commence this new civil disobedience campaign, Gandhi instructed one group from Tolstoy Farm to travel south to the Orange Free State Colony and then cross back over the border into Transvaal Colony. The group consisted of twelve women, six infants, and Hermann Kallenbach. Since the Indian women did not have the requisite permit required for them to enter the Transvaal, they faced potential arrest. Gandhi's goal was to have the women arrested and tried in court in order to draw attention to discriminatory laws that required Indian residents to carry permits that white residents were not required to carry. When this first group of women was not arrested, Gandhi turned to a second group from Phoenix Settlement and instructed them to cross over into the Transvaal from Natal Colony, again without the requisite permit. This group of sixteen residents from Phoenix Settlement included four women and twelve men and was led by Kasturba Gandhi. After crossing the border, they were all arrested, tried, and sentenced to three months' imprisonment with hard labor. Writing in *Indian Opinion*, Gandhi encouraged other Indians to similarly court arrest by defying unjust laws—crossing the border into Transvaal without a permit; hawking goods without licenses; refusing to show a license or permit when requested by authorities; etc. He sought to bring this campaign to the whole of South Africa in this way, calling for volunteers everywhere who were willing to serve time in jail. He also reminded his readers that they could help in other ways, including donating money and food to the families of civil resisters; sending letters to the government in support of the struggle; and sharing copies of *Indian Opinion* throughout the community to publicize the struggle.[79]

The group of women from Tolstoy Farm who had not been arrested next proceeded to Newcastle in Natal Colony, where they began working to educate the Indian community there about the struggle. Heeding this call to action, approximately two thousand Indian laborers who came from indentured families and worked in the Newcastle coal mines decided to go on strike, declaring that they would return to work only after the government repealed the £3 tax. Eleven women from Tolstoy Farm who were in Newcastle were then arrested and sentenced to three months' hard labor. They now joined the Phoenix Settlement members in the Maritzburg jail. Gandhi publicized the suffering the women faced in jail, highlighting the poor quality of the food they received, the laundry labor they were required to perform, and the lack of medical attention. Tragically, one of the women named Valliamma Munuswami Mudaliar was just a teenager when she was sent to prison, and she died from a fever contracted in jail just two days after her release.[80]

Gandhi arrived in Newcastle as the momentum there continued to grow. He quickly realized that a bigger plan was needed, for the striking laborers could no longer reside in their employer-owned housing, and they had no savings. They camped outside and relied on the Indian merchants for food donations. Gandhi came up with a solution: "I must take this 'army' to the Transvaal and see them safely deposited in jail like the Phoenix party."[81] He began to plan what would come to be called the "Great March": a thirty-six-mile walk from Newcastle in Natal Colony into Transvaal Colony. Gandhi explained that the marchers must agree to limited food rations along the way, to nonviolently bearing any abuse from whites along the way, to continuing the march even if Gandhi was arrested, and to the likelihood of being arrested themselves. The large group agreed and then walked to Charlestown, located at the northern tip of Natal, where they halted while Gandhi waited for Kallenbach and other associates from Tolstoy Farm and Phoenix Settlement to join him in order to help take the marchers the remaining several miles across the Transvaal border.[82] Gandhi also wrote to the government, informing them of the plan and offering to call off the strike if they would repeal the £3 tax. In the event that the marchers were not arrested after crossing the border, Gandhi and Kallenbach intended to walk them twenty to twenty-four miles per day for another eight days, until they reached Tolstoy Farm, where they would live in tents and work on the farm for the duration of the struggle.[83]

When no response was received from the government via telegram, Gandhi made a final phone call to General Smuts's office but was told that General Smuts would not speak with him.[84] Gandhi alerted the English-language press that the march would commence.[85] On November 6, 1913, Gandhi led 2,037 men, 127 women, and fifty-seven children on the Great March across the border into the Transvaal at Volksrust. Police were present but allowed the marchers to cross the border. They moved on to Palmford, where they camped for the night. The following morning (November 7), Gandhi was arrested. He sent a telegram to the minister of the interior, stating that there were over two thousand marchers who were without shelter and on starvation rations, including women and children, and that either Gandhi should be allowed to continue leading them or, if the government chose to jail him, they should make a suitable provision for the marchers by sending them by train to Tolstoy Farm with food rations.[86] Gandhi was released on bail and continued to lead the march toward Tolstoy Farm while sending Kallenbach back to Charlestown to ensure that the women and children remaining there had secured temporary housing and to arrange for food provisions to be forwarded along the marching route. The next day (November 8), Gandhi was again arrested in Standerton and again released on bail (though five of his comarchers remained behind bars). On the fourth day (November 9), Gandhi was arrested for a third time as the marchers were en route to Greylingstad. Gandhi asked Henry Polak to assume leadership of the march at this stage and was taken to jail in Heidelberg for the night and then sent to Dundee for trial. Polak led the marchers the afternoon of November 9 and the morning of November 10, until they reached Balfour, where they were informed that there were three trains at the station to arrest all two thousand of the Indian marchers and deport them to Natal. When the marchers refused to board the trains, Polak reminded them that jail was their goal and that only by being peacefully arrested and sent to jail could the *satyagrahis* bring their struggle to a triumphant end.[87]

Henry Polak and Hermann Kallenbach were not initially arrested on the morning of November 10, but separate orders came for their arrest later that afternoon. Kallenbach was uncertain if he would face arrest as a white person, but he was eager to join the other marchers in jail, an experience that he had been training for at Tolstoy Farm. In a long prison diary letter written to his sister Jeanette, Kallenbach describes his growing activism in the cause for racial equality among whites and Indians in South Africa, leading up to his participation in the Great March. He also provides a detailed day-by-day outline of events. In his entry for November 10, 1913, he describes his arrest as "the day of the Lord," writing:

> The heavy prison door closed, the loud rattling of the keys and the sound of the departing steps of the warden were wonderful to my ear. There was now a strange silence. All the prisoners seemed to sleep soundly. In the meantime, also the soft light of the moon entered the courtyard. With all

> my heart I had sent up prayers to God, thanking him that he had deemed me worthy of this experience in my life! Thus began the first night in the prison, which will not leave my memory ever.[88]

Kallenbach seeks to reassure his sister that he is prepared for jail. He comments that he has already been living on a restrictive diet, partaking for the past four months of "only one meal per day, consisting of fruit (tomatoes, cucumbers, included), olive oil, unleavened and unsalted wholewheat bread, and peanuts." He notes that his diet and lifestyle have agreed with him, and he feels "physically and mentally strong and vigorous."[89]

Gandhi was sentenced to a total of twelve months in prison with hard labor; Polak and Kallenbach were each sentenced to three months in prison without hard labor. Kallenbach records that the three of them were housed separately in prison on racial lines, Gandhi sleeping in a room with other Indians, and Polak and Kallenbach sharing a separate room together as whites, but their jailers initially allowed the three of them to spend time together during the day. Kallenbach describes this time together at the start of his prison sentence as a "merry imprisonment," writing almost gleefully about how, after their sentencing, they became a "criminal trio" and were permitted to take turns shaving off one another's hair and moustaches, as the prison sartorial code required.[90]

Gandhi also describes these days in prison together as "happy days," with even more Indians being arrested and joining them day by day.[91] However, their jailers soon decided to separate Gandhi, Kallenbach, and Polak as the leaders of the Great March, and they moved all of them away from Volksrust and to other prisons, where they received harsher treatment: Gandhi to Bloemfontein, Kallenbach to Pretoria, and Polak to Germiston. The Indian indentured laborers who had been imprisoned were forced to work as miners for European mine owners and were physically beaten if they refused. From his prison cell, Gandhi condemned this treatment of the indentured laborers as "slavery, pure and simple."[92] As word spread about this maltreatment of the Indian prisoners throughout the Indian community in South Africa, and also made its way back to India, the civil disobedience movement swelled. In addition to miners, other Indian laborers working on plantations and elsewhere in South Africa also began to go on strike in solidarity. At this stage, nearly all of the residents at both of Gandhi's intentional communities were in prison, leaving only a handful of them (Maganlal Gandhi, Albert West, Albert's sister Ada West, and Sheth Ahmad Muhammad Kachhalia) to coordinate the growing protest movement.

In the pages of *Indian Opinion*, Gandhi and his associates publicized such mistreatment of the indentured laborers. They also publicized the deaths of several nonviolent resisters in the civil disobedience campaign, praising their martyrdom. Some died as a result of their imprisonment. For instance, Gandhi wrote with remorse about the death of one elderly man named Harbatsinh, an ex-indentured laborer who died while in prison after being arrested for his nonviolent participation in the Great March. Gandhi also highlighted the death of the aforementioned teenage woman, Valliamma Munuswami Mudaliar, who protested the declaration of her parents' marriage as invalid, and who died two days after being released from prison. Others died through acts of colonial violence inflicted upon nonviolent protestors. Selvan Guruvadu, for instance, was an indentured laborer who was shot to death when police fired on Indian strikers on November 27, 1913.[93]

Facing growing international pressure, including an inquiry from the British colonial viceroy in India, General Smuts agreed to appoint a commission to conduct an inquiry into the Indians' grievances and released the political prisoners unconditionally. Gandhi, Kasturba, Kallenbach, Polak, and the other marchers were freed from their respective prisons on December 18, 1913. Gandhi now began a period of negotiation with General Smuts, which resulted in the passage of the Indian Relief Act and the Smuts-Gandhi Agreement of 1914. This act repealed the £3 tax on indentured laborers, recognized as legal those marriages performed according to Hindu and Muslim rites of passage, abolished the Asiatic Registration Act (the "Black Act"), and provided for an amelioration of the Immigration Restriction Act. In exchange, Gandhi agreed to end the civil disobedience campaign and to return to his home country.

Closing Tolstoy Farm

Gandhi attributed the success of the Great March, and the broader campaign for Indian civil rights in South Africa, to the dedication of his coresidents from Tolstoy Farm. He emphasized that it was their collective disciplined nonviolence and willingness to serve time in prison and otherwise undergo suffering for the greater good that deserved the credit for bringing about this civil rights victory:

> Tolstoy Farm proved to be a centre of spiritual purification and penance for the final campaign [against the Black Act]. I have serious doubts as to whether the struggle could have been prosecuted for eight years, whether we could have secured larger funds, and whether the thousands of men who participated in the last phase of the struggle would have borne their share in it, if there had been no Tolstoy Farm. Tolstoy Farm was never placed in the limelight, yet an institution which deserved it attracted public sympathy to itself. The Indians saw that the Tolstoy Farmers were doing what they themselves were not prepared to do and what they looked upon in the light of hardship.[94]

Although it was only a temporary intentional community, in operation for just four years from 1910 to 1914, Tolstoy Farm was significant for several reasons.

First, at Tolstoy Farm, Gandhi's philosophy of universal well-being (*sarvodaya*) continued to evolve. In addition to the earlier emphasis on self-discipline, self-sufficiency, equality, and affection, universal well-being now also entailed self-suffering and sacrifice for the collective good. Residents of Tolstoy Farm trained to live as if they were in prison, voluntarily undergoing hardships as preparation for their participation in the broader campaign for Indian civil rights. Second, the residents of Tolstoy Farm served as the leaders of the civil resistance campaign that culminated in the Great March. Whereas Gandhi alone is often credited with leading the civil rights movement on behalf of Indians in South Africa, the success of this campaign was due not only to his leadership but also to the contributions made by Hermann Kallenbach, Kasturba Gandhi, Henry Polak, Harilal Gandhi, and other residents of Gandhi's intentional communities. Finally, Gandhi and the coresidents who returned to India with him would continue to experiment with the values and practices from Tolstoy Farm, as well as the political strategies developed there, evolving them further in the Indian context.

As Gandhi prepared to leave South Africa, the country he had lived in for twenty-one years, he had to make arrangements for the residents of both of his intentional communities before departing for India. The residents of both Phoenix Settlement and Tolstoy Farm were asked to decide if they wanted to remain in South Africa or travel to India with Gandhi. Kallenbach elected to go to India, proclaiming to Gandhi and his coresidents, "You have made me understand better my own religion, you have made me love more my own people, you have helped me to be less arrogant, less slothful, and you have made me become more truthful. . . . I feel in my heart that your country and your people are going to give me more."[95] Gandhi and Kallenbach therefore decided to close Tolstoy Farm. The community members decided that Phoenix Settlement, on the other hand, would remain operational, with enough residents electing to remain to carry on the settlement's mission, including continuing to publish *Indian Opinion*.

Before departing South Africa in July of 1914, Gandhi wrote a farewell letter addressed to the Indian and European communities of South Africa and sent it to the press for publication in multiple newspapers. In the letter, Gandhi thanked his European and Indian friends for their kindness. He asked both sides to uphold the terms of the settlement he had reached with General Smuts, describing it as the Magna Carta of Indian liberty in this land for eliminating legal racial inequality between Indians and Europeans as subjects of the British Crown, and emphasizing that it came about after eight years of nonviolent resistance that entailed strenuous suffering, the loss of material possessions, and the loss of precious lives. He also cautioned both the Indian and the European communities that it would only be by mutual cooperation and goodwill that the settlement would be upheld. Finally, he warned the European community against efforts to forcibly repatriate Indians, reminding them that he was leaving behind an Indian community that was organized, disciplined, and nonviolent, able to "effectively strike in large bodies" and ready to "suffer untold hardships" and even "be martyrs." He concludes that the Indian community should be considered "an honorable part of any nation."[96] Paired with this stern warning to the European community, however, Gandhi also made a friendly gesture to General Smuts, sending him a pair of sandals that he had made at Tolstoy Farm.[97]

Gandhi wanted his coresidents who remained in South Africa and resettled at Phoenix Settlement to continue to live together, emphasizing the ideals of self-sufficiency, equality, and affection that Phoenix was founded upon, but as his farewell letter indicates, he also wanted them to maintain their discipline and be prepared to suffer on behalf of the greater good—as they had learned to do at Tolstoy Farm—should Indian civil rights again be imperiled. After saying farewell, Gandhi looked next to India, where he intended to found a new intentional community in his homeland on the other side of the Indian Ocean to continue evolving and enacting his philosophy of universal well-being.

Interlude 2

Tolstoy Farm after Gandhi

When Gandhi was preparing to leave South Africa and return to India in 1914, the residents of Tolstoy Farm and Phoenix Settlement had to decide if they wanted to remain in South Africa or travel to India with Gandhi. Hermann Kallenbach, the cofounder of Tolstoy Farm and the legal owner of its land, elected to go to India. Gandhi's immediate family was also returning to India, and approximately twenty-five other residents from these intentional communities who were not Gandhi's immediate family members also decided to go to India to undertake the work of establishing a new community there.

As Gandhi left South Africa in July of 1914, he planned to sail first to London to meet with his political mentor, Gopal Krishna Gokhale (who was scheduled to be in London as a representative of the Indian National Congress), and from there on to India. Gandhi booked a direct boat passage to India for the members of the extended Tolstoy and Phoenix "family" who had elected to move to India and appointed his trusted nephew Maganlal Gandhi to look after this communal family for the duration of their trip across the Indian Ocean and after their arrival in India until Gandhi rejoined them. Gandhi, his wife Kasturba, and Kallenbach sailed for London. As their boat entered the English Channel on August 4, 1914, they learned that World War I had begun. The outbreak of war delayed Gandhi and Kasturba's return to India, such that they did not arrive there until January of 1915, and it altered the course of Kallenbach's life.

Kallenbach had lived in South Africa for the past eighteen years. He came from a Lithuanian Jewish family but was technically a German citizen. Before leaving South Africa, Kallenbach had applied to become a naturalized South African citizen and had also submitted paperwork to travel to India. Upon reaching London, however, he was not given his naturalization certificate or permission to enter India as expected. Instead, he was declared an "enemy alien" and sent to a detention camp on the British Isle of Man, where he remained from 1915 to 1917. Kallenbach was released in a prisoner exchange in 1917 and sent to Switzerland, and from there, he traveled to Berlin to reunite with family.[1] Gandhi and Kallenbach corresponded regularly with one another during Kallenbach's internment. Gandhi had taken Kallenbach's possessions with him when he sailed to India, assuming that Kallenbach would soon be released and would join him. In Gandhi's letters to Kallenbach from this period, he encourages him to draw upon the self-discipline he learned at Tolstoy Farm and be a model prisoner for the other detainees. Gandhi also expresses how much he misses Kallenbach and longs for him to join him in India. Kallenbach, however, replied less and less frequently.[2] Once he was released from detainment, Kallenbach decided not to move to India—indeed, he did not travel to India until many years later, visiting Gandhi in 1937 and 1939. Instead, Kallenbach returned to South Africa in 1920.

After returning to South Africa, Kallenbach had to decide where and how he would live. Phoenix Settlement was still an active intentional community, and Kallenbach remained in touch with the residents there, serving as one of its trustees and staying there for two weeks shortly after his return to South Africa. He wrote a letter to Gandhi at the end of this stay at Phoenix, wherein he expressed feeling "lonely, very alone at Johannesburg like an abandoned dog."[3] Though he expressed appreciation for his stay at Phoenix, the communal experience was not the same for Kallenbach without Gandhi there. Tolstoy Farm, of course, was now an empty shell, as Kallenbach and Gandhi had closed it in 1914 when they left South Africa. Kallenbach ultimately made Johannesburg his home base for professional reasons, resuming his work as an architect and growing increasingly active as a member of the Jewish community there and in the Zionist cause.

Kallenbach decided to sell the land at Tolstoy Farm. Today, the land is owned by Corobrik, a South African brick-manufacturing company that uses clay from the land to make bricks. Corobrik has recognized Tolstoy Farm's historic importance and has granted permission for a small piece of the historic farmland to be used as a heritage site. On my visit to Tolstoy Farm, I knew that it was no longer an intentional community and that its original buildings had not been preserved. Nonetheless, I wanted to see the site for myself and to visit the commemorative plaque that I had read had been erected on the site.[4] I contacted Johannesburg-based tourist guides, but none knew anything about Tolstoy Farm or could provide a guide to take me there. I therefore hired a driver to help me find the site, and we set out, with my husband and son joining us for the day, equipped only with GPS coordinates and a map of the terrain around the Lawley train station and the location of the Corobrik office. My driver was curious, willing to go somewhere other than the usual tourist and business destinations with international visitors. Off we went into the countryside beyond Johannesburg, bumping along rough, unpaved roads.

Eventually, we could see on one hillside white rocks forming the words "Gandhi Tolstoy Farm," so we knew we were near. But where was the commemorative plaque? There were no directions or historic signposts, only Corobrik signs saying Private Property, Unauthorized Entry Prohibited. We stopped at a farmer's house to ask for directions. I introduced myself to the elderly farmer over the barking of his dogs and asked if he knew the location of the nearby plaque honoring Tolstoy Farm. He responded, saying something in Afrikaans that I could not understand. I asked him if he spoke English, and he turned around to go back inside his house. My driver then spoke to the farmer in Afrikaans to explain who I was and what I was looking for. The farmer turned back around and addressed my husband and myself, this time speaking in clear English, telling us to exercise caution as white foreigners traveling around with a Black man. He next addressed the driver in Afrikaans, giving him directions to the correct road. We got back into the car and bumped further down the rough road. A bit stunned, I checked in with the driver, who replied that it was not uncommon for white men of that generation to only speak in Afrikaans if Black people were present, that it was part of the racial legacy of apartheid.

At last we came upon the site. Driving down the gravel road, I noted a fenced-in area with meticulously landscaped gardens and—to my surprise—a newly constructed building that was in the process of becoming a Tolstoy Farm museum. The caretakers generously welcomed us inside, even though we were unscheduled visitors, and let us explore the grounds and the museum. Inside the gateway to the site was the plaque commemorating the history of Tolstoy Farm.

Figure 4. Tolstoy Farm site and museum under construction. Photo by Curran Lyons.

Looking down the walkway, one can see the new museum building to the right, and on the left are the stairs leading to the historic foundation of the site where Gandhi and Kallenbach once lived. The plaque opens with a quote from Gandhi about the farm: "The weak became strong on Tolstoy Farm, and labour proved to be a tonic for all." It provides a bit of information about Gandhi and Kallenbach founding the farm, naming it after Leo Tolstoy, and living there with an "eclectic group of some eighty people of diverse cultural, social, and religious backgrounds." At the bottom, the plaque notes that the "Tolstoy Farm was rededicated on May 30, 1997 in deep respect for the ideals of men, women and children who under the leadership of Mahatma Gandhi and the satyagraha movement strove to make our world a better place for all humankind and who inspire us to this day to build upon their selfless foundation."[5]

Following the walkway, one passes newly planted fruit trees—a nod to the abundance of fruit and nut trees that were once on this land—and arrives at the stairs leading to the historic foundation of the site where Gandhi and Kallenbach used to live. On either side of the stairs there is a commemorative bust—the one on the left of Nelson Mandela and the one on the right of Mahatma Gandhi. These busts were added to the site in 2019, commissioned by the Mahatma Gandhi Remembrance Organisation in South Africa, in commemoration of Mandela's 101st and Gandhi's 150th birth anniversary.[6] Climbing the six stairs to ascend the historic foundation, which is all that is extant from the original Tolstoy Farm, one can see, on the hillside beyond, the white rocks that spell out "Gandhi Tolstoy Farm" in large letters. As I stood there, I tried to imagine this space as it was in Gandhi and Kallenbach's time, a space filled with the hubbub of communal labor, with enthusiastic ascetic and ecumenical experimentation, and with the fervor to build a more just and inclusive society.

The museum was not yet open to the public on my visit (in June 2023), though we were permitted to go inside and see its progress. The building construction had recently been finished, and the museum layout was still in the design phase. There was a small bookstore in one corner, with stacks of new books about Gandhi lining its shelves. On another wall was a series of historic photographs from the life of Gandhi. These were grouped into three sections by chronology and location, with the images on the far left from Gandhi's youth and his time in South Africa up until 1914; the middle images from Gandhi's time in London during various visits in his lifetime; and the images on the far right from Gandhi's time in India after his return there in 1915.

On another wall were more photographs of Gandhi from the final decade of his life in India. The rest of the exhibition space was empty, still under development. Thus far, the focus of the museum is on Gandhi's life from beginning to end, rather than on Gandhi's time in South Africa in particular, or on Tolstoy Farm

Figure 5. Inside the museum under construction at Tolstoy Farm. Photo by Karline McLain.

and its many inhabitants and activities during its existence as a living intentional community.

The Mahatma Gandhi Remembrance Organisation in Johannesburg, South Africa, is the organization currently working to transform this site into a heritage museum. The leading figure behind this effort is Mohan Hira (b. 1938), whose family moved to South Africa from India when he was a young boy. Hira is a martial arts expert who spent his career teaching karate. Several decades ago, Hira reportedly came to the former site of Tolstoy Farm, mowed the tall grass that had grown around the historic foundation himself, and decided to try to raise funds for its preservation. He has completed a Johannesburg-to-Durban "Footsteps of Gandhi" fundraising walk on three occasions (1988, 2002, 2005). He has also coordinated with the Johannesburg City Heritage Foundation to have Tolstoy Farm declared a heritage site. In January 2023, Hira received the Pravasi Bharatiya Award, India's highest civilian award for Indians living in the diaspora, for his work to preserve Tolstoy Farm.[7]

Efforts to enrich the museum at Tolstoy Farm are still ongoing. Just months after my visit, a larger-than-life, eight-foot-tall statue of Mahatma Gandhi was installed in the yard in front of the museum. There is also discussion of trying to work with South Africa's robust tourism sector to develop a Gandhi tour circuit in the greater Johannesburg area that could appeal to the Indian community and others interested in the history of Indians in South Africa. Visitors to Johannesburg can already tour Constitution Hill, an impressive museum that is a former prison and military fort, and where Mahatma Gandhi and Nelson Mandela were each imprisoned at different times. In addition to visiting Constitution Hill, I also visited Satyagraha House while I was in Johannesburg. Satyagraha House is a home that was designed and built by Herman Kallenbach in 1907.

Kallenbach was inspired by traditional South African village huts (*kraal*), with their round shapes and thatched rooftops, and built the home to feature two

Figure 6. Satyagraha House in Johannesburg. Photo by Karline McLain.

rondavels joined by a thatched mezzanine. After Gandhi was released from prison in 1908, this is where he lived with Kallenbach to be near the prison and court in Johannesburg, until they decided to move to Tolstoy Farm together in 1910. Today, Satyagraha House has been carefully restored and is privately owned and managed as both a guest house and a small museum. On my visit there, our museum guide was eager to hear an update about the status of the Tolstoy Farm museum and mentioned that they were hopeful that this museum could become another point of attraction for their guests, and presumably, they also hoped that future visitors to the Tolstoy Farm museum could also incorporate Satyagraha House into their itineraries.

Thomas Blom Hansen has pointed out that for Indians living in South Africa, India is an "unwieldy fetish," highlighting how "India features prominently in South African Indian life—through Bollywood films and associated music, fashion, and gossip; a rapidly growing tourism and pilgrimage industry; and Hindu and Muslim religious organizations with roots in the subcontinent."[8] Hansen argues that this fetishization of Indianness is structured by the fact that Indians have historically been seen as completely alien to the land; India was a site of authenticity, "our motherland," but also a site of non-African loyalties. He asks: How can one understand the relationship between South African Indians, India, and "Indianness" in a dynamic fashion that avoids reified notions of Indian culture and Indian religious practice? I think that the efforts of Indians in South Africa to preserve Tolstoy Farm and Phoenix Settlement as heritage sites can be understood as a move toward recognizing this dynamic relationship between Indians, India, and South Africa. Efforts at both Phoenix Settlement and Tolstoy Farm are not only about commemorating Gandhi (a figure who is himself quite fetishized) but also about acknowledging the role of Indians in South African culture and history, and about trying to create a new form of tourism, a "roots tourism" that focuses not (or not only) on returning to India as the motherland but on preserving and visiting important sites central to the history of Indians in South Africa.

3

Sabarmati Ashram

In 1915, Gandhi returned to India. Now forty-five years old, he was returning to his home country after spending twenty-one years in South Africa. The communal lifestyle he lived at Phoenix Settlement and Tolstoy Farm during these years had shaped his outlook significantly. Gandhi brought many members of his extended Phoenix and Tolstoy "family" to India, and he appointed his trusted nephew Maganlal Gandhi to look after this communal family as they sailed directly to India from South Africa, while Gandhi traveled first to England and then on to India.[1] Once in India, one of Gandhi's first meetings was with his political mentor, Gopal Krishna Gokhale, a leading politician in the Indian National Congress. Gokhale was skeptical of some facets of Gandhi's vision for independent India presented in his political treatise, *Indian Home Rule* (*Hind Swaraj*). Gokhale reminded Gandhi of his lack of experience in India and advised him to wait one year before he delved into politics, using this year to listen and learn. Gandhi agreed to this probationary period and spent much of 1915 traveling throughout India and engaging in thoughtful dialogue with Indian leaders, politicians, and activists, but he refrained from becoming politically active at this time.[2] When he wasn't traveling, Gandhi spent the remaining part of 1915 setting up the first of his intentional communities in India.

Gandhi expressed to Gokhale his desire to form an intentional community immediately, ideally in his home state of Gujarat: "I wanted to have an Ashram where I could settle down with my Phoenix family, preferably somewhere in Gujarat, as, being a Gujarati, I thought I was best fitted to serve the country through serving Gujarat. Gokhale liked the idea."[3] Gokhale served as the initial patron for the new community until he passed away later that year. Gandhi settled his communal family near Ahmedabad, the capital city of Gujarat. Here, a friend and fellow lawyer lent them his bungalow in a village called Kochrab. Gandhi and his communal family moved into the two-story bungalow on May 25, 1915, and decided to call their residential community Satyagraha Ashram. *Satyagraha* was the term they had begun using in South Africa to refer to nonviolent civil disobedience. An *ashram*, in classical Hinduism, was a forest hermitage, a place on the outskirts of civilization to which a renouncer could retreat. There, having abandoned society and attachments to householder life, renouncers could practice physical and mental discipline in pursuit of an experiential knowledge of ultimate reality, leading to freedom from the bondage of transmigration. Like traditional Hindu ashrams, Gandhi's intentional communities were similarly located at a remove from urban civilization and emphasized physical and mental discipline; but by contrast, they were places for the pursuit of both spiritual and political liberation. In his autobiography, Gandhi explains the significance of the name Satyagraha Ashram: "Our creed was devotion to truth [*satya*], and our business was the search for and insistence on truth. I wanted to acquaint India with the method I had tried in South Africa, and I desired to test in India the extent to which its application might be possible. So my companions and I selected the name 'Satyagraha Ashram' as conveying both our goal and our method of service."[4]

Gandhi's coresidents from South Africa lived at Satyagraha Ashram in Kochrab for two years and then moved in June of 1917 to a larger spot six kilometers north on the banks of the Sabarmati River, where their community came to be called Sabarmati Ashram. Gandhi made Sabarmati Ashram his primary home for the next fifteen years, until he decided to close it in 1933. Scholarship on Gandhi typically focuses on his political activism during these years, emphasizing his ascendancy within the Indian National Congress political party and his leadership of the Salt March civil disobedience campaign. This chapter focuses on Sabarmati Ashram, arguing that this community was foundational to Gandhi's evolving philosophy of universal well-being, *sarvodaya*, and to his sociopolitical development and anti-colonial activism. At Sabarmati Ashram, Gandhi and his fellow coresidents engaged in further experiments with inclusivity and belonging in the Indian context as they reckoned with untouchability and the Hindu caste system, as well as further experiments with civil disobedience for political self-rule. During these years, as Gandhi continued to engage in residential experiments in the pursuit of utopia, he escalated both the rhetoric and the expectation of suffering and self-sacrifice for communal flourishing and universal well-being.

Daily Life at Sabarmati Ashram

At the founding of this new intentional community in India, Gandhi and his coresidents set forth a constitution with a mission statement: "The object of this Ashram is that its members should qualify themselves for, and make a consistent endeavor towards, the service of the country, not inconsistent with universal welfare [*sarvodaya*]."[5] It enumerated eleven observances as essential for fulfilling this mission. The first and foremost of these was truth: "Truth is God, the one and only Reality. All other observances take their rise from the quest for, and the worship of, Truth." Following truth, the remaining observances included nonviolence, celibacy, control of the palate, nonstealing, nonpossession, physical labor, economic independence, fearlessness, removal of untouchability, and tolerance.[6]

Gandhi wrote the draft constitution and then workshopped it in person with his coresidents, and in correspondence with friends, potential residents, and donors, to arrive at its final form. Comparing the draft constitution with its final form provides insight into the deliberative conversation as the community codified its values. Originally, only the first six observances (truth, nonviolence, celibacy, control of the palate, nonstealing, and nonpossession) were enumerated in the draft constitution, while economic independence and fearlessness were listed as "subsidiary" observances.[7] Through collective input, the latter five observances (physical labor, economic independence, fearlessness, removal of untouchability, and tolerance) were added. This final list of eleven observances reflects a mixed origin of values. The first six observances were standard practice at Indian ashrams in connection with Hindu, Buddhist, and Jain religious traditions of ascetic renunciation. As we have seen in previous chapters, Gandhi and his coresidents at Phoenix Settlement and Tolstoy Farm were increasingly experimenting with these observances. Physical labor and economic independence (self-sufficiency) were inspired by Gandhi's reading of Ruskin and Tolstoy and had also been put into practice in South Africa. In the Indian context, the national movement for economic independence (*swadeshi*) had gained traction in the first two decades of the twentieth century, and the transfer of this from a subsidiary observance in the initial draft to an official observance in the final draft of the constitution indicates the groundswell of support it had among residents. The final three observances—fearlessness, removal of untouchability, and tolerance—were new additions that arose out of this collaborative process, building upon the group's prior experiments with communal living in South Africa and also anticipating some of the challenges they would face in the Indian context. Removal of untouchability would challenge orthodox Hinduism and its caste-based social hierarchy; tolerance was intended to promote a plural community in terms of religion, race, and caste; and fearlessness was intended to encourage residents to actively work against injustices through nonviolent means. As Gandhi explained, through these eleven observances, "the Ashram set out to remedy what it thought were defects in our national life from the religious, economic and political standpoints."[8]

Inclusivity and equity were thus emphasized at Sabarmati Ashram's inception with these eleven observances. Yet the draft constitution simultaneously established a hierarchy of members. Gandhi proposed three classes of residents: controllers, novitiates, and students. Controllers are adult residents who have taken a lifelong vow to follow all observances. They are responsible for the administration of the ashram under the guidance of the chief controller. Novitiates are adult residents who have agreed to temporarily follow all observances while in residence at the ashram but have not yet taken a lifelong vow. Students are minors in residence with the consent of their parents; when they become adults, they can either elect to take a lifelong vow and become a controller or leave the ashram.[9] These categories of membership are not included in the final constitution, suggesting a lack of consensus on this proposed hierarchy. Perhaps some residents questioned the very idea of a hierarchy, given that Phoenix Settlement and Tolstoy Farm had been established with the goal of promoting equality in a multiracial and multireligious communal setting. Perhaps there were concerns about the lack of detail about the chief controller position—presumably, Gandhi intended to fulfill the inaugural chief controller position himself, but who would enact these duties if Gandhi was not available, and how would they be selected? Indeed, the question of leadership in this avowedly equitable community would surface repeatedly, particularly as Gandhi grew more politically active and was away for longer periods of time.

Beyond Gandhi's family (his wife, Kasturba, and his three youngest sons, as his eldest son, Harilal, had rejected communal life), there were approximately twenty-five initial members when the ashram was founded in 1915, most of whom had lived with Gandhi in South Africa and originated from South Indian families. In Kochrab village, everyone lived in the two-story bungalow together as a large family. However, this location was not ideal. They desired a larger plot of land to farm. Gandhi also desired a more rural location because he disliked the proximity to the village and worried about sanitation, a concern that was validated when plague broke out in 1917. In light of the plague, and the rapid growth of the community to sixty residents by 1917, Gandhi purchased thirty-six acres of land on the banks of the Sabarmati River, six kilometers north of Kochrab village, establishing its ownership in a collective trust. The city center of Ahmedabad was across the river and seven kilometers south; Sabarmati Central Jail was three kilometers north. Though the land had no buildings or trees, Gandhi liked the site for multiple reasons: it could be farmed, its location "on the bank of the river and its solitude" were pleasing, and it was not too far from the jail. "As jail-going was understood to be the normal lot of Satyagrahis, I liked this position," Gandhi wrote.[10]

Gandhi recalls how they lived in canvas tents and constructed a temporary shed for a common kitchen as they began building the infrastructure for Sabarmati Ashram: "Our difficulties, before we had permanent living accommodation, were great. The [monsoon] rains were impending, and provisions had to be got from the city four miles away. The ground, which had been a waste, was infested with snakes, and it was no small risk to live with little children under such conditions."[11]

Gandhi also recalls that while the new location was his idea, "the execution was as usual left to Maganlal."[12] Maganlal had joined Gandhi in South Africa as a young man, arriving in 1902 at the age of twenty. Maganlal was one of the first Phoenix settlers, and he took on increasing responsibilities there. In India, Maganlal became Gandhi's right-hand man, leading the community whenever Gandhi was absent. Thomas Weber has discussed how central Maganlal was to Gandhi and to Sabarmati Ashram, writing, "Maganlal designed and supervised the construction of the buildings, he systematized the management of the ashram, introduced discipline and took control of ashram craft work. Maganlal was not just another ashramite who happened to be in charge. It is not an exaggeration to say that the ashram at Sabarmati was Maganlal's creation and that to a large degree he was the 'soul' of the ashram."[13]

Under Maganlal's direction, residents removed prickly shrubs and planted vegetables and fruit trees. They constructed simple yet aesthetically pleasing buildings for communal living with white stucco walls, stone floors, and tile roofs. Gandhi and Kasturba initially resided in the communal living space (known as Udyog Mandir) and then moved into their own house (Hridaya Kunj) in 1918. At Tolstoy Farm in South Africa, Gandhi and Hermann Kallenbach had built gender-segregated, dormitory-style housing for everyone to promote the practice of celibacy. Here at Sabarmati Ashram, dormitory-style housing and communal dining were the norm, but several private houses were also built. Gandhi and Kasturba's house was the largest of these, with a veranda for shaded outdoor meeting space and separate rooms for Gandhi and Kasturba (to facilitate the observance of celibacy), as well as Gandhi's secretariat, a guest room, and a kitchen. Their house faced the Sabarmati River and overlooked the prayer ground. Other private houses included Maganlal's one-room house (Magan Nivas); another small private house (Vinoba/Mira Kutir) that was first occupied by Vinoba Bhave (between 1918 and 1921) and later by Mirabehn (from 1925 to 1933); and a guest house.[14]

At Sabarmati Ashram, weaving and then spinning were added to the expected manual labor of farming, cooking, and sanitation as part of the community's growing emphasis on economic independence. The observance of economic independence entailed a commitment not to buy imported goods when they could be manufactured in India. Gandhi argued that one could serve the world best by serving one's neighbor first.[15] On his return to India in 1915, Gandhi was aware of the *swadeshi* movement, and he became involved in it when he provided legal services and political advocacy to indigo farmers in Champaran in 1917, and then to striking textile mill workers in Ahmedabad in 1918. Gandhi pledged to wear only *khadi*, clothing handwoven by himself or his coresidents, and to refrain from buying imported cloth that threatened the livelihood of Indian workers. Residents learned to grow cotton, to spin cotton, to weave the cotton into cloth, and to dye and print the cloth.[16] Gandhi learned to use a spinning wheel (*charkha*) and decided all residents must spin for one hour each day. Gandhi began traveling with a portable spinning wheel, and he would spin as he gave talks throughout India. Through Gandhi's visible devotion to spinning and the collective work of the ashram residents, *khadi* was embraced by the Indian National Congress in the 1920s and 1930s, and the spinning wheel became the iconic symbol of the Indian independence movement.[17]

In South Africa, the focus on manual labor at Phoenix Settlement entailed running the farm and operating the printing press to publish the weekly newspaper, *Indian Opinion*. In India, the new emphasis on spinning replaced the communal labor of running a printing press, although Gandhi personally remained invested in news media. Gandhi became the editor of the weekly newspapers *Navajivan* (in Gujarati) and *Young India* (in English) in 1919. These were published at a printing press in Ahmedabad, not at Sabarmati Ashram, but Gandhi saw this editorial work as important for introducing Sabarmati Ashram's mission to Indians on a broader scale.[18] In a letter from the editor published in *Navajivan* on September 7, 1919, Gandhi wrote that he felt "proud in describing myself as a farmer and weaver," and he then connected the aim of his communal lifestyle with his aim in publishing the newspaper:

> With much striving I have formulated some principles for my life and put them into practice. The happiness I have found that way, I think, I have not seen in others. . . . In the course of my seeking I have come by innumerable gems, which I want to place before India. *Navajivan* is intended to be a sort of advertisement for them. I saw, during my pursuit of truth, that it was our duty to give willing obedience to laws. But I also saw, while doing this duty, that it was equally a duty to disobey a law if it fostered untruth. What form should such disobedience take? We should suffer the penalty for the breach of law involved in acting according to the truth. This is known as civil disobedience.[19]

Through these newspapers, Gandhi sought to share with a growing community of readers in India his worldview, which encompassed his communal lifestyle and his political activism.

Education was also an important facet of daily life at Sabarmati Ashram, and indeed, the community became an intellectual center in its heyday, drawing in figures like Vinoba Bhave and other scholars and teachers. Gandhi had given significant thought to education at his intentional communities in South Africa, where he first expressed skepticism of colonial education, and he refused to send his children to British-run schools. Gandhi's interest in education intensified in India as he and his coresidents continued thinking through facets of self-rule as well as religious and social philosophy. Gandhi engaged in intellectual talks and debates with many of his coresidents, and during these years, he wrote his *Autobiography* and *Satyagraha in South Africa*, as well as his commentary on the *Bhagavad Gita*. Gandhi and the teachers at Sabarmati Ashram together created a model national school curriculum for primary and secondary education that included physical, intellectual, and religious components; that emphasized instruction in Indian languages (not the language of the colonial master); that sought to educate equally girls and boys, and children from all castes; and that would be free.[20] Gandhi also gave thought to higher education, raising funds to establish a national university, which resulted in the opening of Gujarat Vidyapith. In his inaugural address on November 15, 1920, Gandhi proclaimed that the mission of this university was to educate "with a national aim in view" by cultivating the students' moral strength and character to make "ourselves fit for swaraj [self-rule] in the country."[21]

Gandhi fulfilled his promise to his mentor that he would wait one year before delving into politics in India. In that year, he founded Sabarmati Ashram, which was Gandhi's home base for the next fifteen years; but as Gandhi grew increasingly involved in national politics, he frequently traveled to meet with various Indian leaders, negotiate with the British, and serve time in jail for civil disobedience. By 1924, Gandhi was elected president of the Indian National Congress, after leading several civil disobedience campaigns under its auspices. Though the position of "chief controller" was not formalized in the final constitution for Sabarmati Ashram, Gandhi served as the community's leader. In his absence, Gandhi looked to Maganlal Gandhi to run the community. Gandhi saw Maganlal as an ideal coresident: he accepted the eleven observances as a lifelong vow, in spite of his personal struggles with some of them; and he was quick to learn new skills, like printing press work in South Africa and weaving and spinning in India. To other residents, Maganlal could at times be too strict a taskmaster, and they questioned his role as the de facto leader when Gandhi was away.[22] This tension came to a head in 1919, when several residents complained and threatened to leave the community. Gandhi called a group meeting, where he reminded his coresidents of their mission and the sacrifices that were required of all residents to fulfill it. Gandhi upheld Maganlal as an exemplary resident, praising him for his hard work and sacrifice:

> In South Africa, my best creation was Phoenix. Without it, there would have been no satyagraha in that country. Without the Ashram here, satyagraha will be impossible in India. . . . Do not attribute greatness to me for other works of mine; judge me only by the Ashram. One of my creations here in the Ashram is Maganlal. If I have found from experience five million shortcomings in Maganlal, I have found ten million virtues in him. . . . Maganlal has offered all his work as sacrifice, not for my sake but for the sake of an ideal.[23]

Maganlal remained Gandhi's second-in-command at Sabarmati Ashram until his death in 1928. In the emotional obituary Gandhi wrote and published in *Young India*, he described Maganlal as the person he had "singled out as heir to my all" and as "dearer to me than my own sons." Gandhi highlighted how Maganlal had struggled with two observances, celibacy and the removal of untouchability, yet had persevered and grown ever more committed. Gandhi, who was by then increasingly called "Mahatma" ("Great Soul") in India, acknowledged that his "so-called greatness depends upon the incessant toil and drudgery of silent, devoted, able and pure workers, men as well as women. Among them all Maganlal was to me the greatest, the best and the purest."[24] Gandhi founded Sabarmati Ashram, but Maganlal was central to the day-to-day life of the community, which grew from its initial membership of twenty-five residents in 1915 to a population of 277 members at its height in 1928.

Removal of Untouchability

In South Africa, Gandhi's intentional communities brought together Indians and Europeans to live and labor together as equals, bridging across differences of race and religion to forge a counterworld to the colonialist and capitalist status quo. As discussed in the previous chapters, this utopic vision of inclusivity at the South African communities was simultaneously revolutionary for its time and also limited in scope, in that it did not include native South Africans. At Sabarmati Ashram in India, some white Europeans were again attracted to the multiracial and multireligious communal experiment. Among the European residents were Henry and Millie Polak, who came from South Africa and lived at the ashram until they returned to England in 1917; Madeleine Slade, known as Mirabehn (discussed in chapter 4), who moved from England in 1925 to join the ashram; and Reginald Reynolds, who moved from England in 1929 to join the ashram, drawn to it as a young Quaker and pacifist.[25] However, as the anti-colonial movement gained momentum in India, Gandhi and his coresidents were less focused on bringing together Indians and Europeans at Sabarmati Ashram to set a model for interracial equality and more focused on thinking about caste inclusivity.

As noted above, the "removal of untouchability" observance was not included in the initial draft of the Sabarmati Ashram constitution written by Gandhi. An examination of various editions of the constitution gives insight into how caste in general, and untouchability in particular, were considered in this collaborative process of finalizing the mission and observances of Sabarmati Ashram. By the third edition of the constitution, a "vow against untouchability" had been added as a subsidiary observance. I quote in full the statement about this subsidiary observance because it demonstrates the residents' internal debate about equality and belonging in their community:

> According to the Hindu religion as traditionally practised, communities such as *Dhed*, *Bhangi*, etc., known by the names of *Antyaj*, *Pancham*, *Achhut* and so on, are looked upon as untouchable. Hindus belonging to other communities believe that they will be defiled if they touch a member of any of the said communities and, if anyone does so accidentally, he thinks that he has committed a sin. The founders of the Ashram believe that this practice is a blot on Hindu religion. They believe that the Hindu race will continue to add to its load of sin so long as it regards a single community as untouchable. Some of the consequences of this practice have been terrible. In order to be free from this sin, the Ashram inmates are under a vow to regard the untouchable communities as touchable; actually one *Dhed* family was staying in the Ashram, and it is still there, when the third edition of these rules was being drawn up. It lives exactly in the same condition as the others in the Ashram do. This vow does not extend to association for purpose of eating.[26]

In this statement, the ashram members resolutely condemn the practice of untouchability. They view untouchability as wrong because it treats a subset of Indians as defiled and unequal based upon their ascribed status. They also view untouchability as a corruption of Hinduism. The members commit to regarding Dalits, or so-called "untouchables," as touchable.[27] At the time of this third edition of the constitution, they note that they have admitted one Dalit family into the community. However, they also note that this vow to eradicate untouchability "does not extend to association for purpose of eating." Here, we have evidence of dissent among the residents about the place of this family in the ashram's communal life. This line gives residents who do not want to dine with lower-caste members the permission to refrain from associating with them in this way, suggesting that there were upper-caste Hindus in the community who were not willing to defy conservative tradition by interdining with lower-caste members.

When the final edition of the constitution was approved, "removal of untouchability" became one of the eleven observances all residents had to vow to uphold (no longer a subsidiary observance). The constitution also eliminated any discussion permitting a limit to associating with lower-caste coresidents (i.e., while dining):

> Untouchability, which has taken such deep root in Hinduism, is altogether irreligious. Its removal has therefore been treated as an independent principle. The so-called untouchables have an equal place in the Ashram with other classes. The Ashram does not believe in caste which, it considers, has injured Hinduism, because its implications of superior and inferior status, and of pollution by contact are contrary to the law of Love.[28]

In the process of finalizing the constitution for Sabarmati Ashram, significant debate took place among members about caste in general and untouchability in particular, with one subset of residents advocating for the inclusion of Dalits as equal members, and another subset of residents resisting this. It is impossible to determine who all of the members of each subset were from the archive, but a few key voices can be identified.

One voice advocating to include Dalits as equal members was Gandhi. Gandhi was eager to join the Servants of India Society, which had been founded by Gandhi's mentor, Gokhale. The society's mission was one of nation-building, emphasizing self-governance within the framework of the British Empire and unity across religious and caste divides. Two of their principal efforts emphasized caste reform: assisting educational movements for women and "backward classes"; and the "elevation of the depressed classes."[29] To be admitted into the society, one had to commit to seven vows, the third of which required the member to regard "all Indians as brothers" and to actively work for "the advancement of all, without distinction of caste or creed."[30] Gandhi was in regular communication with members of this society during his first years back in India, especially V. S. Srinivasa Sastri, an educator who became the society's president after Gokhale's death, and Amritlal Vithaldas Thakkar (known as Thakkar Baba), a civil engineer. Both Sastri and Thakkar encouraged Gandhi to consider how Sabarmati Ashram could be more proactive in contributing to the effort to end untouchability. It was Thakkar who suggested that Gandhi should admit a Dalit family to live at Sabarmati Ashram, even recommending a particular "humble and honest untouchable family."[31]

Thakkar's suggestion put Gandhi and his coresidents to the test. They had already agreed that they would not employ any servants, in order to promote the ideal of self-sufficiency, to emphasize the value of manual labor, and to eliminate hierarchical notions of labor. All residents were expected to engage in three forms of manual labor that were traditionally deemed the work of Dalits: sanitation, weaving, and tanning. Everyone must take their turn cleaning latrines; everyone must learn handloom weaving (later, spinning); and everyone must learn to tan the hides of the ashram's dairy cows (after they die a natural death, in keeping with the vow of nonviolence).[32] By doing this work that was viewed as ritually polluting by upper-caste Hindus, residents of Sabarmati Ashram would ideally learn to value members of all castes and their contributions to society equally. While the community had noble intentions to connect manual labor with social equality in this way, there was no direct effort to improve the daily life of Dalits—a fact that Thakkar and Sastri pointed out as they encouraged Gandhi to consider what more the community could do to help eradicate untouchability.

Gandhi shared Thakkar's suggestion to admit a Dalit family with his coresidents. Gandhi records the reaction, writing, "I was perturbed. I had never expected that an untouchable family with an introduction from no less a man than Thakkar Baba would so soon be seeking admission to the Ashram. I shared the letter with my companions. They welcomed it."[33] The family Thakkar recommended joined the community in September of 1915: a man named Dudabhai Dafda, from the Dalit subcaste known as Dhed, which is traditionally associated with the occupation of weaving; his wife, Danibehn; and their young daughter, Lakshmi. However, residents' responses to this Dalit family were not universally welcoming. Gandhi's terse diary entries from 1915 point to some tensions: he notes on September 11 that Santok, Maganlal's wife, fasted in protest, and so Gandhi undertook a counterfast: "Dudabhai came from Bombay. There was quite a scene. Santok refused to eat, and I, too, therefore." On October 8, he writes about Kasturba, "Got excited again and lost temper with Ba [Kasturba]."[34] In a letter to Sastri, Gandhi reported more details about the fallout from his wife's rebellion against the admission of the Dalit family:

> I have told Mrs. Gandhi she could leave me and we should part good friends. The step is momentous because it so links me with the suppressed classes mission that I might have at no distant time to carry out the idea of shifting to some *Dhed* quarters and sharing their life with the *Dheds*. It would mean much even for my staunchest co-workers. I have now given you the outline of the story. . . . Please share this with any other member [of the Servants of India Society] you please.[35]

Kasturba and Santok did not keep a diary, so we do not have their unmediated thoughts on the situation. But from Gandhi's correspondence to Sastri and to his friend Hermann Kallenbach, we know that Gandhi gave an ultimatum to Kasturba, Maganlal, Santok, and other residents who were unwilling to accept the Dalit family: they could either accept the family as equal members or leave. Kasturba stayed, but Maganlal and Santok left with their children. They returned, briefly, a week later to meet with Gandhi, at which time Gandhi gave them an alternative option: they could travel south to Madras, living there for six months to improve their weaving skills, and then teach weaving in the ashram upon their return.[36] For Gandhi, the idea of Maganlal permanently leaving Sabarmati Ashram was unthinkable. Maganlal and Santok agreed to this option, and Gandhi wrote that they "mastered the art of weaving and after mature consideration also washed their hearts clean of untouchability."[37]

Sharing the common kitchen was a sticking point for those who objected to the admittance of the Dalit family. Keeping the kitchen ritually pure was the domain of women in the typical Hindu home, where cooking was done for the family and for the daily worship of the domestic gods. Kasturba and Santok would have been raised in orthopraxy to believe that sharing the kitchen space, dishes, and utensils with Dalits would mean risking ritual pollution and inauspiciousness. By the time of the third edition of the Sabarmati Ashram constitution, the Dalit family had been admitted, but there was still significant resistance to interdining, as can be seen by the stipulation that the vow to eradicate untouchability "does not extend to association for purpose of eating." This third edition of the constitution also included a brief discussion of caste more generally as benign, and it commented further on interdining: "There is no reason to believe that eating in company promotes brotherhood ever so slightly."[38] Although Kasturba chose to stay at the ashram, she apparently continued to protest the common kitchen. Gandhi wrote to Hermann Kallenbach that Kasturba had tried his temper too much over the admittance of the Dalit family, and she was "not allowed to take part in the kitchen."[39]

By the time the constitution for Sabarmati Ashram was finalized, "removal of untouchability" became one of the eleven formal observances, and no discussion remained that permitted a limit to associating with lower-caste members of the community. In writing about the observances, Gandhi emphasized that interdining was permitted but not publicly promoted:

> There are no restrictions on interdining and all Ashramites sit to dinner in the same line. But no propaganda in favour of interdining is carried on outside the Ashram, as it is unnecessary for the removal of untouchability, which implies the lifting of bans imposed on Harijans in public institutions and discarding the superstition that a man is polluted by the touch of certain persons by reason of their birth in a particular caste. This disability can also be removed by legislation. Interdining and intermarriage are reforms of a different type which cannot be promoted by legislation or social pressure.[40]

From Gandhi's correspondence, it seems that Maganlal embraced the common kitchen in time, but Santok continued to struggle with it. In a letter from 1929 (after Maganlal's death), Gandhi comments that Santok "never liked the common kitchen, nor the inmates of the Ashram."[41] Kasturba and Santok's resistance to interdining with Dalits is part of the reason that, as the community transitioned from the bungalow in Kochrab Village and built their new dormitory quarters and common kitchen at Sabarmati Ashram, Gandhi and Maganlal each built private residences for their families, which included a small kitchen for private cooking and dining.

In the final edition of the constitution, there is a brief discussion of caste more generally following the discussion of the removal of untouchability. Here, the Hindu concept of *varna-ashrama-dharma*—a person's social and religious duties (*dharma*) according to their ascribed caste (*varna*) and stage of life (*ashrama*)—is reinforced:

> The Ashram however believes in *varna-ashrama-dharma*. The division of *varnas* is based upon occupation, and therefore, a person should maintain himself by following the hereditary occupation, not inconsistent with fundamental morals, and should devote all his spare time and energy to the acquisition and advancement of true knowledge. . . . Though, therefore, the Ashram believes in *varna-ashrama-dharma*, there is no place in it for distinction of *varnas* as the Ashram life is conceived in the light of the comprehensive and non-formal *sannyasa* [renouncer stage of life] of the *Bhagavad Gita*.[42]

Through these deliberations, the residents arrived at a moderate reform stance with regard to caste. Untouchability was explicitly rejected, as was the hierarchical ordering of castes into superior and inferior statuses; but caste as entailing ascribed hereditary occupations was reinforced for the well-being of society at large, outside of Sabarmati Ashram.

Gandhi's desire to join the Servants of India Society challenged him and his coresidents at Sabarmati Ashram to think through their principles of inclusivity and equity as they pertained to Dalits, and to put those principles into action. Gokhale endorsed Gandhi to join the Servants of India Society prior to his passing, but not all of the society's members were willing to accept Gandhi's membership application. Gandhi records that some members felt there was "a great difference between my ideals and methods of work and theirs."[43] When it became clear that he would not easily gain acceptance into the group, Gandhi withdrew his application, writing that though he did not officially become a member, he was a "member in spirit" of the society.[44]

The Case of Lakshmi Dafda

What was life like for the Dalit family that joined Sabarmati Ashram? There's no memoir from Dudabhai or Danibehn Dafda, nor have their letters to Gandhi been preserved. But reading the archive carefully, I can extract some details and make some educated extrapolations.[45] The family was recommended to Gandhi by Thakkar, who trained Dudabhai to teach basic literacy to other Dalits. Gandhi wanted to expand educational opportunities for women and Dalits, and Dudabhai may have welcomed the opportunity to contribute to this outreach. Dudabhai and Danibehn may have also welcomed the promise of living as equals in a community committed to abolishing untouchability, and raising their young daughter there. However, after joining Sabarmati Ashram, they would have quickly become aware that there was ongoing debate among the residents about untouchability and that the community was not entirely free from caste prejudice. Gandhi notes in his autobiography that he detected the women's "indifference, if not their dislike, towards Danibehn" and that he pleaded with Dudabhai to "swallow minor insults" and ask his wife to do likewise.[46] Dudabhai and Danibehn arrived with their daughter, Lakshmi, at Sabarmati Ashram in September of 1915, but they stayed for less than a year before leaving. Four years later, however, they returned to leave Lakshmi—then approximately six years old and ready to begin formal schooling—to be raised and educated by the community, as they returned to Dudabhai's native village of Botad, where he would open a school for Dalits.

When Gandhi accepted Lakshmi into Sabarmati Ashram in 1920, he insisted that Dudabhai and Danibehn must give up all parental claims while Lakshmi lived there. In exchange, Gandhi and his coresidents would provide free room, board, and education, raising Lakshmi alongside and as equal to the other children of the community.[47] Gandhi often spoke of Lakshmi as his adopted daughter, though he increasingly relied upon several other residents to help raise her as he became more involved in politics. Kasturba was resistant to raising Lakshmi, and Gandhi spoke openly about disputes they had over this. For instance, in a speech Gandhi gave in November of 1925, he called upon upper-caste Hindus to treat Dalits with love as their brethren, and he admitted that he knew how challenging this could be, for it had divided his own household: "I told my wife that if my dharma [duty] were distinct from hers, it was only proper that we should live in separate huts; but she should not insist on my sending away Lakshmi and I, on my part, should not insist on her having Lakshmi with her."[48] Gandhi did not insist that Kasturba help raise Lakshmi, but he did insist that Maganlal do so, writing to him, "To me she is like a daughter. Though she is not well bred, we have got to bear with her. The only unhappy part of the business is that I have invited the burden and you have to bear it. Well, that has been my way, and there is nothing for you to do but to put up with it. In this lies your training."[49]

Gandhi sought to educate and "refine" Lakshmi and thereby demonstrate her equality with upper-caste members of society. In a speech at a new school for Dalit boys in 1925, Gandhi encouraged them to be model students, stating, "There is a girl named Lakshmi accompanying me. I would tell her that a great responsibility lies on her, that other *Antyajas* ["untouchables"] would be judged through her. You have to show the world, which at present holds down the *Antyajas*, that there is no difference between them and others."[50] Gandhi asked Maganlal to raise Lakshmi alongside his own children whenever Gandhi was away from Sabarmati Ashram. After Maganlal's death, this responsibility shifted not to Santok—who instead decided to leave Sabarmati Ashram—but to Narandas Gandhi (Maganlal's younger brother) and the women in charge of the girls' education, Gangabehn (Ganga Vaidya, an upper-caste widow who joined the community in 1924, along with two grandchildren) and Premabehn (Prema Kantak, a Brahmin woman who joined the community in 1929).

Gandhi and Dudabhai corresponded regularly about Lakshmi as she grew up. In her teenage years, Lakshmi was routinely sent back to her parents' village whenever she disobeyed the rules. As Lakshmi approached adulthood, she had little interest in taking a lifelong vow to uphold the eleven observances, which frustrated Gandhi. In a letter to Dudabhai in 1929, Gandhi wrote that Lakshmi's "pranks are once again on the increase" and that she "cannot keep her mind under control for a long time," and he asked Dudabhai to again "take her away, educate and send her back."[51] By 1933, Gandhi's frustration had grown to such an extent that he questioned his decision to accept Lakshmi into the community in the first place, which he expressed in a letter to Premabehn:

> I feel now that I should not have accepted Lakshmi at all. But who was I to decide? I am but a servant of God. I did not seek Lakshmi. God sent her. Let Him, then, look after her. She was under the charge of Ba [Kasturba] first, then of Santok, then of Gangabehn, and now she is under your charge. None of you have asked to have charge of her. . . . God will ultimately solve the problem. She has come to us as a representative of Harijans to claim payment of the debt which we owe to them. If she is full of shortcomings and indolent, the responsibility for that lies on you, me and on the caste Hindus. We reap as we sow. I am trying to get her married off.[52]

Gandhi began trying to arrange a marriage for Lakshmi in 1931, when he consulted with several coresidents and then wrote to Dudabhai to inform him that he had "decided to give Lakshmi in marriage to a non-*Antyaja* [a non-"untouchable"]."[53] Dudabhai replied, asking for more information about the proposed intercaste marriage and cautioning that Lakshmi was not in a hurry to marry.[54] Gandhi had identified a young man known as Maruti (Marutidas Sharma) as the potential bridegroom, a Brahmin from South India who was orphaned as a boy and then raised by Lakshmidas and Velabehn Asar. Lakshmidas was a businessman and ally of Gandhi. From the correspondence, it is clear that Dudabhai expressed hesitation about this match, though it is not clear if his hesitation was about the bridegroom in particular or the idea of an intercaste marriage more generally.[55] In February of 1933, Gandhi declared to Narandas that when Dudabhai visited Sabarmati Ashram that month, they must come to a final decision about the marriage of Lakshmi and Maruti, and he instructed Narandas to give Dudabhai an ultimatum: "If he agrees, let the marriage take place as soon as possible. If he does not give his consent, tell him that we shall not be able to look after Lakshmi any longer."[56]

The marriage of Lakshmi and Maruti took place on March 14, 1933. Because the community was committed to observing celibacy, Gandhi insisted the marriage not take place at Sabarmati Ashram, so it was held at a neighbor's property. Gandhi sent a letter to the community to be read aloud to convey his blessing of the marriage and to express his regret that neither he nor Kasturba could be there (both were then imprisoned for civil disobedience). In this same letter, Gandhi included a lengthy statement about intercaste marriage:

> There can be no doubt that, if this marriage is successful, it will benefit both Harijans and Hinduism a great deal. . . . The Ashram believes in the principle of varna-ashrama and tries to follow it as well as it can. I cannot speak for all, but I have often stated that I myself believe that in the present age all Hindus can, and do, belong to one varna only. If we wish to revive the varna-ashrama system, we shall have to start with a clean slate. This being my view, it was my duty to find a suitable husband for Lakshmi. . . . Mixed marriages like this one are in no way a part of the movement for the removal of untouchability. This marriage is a recognition of the point of view of one who believes in all the various ideals of the Ashram. I hope that no one will misunderstand its significance because it is taking place at the present time when the movement for the removal of untouchability is going on and because it is inspired by one who is the chief leader of that movement. I do not hold up this marriage as an example for anybody to follow. I regard marriage as a matter of the parents' and their children's free will.[57]

Gandhi used Lakshmi's wedding to reiterate the moderate caste reform stance that he and his coresidents had arrived at when they drafted their constitution nearly two decades earlier. Untouchability is rejected as unethical and a corruption of "true" Hinduism. But the institution of caste itself (*varna-ashrama-dharma*) is reinforced, even as the hierarchical ordering of castes into superior and inferior statuses is collapsed. While Gandhi upholds this intercaste union as beneficial for Dalits and for Hinduism, he simultaneously insists that intercaste marriage is not essential for the removal of untouchability.

After her wedding, Lakshmi left Sabarmati Ashram, moving to live with Maruti and eventually becoming the mother of two children. What was the impact of growing up at Sabarmati Ashram, both for Lakshmi and for the community? Lakshmi received an education enabling her to read and write, which was rare for Dalit girls at that time, in addition to learning the forms of manual labor that were the collective work at Sabarmati Ashram. Through her coresidents, she grew up in a network of upper-caste connections that went beyond the Dalit connections of her natal village and resulted in a marital union with Maruti. In spite of the commitment to the removal of untouchability at Sabarmati Ashram, one can imagine that Lakshmi must have questioned at times whether she truly belonged there or was simply the token Dalit member of a predominantly upper-caste institution. As a teenager she must have felt—and perhaps chafed under—the microaggressions she experienced, along with the heavy weight of Gandhi's expectation that she constantly behave as a model Dalit. Lakshmi's presence at Sabarmati Ashram had a significant impact upon her coresidents, challenging these upper-caste members of the community to think through their commitment to inclusivity and equity in a way that rhetoric alone (i.e., drafting the constitution) could not. They had to wrestle with practical questions of day-to-day life in a mixed-caste community, such as whether a commitment to equity also entailed intercaste dining and marriage. Lakshmi's presence at the ashram challenged Gandhi to articulate more clearly—to himself, to his coresidents, and to the public—his stance on caste reform. As Gandhi reckoned with caste reform, he returned again and again to the concept of suffering for the greater good.

Suffering and Sacrifice

In addition to the internal dissent that arose among residents over the decision to admit a Dalit family into Sabarmati Ashram, members faced external pressures as well. Monetary donations from upper-caste Hindus dried up, including from their primary patron, the textile magnate Mangaldas Girdhardas—although, in his absence, the Jain industrialist Ambalal Sarabhai eventually stepped up and funded the community for the next two years. Beyond finances, even routine chores like drawing water from the village well at Kochrab were suddenly challenging. In his autobiography, Gandhi recalls, "The man in charge of the water-lift objected that drops of water from our bucket would pollute him. So he took to swearing at us and molesting [hitting] Dudabhai. I told everyone to put up with the abuse and continue drawing water at any cost. When he saw that we did not return his abuse, the man became ashamed and ceased to bother us."[58] Gandhi gave considerable thought to this incident over the years, recounting it on many occasions and taking inspiration from Dudabhai's silent suffering at the hands of the upper-caste villager. One occasion when Gandhi recounted this incident was during a speech given to Dalits in 1920:

> After I had started the Satyagraha Ashram in Ahmedabad, I admitted to it an *Antyaj* ["untouchable"] friend, named Dudabhai, and his wife. How did our Hindus behave at that time? Dudabhai's wife was not allowed to draw water from the well which we had been using. I told them that, in that case, I, too, would not avail myself of that well. I had a share in the use of that well. But I let it go. How did Dudabhai behave? He remained perfectly calm, bearing the abuse in silence. With this *tapascharya*, the difficulty was overcome in three days, the people having realized that Dudabhai, too, was free to draw water from that well. This same Dudabhai's daughter, Lakshmi, lives in my house, moving like [Goddess] Lakshmi indeed. If all of you learnt to do the *tapascharya* which Dudabhai did, your suffering would be over this very day.[59]

Gandhi makes several moves in retelling this incident that are noteworthy. First, he connects Dudabhai's silent suffering with *tapas*. In Indian religions, *tapas* (and its variants, *tapasya* and *tapascharya*) refers to a variety of austere meditation practices undertaken by some renouncers. These practices entail bodily control, deprivation, and hardship. Classic examples include undertaking very restrictive fasts and meditating while seated in the midst of five blazing fires.[60] Gandhi refers to Dudabhai's behavior as a form of *tapas*, for he exerts bodily control in receiving physical abuse from the upper-caste villager and enduring it without reacting physically (fighting back, running away, etc.) or verbally (crying out in pain, asking his abuser to stop, swearing at him, etc.). People who undergo *tapas* are typically viewed as holy figures; thus, Gandhi elevates Dudabhai's status by likening his behavior to that of a renouncer. Second, Gandhi suggests that such suffering for a moral cause can have an effect on one's adversary. In traditional religious thought, *tapas* is understood to help transform the individual who undertakes the rigorous discipline, enhancing their meditation and burning up their karma so that they may progress toward liberation. Gandhi, however, suggests that through *tapas*, both parties in a conflict—the person who bears the suffering and the person who causes the suffering—will be changed. In this example, Dudabhai's inner strength and discipline are enhanced, while his abuser becomes ashamed of his behavior and stops the abuse, ultimately allowing Dudabhai to use the well. Third, Gandhi suggests that his audience should learn to do *tapas* like Dudabhai.[61]

Gandhi gave this speech to a Dalit conference in Nagpur, Maharashtra, where he had traveled to attend the annual meeting of the Indian National Congress. The Dalits were lobbying the Indian National Congress to take up their cause for equal rights and were specifically advocating for the legal right to enter Hindu temples. In his speech, Gandhi emphasized his support for eradicating untouchability, stating that political self-rule would be impossible until Hindu society was purged of untouchability. However, Gandhi did not endorse the temple-entry resolution, stating that society "is not prepared for this yet." Gandhi also told the group that he could not support their other resolutions: "I cannot tell a Hindu—for I do not believe in it—that he may freely eat and drink in the company of any other Hindus or that all Hindus should freely intermarry. This is not necessary."[62] Enacting new laws to guarantee the rights of Dalits, Gandhi believed, would only foment discord. Instead, he argued, Dalits should focus on *tapas*:

> I ask you to make yourselves fit for the rights which you demand. By saying so, I do not wish to suggest that you are not already fit. When I ask the country to be fit for *swaraj* [self-rule], I do not imply that it is unfit. I only ask it to be fitter than it is. I tell the *Antyajas* ["untouchables"], likewise, that they have a right to be free, to be the equals of any other Hindu; I ask them, however, to do *tapascharya* and be fitter for these things.[63]

It is at this point in his speech that Gandhi launches into the story of Dudabhai at the well. Like Dudabhai, who silently suffered the abuse of the upper-caste villager, so too should the Dalits gathered before Gandhi learn to suffer in silence when they are abused by upper-caste Hindus. In Gandhi's logic, such *tapas* will make the Dalits more morally fit for the equality they seek; and it will eventually transform their upper-caste adversaries, enabling them to recognize the full humanity of Dalits and embrace them as fellow Hindus. In another speech at a Dalit conference in Ahmedabad in 1921, Gandhi reiterated this message, telling the Dalits there, "You must not ask Hindus to emancipate you as a matter of favour. Hindus must do so, if they want, in their own interests. You should, therefore, make them feel ashamed by your own purity and cleanliness."[64]

Not all Dalits were content to suffer in silence. One of Gandhi's harshest critics on this matter was Dr. Babasaheb Ambedkar, a Dalit who had received scholarships to pursue undergraduate and graduate study in economics and law, eventually earning doctorates from Columbia University and the London School of Economics. When Ambedkar returned to India, he began leading efforts against untouchability in the 1920s, mobilizing Dalits in protest campaigns and fighting legal battles for Dalits' right of access to public water, right of entry into Hindu temples, and right of admission into village schools. Eventually, Gandhi and Ambedkar clashed with one another over their differing approaches to the removal of untouchability.

From 1930 to 1932, the Round Table Conferences took place in London over three sessions. The purpose of these conferences was to gather prominent Indian and British leaders together to discuss the next stage of India's constitutional development. Gandhi was invited to attend the second session as a representative of the Indian National Congress, and Ambedkar was invited to attend as a Dalit representative. At that conference, Gandhi and Ambedkar disagreed over the question of separate electorates. Ambedkar insisted that Dalits should receive separate electorates (which were also being considered for Muslim and Sikh religious minorities) to ensure they could elect their own representatives. Gandhi opposed separate electorates for Dalits, arguing that they were Hindus and should not be treated as a minority group. They also disagreed over the question of who truly represented the Dalits. As Harold Coward has pointed out, Gandhi was quite surprised to learn that Ambedkar, a well-educated lawyer, was himself a Dalit: "Gandhi admitted that he had at first taken Ambedkar to be a Brahmin obsessed with helping the Untouchables. It was not until their clash in London that Gandhi realized that Ambedkar was an Untouchable—which says much about Gandhi's stereotype of Untouchables as the 'dumb millions' that he and Congress maintained they represented."[65] When British Prime Minister Ramsay MacDonald decided in 1932 that separate electorates would be granted to Dalits ("Depressed Classes"), among other minorities (Muslims, Sikhs, Indian Christians, and Anglo-Indians), Gandhi announced that he would fast unto death in protest. In his opinion, a separate electorate for Dalits was "harmful for them and for Hinduism" because it would divide "untouchable" and "touchable" Hindus and thereby "vivisect and disrupt" Hinduism.[66]

Gandhi was then already in Yeravda Central Prison in Pune, Maharashtra, for nonviolent civil disobedience. He sent numerous letters about his intended fast to British colonial officials, Indian newspapers, and his coresidents at Sabarmati Ashram. In his letter to Prime Minister MacDonald, which was also published in the newspaper, Gandhi wrote that he had to resist the decision about separate electorates for Dalits with his life, declaring:

> This fast will cease if during its progress the British Government, of its own motion or under pressure of public opinion, revise their decision and withdraw their scheme of communal electorates for the "depressed" classes, whose representatives should be elected by the general electorate under the common franchise no matter how wide it is. . . . It may be that my judgment is warped and that I am wholly in error in regarding separate electorates for the "depressed" classes as harmful to them or to Hinduism. If so, I am not likely to be in the right with reference to other parts of my philosophy of life. In that case my death by fasting will be at once a penance for my error and a lifting of a weight from off those numberless men and women who have childlike faith in my wisdom. Whereas if my judgment is right, as I have little doubt it is, the contemplated step is but the due fulfilment of the scheme of life, which I have tried for more than a quarter of a century, apparently not without considerable success.[67]

In private letters, Gandhi described his fast-unto-death as a *yajna*, a sacrifice, using the Hindu religious term that typically refers to the material offerings sacrificed upon the fire altar to seek divine blessings. Rather than a ritual sacrifice in a liturgical context, Gandhi believed he was offering his life as a sacrifice for the greater good. On the eve of commencing the fast, Gandhi wrote to his brother, asking him not to grieve upon his death but to "rejoice that you had a younger brother whom God had granted the strength to complete such a *yajna*."[68] Gandhi wrote to Gangabehn at Sabarmati Ashram, "Do not be alarmed or upset by the *yajna* I have in mind. I am going to have you all undertake similar sacrifices. I will leave this body—if I have to—with the faith that you will all be able to do it. This is the only way to atone for the sins accumulated through generations."[69] In a letter to the whole community, Gandhi wrote, "I hope none of you has got perturbed by this *yajna* of my fast. God has inspired me to undertake it and may He carry it successfully to its end. None knows how many such *yajnas* we shall have to perform in order to eradicate this evil of untouchability. Get ready to perform such a *yajna* yourself."[70]

In these letters, Gandhi emphasizes that he is prepared to offer his life as a sacrifice, and he instructs his coresidents to prepare to sacrifice their own lives when he calls upon them to do so. Gandhi had already been instructing the community about sacrifice for several years. In 1926, he took a sabbatical year from political work to remain fully present at Sabarmati Ashram. During this year, he intensified his study of the *Bhagavad Gita* scripture, reading multiple translations and giving talks on its meaning after the daily morning prayers. Two residents, Mahadev Desai and Punjabhai, wrote down these talks, which were published as *The Bhagavad Gita According to Gandhi.*[71] In Gandhi's commentary on the *Bhagavad Gita*, it is well-known that he emphasizes nonviolence as a key lesson of this scripture, interpreting its war as metaphorical. But it is noteworthy that Gandhi also emphasizes self-discipline, suffering, and sacrifice in his interpretation. In response to the mention of "*yajna*" in verse 3.9 of the *Bhagavad Gita*, Gandhi states, "We accept a broad definition of *yajna*. *Yajna* means any activity for the good of others. A man works for the good of others when he spends his body in their service. This should be done in a spirit of dedication to God."[72] Gandhi is aware that he is broadening the definition of *yajna* when he redefines it from a liturgical sacrifice to a sacrifice of the body; indeed, he states, with reference to Vyasa as the legendary composer of the *Bhagavad Gita*, "There is no harm in our enlarging the meaning of the word *yajna*, even if the new meaning we attach to the term was never in Vyasa's mind."[73] Gandhi emphasizes that just as within the *Bhagavad Gita* Krishna goads Arjuna to act, to fight, and even die on the battlefield, so too must the residents of Sabarmati Ashram put the message of this holy book into action in their lives—through their physical labor, self-discipline, voluntary suffering, and willingness to sacrifice themselves for the greater good.

Some of Gandhi's allies questioned the idea of a "fast-unto-death" out of concern for Gandhi's personal well-being as well as for the practicality and even the ethics of this tactic. Jawaharlal Nehru, Gandhi's political protégé and a fellow Hindu, expressed concerns about how Gandhi injected religion into politics with this fast. In his autobiography, Nehru records his feelings at the moment when Gandhi announced his fast, writing, "I felt angry with him at his religious and sentimental approach to a political question, and his frequent references to God in connection with it. He even seemed to suggest that God had indicated the very date of the fast. What a terrible example to set!"[74] Nonetheless, Gandhi began his fast on September 20, 1932.

Gandhi gave an interview from prison the following day, September 21, stipulating his negotiating position. At this time, Gandhi came out publicly in favor of legislation to secure Dalits' right of entry into Hindu temples, reversing his earlier position, but he remained staunchly against separate electorates for Dalits, though he conceded that he would consider the idea of reserved seats for Dalit legislators if they were elected by the general electorate:

> If I had my way I would insist on temple-entry and the like being included in any pact that may be concluded and I would invite all reformers and untouchables to do so. I am aware that temple-entry is a difficult thing to accomplish in the very limited time that my life can hold out against the fast, but all the parties to the pact should pledge themselves to realize this elementary right of human beings at the earliest opportunity. . . . I would accept any pact that has not a tinge of separate electorate about it. I would, with the utmost reluctance, tolerate reservation of seats under a joint electorate scheme.[75]

Gandhi believed he was acting on behalf of Dalits and in their best interest, and he reiterated that he was willing to sacrifice himself for their cause, stating that if he did not do this, "I would be guilty of betraying God in whose name I have taken this great fast and the interest of untouchables for whose sake it has been taken."[76]

As coverage of Gandhi's fast-unto-death spread throughout India, more upper-caste Hindus made public vows to grant Dalits access to temples, wells, and public roads.[77] Ambedkar came under increasing pressure to compromise and thereby save Gandhi's life. Ambedkar and several other Dalit leaders traveled to meet Gandhi in Yeravda prison, where they negotiated for several days. Ultimately, they reached an agreement (called the Yeravda Pune Pact), whereby Ambedkar gained more reserved legislative seats for Dalits, while Gandhi gained his stipulation of no separate electorates. The agreement also specified that upper-caste Hindus would actively work toward the removal of untouchability in social and religious realms. The British cabinet accepted this agreement, and Gandhi broke his fast on September 26, issuing a press statement from his prison cell that celebrated the agreement as a win for all.[78] The following week was declared "Untouchability Abolition Week" throughout India.

While Gandhi celebrated this agreement, Ambedkar initially felt ambiguous about this compromise. He later wrote that Gandhi's fast-unto-death was "the worst form of coercion against a helpless people to give up the constitutional safeguards of which they had become possessed. . . . It was a vile and wicked act."[79] Arundhati Roy describes the impact of the compromise upon Dalits in this way: "The number of seats they were allotted in the provincial legislatures increased (from 78 to 148), but the candidates, because they would now have to be acceptable to their privileged-caste-dominated constituencies, lost their teeth. Uncle Tom won the day. Gandhi saw to it that leadership remained in the hands of the privileged castes."[80] If, as Gandhi claimed, *satyagraha* is a moral way to fight against injustice that entails not only nonviolence but also noncoercion, then one can raise legitimate questions about whether Gandhi's fast-unto-death aligned with his method of *satyagraha*.[81] Ambedkar came to the conclusion that it did not, that it was coercive, for he did not have free choice—his only choice was to either strike a compromise or to let Gandhi die.

Whereas Gandhi sought to create an ideal village where all residents could live and labor together as equals, Ambedkar described villages as places where casteism flourished and where residents were geospatially divided into "touchables," the community at the center who act as overlords, and "untouchables," the community at the periphery who function as a "subject race of hereditary bondsmen."[82] Ambedkar did not view Sabarmati Ashram as an exception, nor was he tempted to live there. Ambedkar did not want to suffer silently at the village well as Dudabhai had suffered while upper-caste Hindus abused him, and he did not want to wait patiently for Hindus to have a change of heart and recognize his full humanity. In the years following Gandhi's fast-unto-death, Ambedkar increasingly challenged Gandhi and his methods, arguing that Dalits had suffered and sacrificed enough and that the only way to eliminate untouchability was to legally abolish caste entirely. Ambedkar wrote multiple treatises on this topic, including *The Annihilation of Caste* (1936) and *What Congress and Gandhi Have Done to the Untouchables* (1945). Ambedkar also played a vital role in drafting the Indian Constitution as a member of the Constituent Assembly, and he helped to ensure that untouchability was legally abolished, though he was not able to put in place all the safeguards for subordinated castes and women that he hoped to.[83] In 1956, shortly before his death, Ambedkar publicly converted to Buddhism, along with five hundred thousand of his Dalit followers, as a final repudiation of caste and Hinduism. Gandhi, however, intensified his usage of the terms *tapas* and *yajna*, suffering and sacrifice, insisting that his coresidents must embrace these ideals in their daily life, and amplifying these ideals in connection with civil disobedience campaigns.

The Salt March

In South Africa, Gandhi had begun emphasizing self-discipline and voluntary suffering in the context of communal living, and he began connecting sacrifice to nonviolent civil disobedience by calling upon his coresidents to be willing to serve time in jail, and even die, in pursuit of Indian civil rights. In India, at Sabarmati Ashram, Gandhi escalated both his rhetoric and his expectation of voluntary suffering and sacrifice for universal well-being, on both the micro (ashram) and macro (nation) scales. Aside from his two sabbaticals (1915 and 1926), Gandhi was deeply involved in politics during his Sabarmati Ashram years, leading multiple nonviolent civil disobedience campaigns. The most famous of these was the Salt Satyagraha. On March 12, 1930, Gandhi (now sixty years old) led a group of coresidents from Sabarmati Ashram on a twenty-four-day march to the coast of western India. On April 6, the marchers reached the seashore, where they collected natural salt. In so doing, they broke the British salt tax law and sparked a nationwide civil disobedience campaign.

The Salt March has been memorialized in paintings and statues that depict Gandhi, wearing a homespun loincloth and carrying a walking stick, leading his band of marchers to the seashore. Political scientists and historians have discussed the Salt March, emphasizing Gandhi's transformative leadership and his idealism in action, highlighting not only how his nonviolent campaign contributed to securing India's freedom but also how it inspired other civil disobedience movements around the world.[84] Such analyses overlook the central role of the Sabarmati Ashram community in the Salt March, and the impact that the Salt March had upon the ashram community. Gandhi's success was indebted to the core circle of residents from Sabarmati Ashram, who were at his side throughout the march and who helped to plan and carry out the campaign. Ultimately, this campaign took a toll upon the members of the ashram community, who had to endure significant suffering and sacrifice—culminating in the sacrifice of Sabarmati Ashram.

Gandhi began thinking about salt in South Africa, where he restricted his intake of salt for health reasons. In India, he continued to minimize his salt intake and advised his coresidents to also do so to improve their health and control their passions. Gandhi also became aware of the politics of salt.[85] In speech after speech, he emphasized that the poor can often only afford one meal of bread and salt per day. The India Salt Act of 1882 made the collection and manufacture of salt a monopoly of the British colonial government, providing that salt could only be manufactured at government salt depots and levying a tax upon salt. As World War I drew to a close, some British politicians advocated doubling the salt tax to pay for war expenses. Gandhi urged politicians to reconsider, emphasizing the toll the salt tax placed upon the poor: "The monopoly has artificially raised the price of salt and today the poor find it most difficult to procure salt at a reasonable price. To them salt is as necessary as water and air."[86] Salt, Gandhi argued, was a basic need. To monopolize and tax it was an unjust law that served colonialism and capitalism at the expense of India's poor.

Throughout the 1920s, Indian politicians lobbied for political reforms and rights but to little avail. Ultimately, on January 26, 1930, the Indian National Congress released their declaration of independence, publicly asserting the goal of complete independence through nonviolent means. Gandhi wrote to the viceroy, Lord Irwin, stating that if the British cabinet would agree to eleven reforms, one of which was the abolition of the salt tax, then civil disobedience would end and they could together determine the path forward.[87] When the British did not agree, Gandhi returned to Sabarmati Ashram to plan a civil disobedience campaign.

Many members of the Indian National Congress who had endorsed a campaign to be led by Gandhi were skeptical after they learned that he planned to focus on the salt tax, fearing this issue would not suffice for mobilizing a nationwide campaign.[88] Mirabehn, one of the residents at Sabarmati Ashram, recalled that members of the Congress Working Committee who were meeting at the ashram were incredulous and exclaimed, "Salt! Do you expect us all to go out and just make salt?"[89] Gandhi wrote to Jawaharlal Nehru, then president of the Indian National Congress, informing him that he intended to carry out the campaign with his coresidents, not members of Congress, and that he would "think out what part the Congress can play in that event."[90] As Gandhi planned the Salt March, he looked back to the "Great March" he and his Tolstoy Farm coresidents had led in South Africa in 1913 for Indian civil rights (discussed in chapter 2) and decided that his companions in the march must be coresidents from Sabarmati Ashram, for only they were committed to nonviolence as a lifelong observance, rather than a temporary political strategy.

Gandhi anticipated that the marchers would meet with physical violence and, quite possibly, death. He carefully handpicked the coresidents with whom he wanted to march, choosing seventy-eight Indian men who came from a cross-section of regional, caste, and religious backgrounds to represent the diversity of India. These coresidents had already taken lifelong vows of celibacy and nonviolence, and Gandhi emphasized that they must be willing to serve time in jail for breaking the law and must be willing to sacrifice their lives if needed. To the other residents who wanted to march but weren't selected, including female and European-heritage residents, Gandhi emphasized that they would have a role in this campaign in due time.[91] Gandhi did, however, shrewdly dispatch one European coresident—the Quaker pacifist Reginald Reynolds—to hand deliver a letter to Lord Irwin, informing the viceroy of the terms of the march and stating that, to demonstrate that he did not consider the British as enemies, he was having the letter "specially delivered by a young English friend who believes in the Indian cause and is a full believer in non-violence."[92]

The night before the march began, Gandhi gathered the Sabarmati Ashram community together and gave a motivational speech. Using strong rhetoric, he described the Salt March they were about to embark upon as a "life-and-death struggle" and declared that the marchers would not return to the ashram until they had either attained independence or died trying:

> This fight is no public show; it is the final struggle—a life-and-death struggle. If there are disturbances, we may even have to die at the hands of our own people. . . . We hope to become the representatives of the poorest of the poor, the lowest of the low and the weakest of the weak. If we do not have the strength for this, we should not join the struggle. .

> . . I do ask you to return here only as dead men or as winners of swaraj [independence]. . . . We are entering upon a life-and-death struggle, a holy war; we are performing an all-embracing sacrifice in which we wish to offer ourselves as oblation.[93]

Gandhi expected the coresidents who marched alongside him to serve as the vanguard for this civil disobedience movement, viewing the march as a nonviolent "holy war" and willing to sacrifice their homes and their lives in pursuit of independence.

During the Salt March, Gandhi demanded that his coresidents-turned-comarchers continue to maintain their simple standard of living. They were instructed to accept only the simplest of food from the villages they passed through. Gandhi also published essays requesting that residents of the villages they would pass through should "be miserly rather than lavish" in their hospitality and should only provide bread, vegetables, or goat milk if doing so did not deprive their families.[94] Gandhi only allowed reporters to travel alongside the marchers on the condition that they live on the same simple alms for the duration of the march. Gandhi emphasized that "hundreds of thousands will follow this batch of seventy-eight in whatever they do"; thus, they must cultivate nonviolence and self-sacrifice.[95]

After collecting salt from the ocean on April 6 and gaining international media attention through the Salt March, Gandhi expected to be arrested immediately. When he was not, he began planning the next steps. On April 9, he called upon the female residents of Sabarmati Ashram to lead boycotts against foreign cloth and liquor.[96] The following day, Gandhi published an essay, "To the Women of India," in *Young India*, wherein he acknowledged the impatience of women to join the civil disobedience campaign and asked them to picket stores selling foreign cloth and liquor, writing, "When the women of the Ashram insisted on being taken along with men something within me told me that they were destined to do greater work in this struggle than merely breaking salt laws. I feel that I have now found that work. . . . Let the women of India take up these two activities, specialize in them; they would contribute more than man to national freedom."[97] Gandhi also set his sights on the government-run Dharasana Salt Works in Gujarat. Gandhi now expanded beyond the ashram community and invited Congress members and the Indian masses to join him if they would wear homespun cloth, be sober, and commit to nonviolence. After writing to the viceroy to share his intention to raid the Dharasana Salt Works, Gandhi was arrested on May 5, 1930, and sent to Yeravda Central Prison. The raid went forth as planned, led initially by Kasturba Gandhi and the Gujarati leader Abbas Tyabji; after their arrest, Congress members Sarojini Naidu (who was elected the first female president of the Indian National Congress in 1925 and 1926) and Maulana Abul Kalam Azad took the lead. At this raid, hundreds of nonviolent protestors were brutally beaten by colonial forces before being arrested.

To the surprise of many members of the Indian National Congress, the Salt Satyagraha galvanized the masses, bringing working classes, the youth, and women into the movement for independence on an unprecedented scale.[98] In total, over eighty thousand Indians were arrested. The raid on Dharasana Salt Works was covered by the international press and resulted in an outpouring of global sympathy; as Dennis Dalton points out, descriptions of the rows of nonviolent Indian protestors courageously facing violent beatings spread quickly through the news, and direct comparisons of Gandhi with Christ became common in popular commentary in Britain and the United States.[99]

In the 1970s and 1980s, Dennis Dalton and Thomas Weber each interviewed a number of former Sabarmati Ashram residents, including several of the seventy-eight marchers who led the Salt Satyagraha alongside Gandhi. These interviews showed that developing the level of self-discipline advocated at the ashram was met with a range of responses. Some younger members who came from wealthy, high-caste families found the manual labor requirements onerous. Others recounted that the disciplined lives they led at Sabarmati Ashram were crucial not only for their experience along the 240-mile march but for the months of rigorous imprisonment that followed. Satish Kalelkar, who joined Sabarmati Ashram in 1929 as a nineteen-year-old, reflected to Dalton that a highlight of such disciplinary training was a discovery of unexpected personal reserves, which in turn produced a fearlessness in the face of government assault.[100] Another of the seventy-eight marchers, Haridas Muzumdar, reported that Sabarmati Ashram residents were trained in the months leading up to the Salt March to learn to "joyfully suffer even unto death"; to "put up with assaults from the opponent, never retaliate" physically or verbally; to "voluntarily submit to arrest"; to "behave courteously toward prison officials"; and to "joyfully obey all orders issued by the leader of the [satyagraha] corps, whether they please him or not."[101] Residents were trained in nonviolent tactics, nonviolent philosophy, and in the expectation that they would have to voluntarily—even joyfully—suffer and possibly die for the greater good.

After Gandhi was arrested, he was sent to Yeravda prison, where he was housed separately from other protestors and had limited contact with them. While serving time, Gandhi exchanged weekly letters with the residents remaining at Sabarmati Ashram (those not imprisoned), providing detailed input on daily life and asking regularly about Lakshmi. Gandhi emphasized that he and the other marchers now imprisoned had made a sacrifice of themselves for the cause of independence; those remaining at the ashram should similarly make a sacrificial offering of themselves by continuing to support the struggle in nonviolent ways and with an attitude of joy. In a long letter to Narandas, Gandhi wrote, "A life of sacrifice is the pinnacle of art and is full of true joy. Such life is the source of ever fresh springs of joy which never dry up and never satiate. *Yajna* is not *yajna* if one feels it to be burdensome or annoying."[102] Gandhi continued thinking about suffering and sacrifice in prison and also after his release.

When Gandhi was released from prison on January 26, 1931, he negotiated a temporary settlement with Lord Irwin and then sailed for London to negotiate with the British government at the second Round Table Conference (where he and Ambedkar would reach their stalemate over the issue of separate electorates for Dalits). Gandhi gave a speech at the conference plenary, stating:

> I shall strain every nerve to achieve an honorable settlement for my country, if I can do so without having to put the millions of my countrymen and countrywomen, and even children, through this ordeal of fire. [But] if a further ordeal of fire has to be our lot, I shall approach that with the greatest joy and with the greatest consolation that I was doing what I felt to be right, the country was doing what it felt to be right, and the country will have the additional satisfaction of knowing that it was not at least taking lives, it was giving lives—it was not making the British people directly suffer, it was suffering. . . . I want you to suffer because I want to touch your hearts, and when your hearts have been touched, then will come the psychological moment for negotiation.[103]

In this speech, a willingness to sacrifice oneself and undergo suffering is central to Gandhi's evolving concept of universal well-being. We see this at work first at the microlevel, when Gandhi urged Dudabhai and his coresidents to endure the village neighbor's abuse to secure equal access to well water, and then at the macrolevel, when Gandhi urged Dalits throughout India to endure suffering to secure recognition of their full humanity from upper-caste Hindus, and again when Gandhi urged his fellow protestors to endure beatings and imprisonment to secure national independence. Such voluntary suffering and sacrifice, Gandhi believed, had the power to bring about change by opening the heart of the oppressor.

Sacrificing Sabarmati Ashram

After the Round Table Conference sessions concluded without an agreement, it was clear that India's independence was still some years away. Yet Gandhi had vowed in 1930, when embarking upon the Salt March, that he would not return to Sabarmati Ashram unless they had won independence. Gandhi therefore decided to close Sabarmati Ashram on July 22, 1933. At this time, 107 residents remained—mainly women and children, as a majority of the male residents and some female residents were in prison. Gandhi began making preparations for these remaining residents, including arranging the marriage of his "adopted" daughter, Lakshmi. Gandhi encouraged as many of the remaining residents as could do so to court arrest, and he made preparations for the remaining women and children to relocate to a satellite ashram in Wardha that was run by a former resident of Sabarmati Ashram, Vinoba Bhave.[104]

There are several theories about why Gandhi made this decision to close and disband Sabarmati Ashram. Mark Thomson suggests that the major reason was the residents' lack of discipline and Gandhi's inability to restore order due to his prolonged absences. The school-age children were ill behaved and did not always perform their manual labor; and the adults did not always sublimate their sexual urges in keeping with their vow of celibacy. Thomson writes, "Gandhi found himself unable to supervise either the internal workings or the external constructive activities of Sabarmati, with the result that he devolved responsibility on men and women who lacked his charismatic authority and organizational ability. . . . Gandhi realized that the Ashram had outlived its usefulness and disbanded it."[105] Gandhi's letters to Narandas and other residents from this period are a testament to his concerns over the residents' behavior and lack of discipline.[106] Thomas Weber, on the other hand, suggests that the major reason for closing Sabarmati was Maganlal Gandhi's death. Gandhi had relied upon Maganlal to look after this communal family during his prolonged absences and to ensure that the community upheld their disciplined labor and their moral commitment to the eleven observances. Weber writes that after Maganlal's passing in 1928, "the soul of the establishment had, as he claimed, to a large extent departed. The ashram was now little more than a collection of buildings with all too frequently squabbling inmates. It seems that this made it far easier to leave, and the time had come to set up new headquarters in a place where the void left by Maganlal's passing was not as evident."[107] Added to these factors, Sabarmati Ashram had not paid land taxes for the previous two years as part of their boycott of colonial governance. Gandhi feared that the government would soon seize the property. In a letter to Jamnalal Bajaj, wherein Gandhi discusses some of his arrangements for closing Sabarmati Ashram, Gandhi discloses this concern, writing, "The reason for handing over control of the Ashram is that it is better to hand over ourselves what the Government is sure to take by force in due course."[108]

All of these reasons were likely on Gandhi's mind as he made this momentous decision. I argue that there was yet another motivation behind Gandhi's decision to close Sabarmati Ashram: Gandhi had not yet succeeded in attaining complete independence, and so by his logic, a greater sacrifice was needed to open the heart of the oppressor. In a long letter to the home secretary, Gandhi offered Sabarmati Ashram to the colonial government. He did so to repay the tax debt but also described the ashram's closing as a sacrifice for independence, writing, "Time has now arrived for the Ashram to make a greater sacrifice in the face of the existing situation—on the one hand the growing terrorism by the Government and on the other the equally growing demoralization among the people."[109] He explained that since the viceroy had rejected Gandhi's proposal for independence, the struggle must continue, with greater sacrifices:

> The struggle therefore is bound to be prolonged and calls for much greater sacrifice than the people have hitherto undergone. It follows that the greatest measure of sacrifice is to be expected of me as the author of the movement. I can therefore only offer that which is nearest and dearest to me and for the building of which I and many other members of the Ashram have labored with infinite patience and care all these eighteen years. Every head of cattle and every tree has its history and sacred associations. They are all members of a big family. . . . It will not be without a tear that we shall break up the family and its activities.[110]

Gandhi felt he had to offer that which was dearest to him as a sacrifice for independence, and nothing was dearer to him than Sabarmati Ashram. Gandhi reiterated this in an interview to the Associated Press, stating, "Hundreds or thousands who took part in the struggle have lost their all. Having heard the story of the brave suffering of the villagers, I felt that some drastic action was necessary on my part. What was it that I could sacrifice?" He explained that Sabarmati Ashram was the most precious thing he could offer.[111] Gandhi encouraged the residents of Sabarmati Ashram to embrace this sacrifice and to constitute a "walking ashram": "The disbandment of the Ashram would mean that every inmate would constitute a walking ashram, carrying with him or her the responsibility for realizing the Ashram ideal, no matter where situated, whether in prison or outside."[112] From his prison cell, Gandhi sacrificed Sabarmati Ashram upon the altar of the independence struggle, hoping that just as his coresidents had taken the ashram's values on the road during the Salt March, so would they continue to put them in practice in their lives as they left their communal home behind forevermore.

Interlude 3

Sabarmati Ashram after Gandhi

On my first visit to Sabarmati Ashram, I stood barefoot on the sandy square plot demarcated as the prayer ground, which the historical signpost proclaimed as "the place consecrated for morning and evening prayers of the inmates of the Ashram, where the hallowed voice of many a sermon of Gandhi-ji still lingers."[1] There, as I felt the warm sand between my toes and the sun on my head, I reflected upon the deliberate choice Gandhi and his coresidents made to refrain from erecting any building or walls for their prayer space at their intentional communities— instead, they privileged nature over any human-designed and potentially communally exclusive architectural form, choosing to demarcate a central plot of land as sacred and making it accessible to all. I watched a fishing boat drift on the Sabarmati River, and two green parrots descend on the riverbank. The other visitors on that day were quiet and respectful, whispering to one another as they walked the grounds. At the time of its founding, the ashram farmland was in the rural countryside, across the river and a ways north from the city of Ahmedabad. But over the past century, the city has sprawled across the Sabarmati River, enfolding the ashram grounds within it, and "Sabarmati" is now a suburb of western Ahmedabad city. Although I had been forewarned by Arun Gandhi (grandson of Mahatma Gandhi, who graciously showed me around the site on my first visit in 2015, along with his son Tushar Gandhi) that Sabarmati Ashram was now just a noisy place where tourists come to take photos, and local children come on school field trips to traipse through the museum, I found it to be a comparatively tranquil oasis in the midst of the bustling city.

Gandhi tried to sacrifice Sabarmati Ashram to the British colonial government in 1933, but the British had no desire to take possession of it. Gandhi consulted with the ashram trustees, and they decided to hand over the ashram grounds to the Harijan Sevak Sangh ("Servants of Untouchables

Figure 7. Hridaya Kunj, the house of Gandhi and Kasturba at Sabarmati Ashram. Photo by Karline McLain.

Society"), a nonprofit organization headquartered in Delhi and dedicated to the removal of untouchability, to serve as a hostel for Dalit families and a place to provide an education and professional training to Dalit children.[2] Following India's independence in 1947 and Gandhi's assassination in 1948, the ashram was divided into a handful of trusts dedicated to Gandhian pursuits (including Sabarmati Ashram Preservation and Memorial Trust; Sabarmati Harijan Ashram Trust; Sabarmati Ashram Gaushala; Khadi Gramodyog Prayog Samiti; and Khadi Gramodyog Mandal). The trustees of the Sabarmati Ashram Preservation and Memorial Trust made the decision to preserve part of the ashram as a heritage site and to build a museum there. Visitors to Sabarmati Ashram today can tour several historic edifices, including Gandhi and Kasturba's house ("Hridaya Kunj"), where they can step onto the veranda and see one of Gandhi's spinning wheels and read a list of the eleven observances hanging on the wall. A sign on the house proclaims, "From here were inspired all his [Gandhi's] national activities. It was from here that the famous Dandi [Salt] March" began.[3] Visitors can also tour the house that was first occupied by Vinoba Bhave, and later by Mirabehn ("Vinoba/ Mira Kutir"), and see the prayer ground. Beyond these historic sites, the Gandhi Memorial Museum serves as the primary attraction for most visitors.

Indian architect and urban planner Charles Correa was hired to design the Gandhi Memorial Museum, which was completed in 1963. Correa used a modular design, and he gave significant thought to the form the museum should take to

Figure 8. Gandhi Memorial Museum at Sabarmati Ashram. Photo by Karline McLain.

honor Gandhi's legacy, concluding that like Gandhi, the museum should also be "human-scaled, unpretentious, modest." He wrote:

> With this as a starting point, the building very soon designed itself—as a series of pavilions, some open and some enclosed, interspersed with courtyards and a water pool. The mood is one of calmness and contemplation, qualities that the Mahatma exemplified and that are essential to any scholar attempting to understand his world. Of decisive importance to the creation of this mood are, the "rest" spaces—those open areas that interlock with the closed ones.[4]

The museum was inaugurated by Prime Minister Jawaharlal Nehru on May 10, 1963. Nehru had visited Gandhi at Sabarmati Ashram on many occasions to discuss political strategies in the quest for independence, though he never chose to live there, preferring city life. In his inaugural speech, Nehru commented on the beautiful modesty of the museum, saying, "I thank you for inviting me to this old place, full of memories. It is good that you have built here a museum—a beautiful museum. Beautiful not because somebody has put up a huge building using marble and such things—for that is not proper. . . . There is nothing pretentious here, but in itself shows that is a very simple and lovely thing. And that is why I am pleased to see it."[5] Walking through the museum, visitors move through a series of square rooms, each constructed of brick and wood, with stone floors and tile roofs to align with the aesthetic of the earlier buildings. There is ample natural light, cooling breezes flow across the water tank into the open-air pavilions, and there are wide benches to sit on.

The focus of the museum's permanent exhibit is Gandhi's political leadership in the anti-colonial struggle during the years he was in residence at Sabarmati Ashram (1915–1933). The exhibit begins with the following statement:

> The Ashram was the focal point of Gandhi-ji's initial activities on his return to India. Leaders and intellectuals from all parts of the country came here to seek his guidance. Between 1915 and 1930, the year of the Dandi [Salt] March, the ashram witnessed many events of local as well as national importance. Gandhi-ji's experiments in the fields of truth and action originated here. Thus, his stay in Ahmedabad is an important phase of his life.[6]

Display cases feature historical black-and-white photos, with text in Hindi, Gujarati, and English languages to provide historical context, focusing on Gandhi's nonviolent civil disobedience campaigns during these years, culminating in the Salt March. A secondary focus of the exhibit is the ashram itself, with display cases that highlight the community's eleven observances, daily activities, Gandhi and Kasturba as the "father" and "mother" of the community, and the controversial decision to admit an "untouchable" family—Dudabhai and Danibehn Dafda and their daughter, Lakshmi—into the community.

Two large paintings serve as the visual anchors for the exhibit. Each painting is approximately five feet tall by six feet wide. One is titled "Satyagraha: Dandi March" and features Gandhi leading the Salt March. It is based on a historic photo, taken on March 12, 1930, at the start of the march, when Gandhi left Sabarmati Ashram accompanied by seventy-eight of his coresidents to begin the twenty-four-day-long march to Dandi on the coast of western India. When they arrived at Dandi on April 6, Gandhi and his fellow marchers bent down and collected natural salt from the seashore. In so doing, they broke the British salt tax law and sparked a nationwide anti-colonial campaign. In the painting, Gandhi is featured at the center, wearing his homespun loincloth and carrying a walking stick. He is flanked on either side by his coresidents, all dressed in white homespun cloth, symbolizing their commitment to economic and political self-rule. The Salt March is the most famous of Gandhi's civil disobedience movements. Political scientists and historians often highlight Gandhi's leadership of this movement but overlook the central role of Sabarmati Ashram members. In foregrounding this painting, the museum seeks to rectify this oversight, emphasizing that this civil disobedience campaign was the work of Gandhi *and* the community.

Figure 9. "Removal of Untouchability: Intercaste Harijan Marriage," Gandhi Memorial Museum at Sabarmati Ashram. Photo by Karline McLain.

The other painting is titled "Removal of Untouchability: Intercaste Harijan Marriage." It depicts a bride and groom dressed in white homespun cloth, seated before the sacred fire and a Hindu priest, making their marital vows. Gandhi and Kasturba are seated next to the bride and groom, and other attendees are in the background. This painting is also based on a historic photo, this one taken in 1940, when an intercaste and interreligious marriage ceremony was held at Sevagram Ashram—not Sabarmati Ashram—under the auspices of Gandhi and his wife. On each of my visits to the museum, I have paused at length before this painting, wondering: What is at stake in the decision to include this anachronistic image so prominently in this exhibit? After all, during his years at Sabarmati Ashram, Gandhi did not allow any weddings to take place on its grounds due to the communal observance of celibacy. As discussed in chapter 3, during his years at Sabarmati Ashram, Gandhi did arrange one intercaste marriage, which took place in 1933 (at the nearby bungalow of Gandhi's associate Dr. Pranjivandas Mehta) between Gandhi's "adoptive" daughter, Lakshmi Dafda, a Dalit, and an upper-caste Brahmin, Maruti Sharma. Neither Gandhi nor Kasturba was in attendance at this wedding, as they were both in prison for civil disobedience. In the letter Gandhi sent to the Sabarmati Ashram community to convey his blessings to the couple, he emphasized that while the marriage was of symbolic importance, he did not endorse intercaste marriage as part of the movement to abolish untouchability, writing, "I do not hold up this marriage as an example for anybody to follow. I regard marriage as a matter of the parents' and their children's free will."[7]

Gandhi and his coresidents at Sabarmati Ashram had arrived at a moderate reform stance with regard to caste. "Removal of untouchability" was one of the eleven observances all residents were committed to upholding, and it entailed rejecting the practice of untouchability as unethical and a corruption of "true" Hinduism. However, they reinforced the institution of caste itself (*varna-ashrama-dharma*), even as they sought to collapse the hierarchical ordering of castes into superior and inferior groups. Due to resistance from upper-caste Hindus, which arose both internally and externally to the ashram community, Gandhi maintained during his years at Sabarmati Ashram that neither intercaste dining nor intercaste marriage was essential to the abolition of untouchability.

One of Gandhi's harshest critics on his stance regarding caste reform was the Dalit lawyer and activist Dr. Babasaheb Ambedkar. As discussed in chapter 3, Gandhi and Ambedkar clashed publicly in 1931 and 1932 over the question of whether Dalits should be granted separate electorates, with Gandhi embarking upon a "fast-unto-death" in 1932 to protest a separate electorate for Dalits, which he argued was "harmful for them and for Hinduism" because it would "vivisect and disrupt" Hinduism.[8] Ambedkar later renounced Hinduism, arguing that Dalits would never be included as equals within Hinduism unless Gandhi and all other upper-caste Hindus were willing to eradicate not just untouchability but caste entirely.[9] Gandhi has posthumously continued to receive criticism for his moderate stance with regard to caste reform. Arundhati Roy, for instance, writes, "Notwithstanding stories and anecdotes from Gandhi's followers about Gandhi's love for untouchables and the inter-caste weddings he attended, in the 98 volumes of his writing, he never decisively and categorically renounced his belief in chaturvarna, the system of four varnas [castes]."[10] Other scholars, however, have pointed out that Gandhi's attitude toward caste shifted over time. Harold Coward writes, "In the 1940s, Gandhi's emphasis seemed to change, perhaps as a result of his continually having to contend with Ambedkar's critique. Rather than continuing to exalt a purified caste order purged of untouchability, he began to call for the full repudiation of caste."[11]

The museum exhibit is noticeably silent about Gandhi's dispute with Ambedkar and his controversial fast-unto-death. It does not make reference to these historical events in either text or image, in spite of the fact that they took place during Sabarmati Ashram's active years, prior to its closure in 1933. Display panels do, however, acknowledge the internal tension that arose within the Sabarmati Ashram community after the Dalit family was admitted into the ashram. One text-heavy display panel (featuring handwritten letters by Gandhi but no photographs) describes this moment in the ashram's history: "A Harijan teacher, Dudabhai, and his family, came to stay at the ashram on September 26, 1915. It marked the formal beginning of Gandhi-ji's effort to get Harijans accepted by society. This created many problems for him in the ashram and in society which occupied a lot of his attention."[12] The following panel details how some residents, including Gandhi's wife, Kasturba, and his nephew Maganlal, initially protested the decision to admit Dudabhai and his family, and how Gandhi had to work to procure donations for the community after some Hindu patrons withheld their financial support in protest. Discussing Gandhi's decision to "adopt" Lakshmi, another text-heavy display panel (also without photographs) includes the following question-and-answer statement:

> Did Gandhi-ji adopt a Harijan girl to teach Kasturba a lesson? Kasturba did not dislike Dudabhai's wife Danibehn, but she was indifferent to her. Later, when Dudabhai and Danibehn left the ashram for some other reason Bapu [Gandhi] persuaded them to leave their daughter Lakshmi behind. He adopted her and made Ba [Kasturba] responsible for looking after Lakshmi. In the beginning she did not like the idea but she soon accepted her.[13]

The "Removal of Untouchability: Intercaste Harijan Marriage" painting represents a later phase in Gandhi's intentional communities and in Gandhi's thinking about caste reform. In the decades after closing Sabarmati Ashram in 1933, Gandhi continued to think deeply about caste matters and work for the eradication of untouchability: he handed over the Sabarmati Ashram land to the Harijan Sevak Sangh to provide homes and educations to Dalits; he founded a newspaper called *Harijan*, dedicated to the abolition of untouchability; and he began to defy Hindu orthopraxy by publicly endorsing intercaste dining and marriage. The 1940 photo that inspired the "Removal of Untouchability: Intercaste Harijan Marriage" painting was taken by Gandhi's grandnephew, Kanu Gandhi (son of Narandas Gandhi), who lived with Gandhi at his last intentional community, Sevagram Ashram, located in Maharashtra. It documented the wedding of Dakshayani, a Hindu Dalit (Pulayar caste) woman, and Velayudhan, a Christian Dalit (Ezhava caste) man. The wedding was performed by Parchure Shastri, an upper-caste Hindu who had been outcaste because he suffered from leprosy but who came to live at Sevagram Ashram at Gandhi's invitation. Gandhi and Kasturba attended this wedding as the witnesses, giving the married couple their blessing. A few years later, in 1945, Gandhi decided that he would now only attend weddings if they were intercaste and entailed marrying a Dalit to an upper-caste Hindu.[14]

The inclusion of the "Removal of Untouchability: Intercaste Harijan Marriage" painting alongside the "Satyagraha: Dandi March" painting as the two visual anchors of the Gandhi Memorial Museum exhibit has the effect of keeping Gandhi centered as the hero of the history presented therein, and it preserves the Sabarmati Ashram community as his supporting cast. One painting shows that Gandhi led the Salt March and launched a nationwide anti-colonial campaign for independence, accompanied by seventy-eight Sabarmati Ashram coresidents. The other painting shows that Gandhi worked to challenge casteism by encouraging intercaste marriages and breaking down other caste taboos, with his wife at his side and other residents celebrating the occasion in the background. The inclusion of this second, anachronistic painting (that depicts an event from a later time and at a different intentional community) allows the exhibit to look beyond the Sabarmati Ashram years (in spite of its stated focus on these years), wherein there was significant tension over the admission of a Dalit family into the community and over Gandhi's politics surrounding caste reform, and to highlight in a more positive way the evolving, increasingly more anti-casteist attitude of Gandhi, Kasturba, and other residents in Gandhi's intentional communities.

On March 12, 2024, Narendra Modi, the prime minister of India, visited Sabarmati Ashram. It was the ninety-fourth anniversary of the Salt March, and the prime minister used the occasion to ceremoniously lay the foundation stone for a new redevelopment project for the ashram.[15] This act formally inaugurated a new plan by the government of India and the state of Gujarat (both Gandhi's and Modi's home state) to expand Sabarmati Ashram and transform it into a world-class memorial and heritage site. Ahmedabad is the largest city in the state of Gujarat and is an important economic and industrial hub in India today. It is also a historic city, with many layers of habitation and architecture, and it was recognized as such by the UNESCO World Heritage Convention in 2017. Leading up to the UNESCO decision, plans to redevelop the riverfront around the Sabarmati River, which flows through the city, were launched in phases. One phase, completed in 2017, included the creation of a pedestrian promenade expansion of the riverfront at Sabarmati Ashram. It also entailed the demolition of informal housing and the displacement of impoverished residents who had made their homes along the riverfront. Now, the attention is on (re)developing the historic ashram itself.

At present, Sabarmati Ashram occupies only five acres of its original land. Several of the ashram's original buildings have been torn down in the past century due to urban encroachment, while others are extant that are not within the boundary of the current heritage site. The mission of the redevelopment plan is to "give the world Gandhi-ji's ashram back in its truest form."[16] Its vision entails restoring, unifying, and expanding the current heritage site: restoring thirty-six extant buildings from Gandhi's time at Sabarmati Ashram, unifying them into the formal grounds of the heritage site, and expanding the footprint of Sabarmati Ashram from its current five acres to a total of fifty-five acres. Part of this expansion plan entails incorporating additional educational exhibits and displays, expanding the archive and adding more research facilities, and adding an amphitheater, food court, VIP lounge, and shopping area. As Sarosh Anklesaria points out, this plan for a "world class" transformation of Sabarmati Ashram "starkly contrasts with Gandhi's commitment to frugal living rooted in localism and his profound skepticism of centralized power. It also signifies a significant effort in the Hindu right's effort to appropriate Gandhi's narrative and legacy."[17]

Notably, this redevelopment plan also entails tearing down homes and businesses that were not part of the original ashram. The plan, funded by the government of India in the amount of twelve billion Indian rupees, includes funding earmarked to relocate impacted residents. Many of these residents do not have legal titles to the land but are Dalit descendants of families that lived at the ashram as residents of the Harijan Sevak Sangh. When the redevelopment plan was initially announced in 2021, some of these residents wrote a letter to the government, asking that they be allowed to remain, noting that they "still follow the Gandhian tenets of spinning, weaving and wearing *khadi* [homespun cotton], cleanliness, women's education, the abolition of untouchability, and communal harmony."[18] That is, they argued that Sabarmati Ashram was not just a heritage site and museum but was still a living community, and that they should be granted the legal right to remain in their houses based not only on their intergenerational residency at the ashram but also on their ongoing commitment to its original observances. Several hundred activists submitted a public letter opposing the redevelopment plan, and Tushar Gandhi filed a court case in 2022 seeking to halt it, including the forced relocation of impacted residents.[19]

After the Gujarat high court ruled in favor of the redevelopment plan, the government of India gave nearly three hundred households an ultimatum: they could choose to leave and accept a monetary compensation package, or they could choose to relocate to a government-built house or apartment beyond the perimeter of the soon-to-be-expanded heritage site. With this redevelopment plan, a very different interpretation of the "removal of untouchability" observance is unfolding at Sabarmati Ashram, such that Dalits are being physically removed from the historic site. Yet alternative plans could have been put in place, plans that would honor the legacy of the residents of Sabarmati Ashram from Gandhi's time and their communal values, and also honor the dignity of the residents living in and around this heritage site today.[20]

4

Sevagram Ashram

When Gandhi was released from prison in 1933, the sixty-three-year-old man suddenly found himself homeless. He had been imprisoned for civil disobedience after leading the Salt March, and while in prison, he had decided to close and disband Sabarmati Ashram, the intentional community that had been his home in India. Gandhi published a brief statement in his new newspaper *Harijan* ("Children of God," named after the term Gandhi used to refer to Dalits, or so-called "untouchables"), expressing surprise at his unexpected freedom and pondering his next steps: "How I shall use this life out of prison, I do not know. But I must say this that whether in prison or outside prison, Harijan service will be always after my heart and will be the breath of life for me, more precious than the daily bread."[1] Privately, Gandhi confessed to friends that he did not have a plan for where he would go or what he would do next, but he was sure that "God will clear the way."[2]

In the months after his release from prison, Gandhi decided to stop his civil disobedience activities, step away from politics, and settle down in rural India. Gandhi declared in the press that it was time for him to retire from politics, citing a "growing and vital difference of outlook" between many members of the Indian National Congress and himself over fundamental issues, including Gandhi's insistence upon the commitment of Congress members to spinning for one hour every day and wearing only homespun cloth (*khadi*); the prioritization of the abolition of untouchability; and the commitment to nonviolence as a fundamental creed.[3] Gandhi decided to turn his energy away from politics and toward rural India, writing in *Harijan*, "For the city-dweller, the villages have become untouchable. He does not know them, he will not live in them, and if he finds himself in a village, he will want to reproduce the city life there."[4] Gandhi argued that the revivification of India's villages was essential for the benefit of all Indians. He undertook what he called a "Harijan pilgrimage" in 1933 and 1934, traveling twelve thousand miles throughout India to promote the abolition of untouchability, and he determined from this pilgrimage that the only way to address the inequality and poverty of the masses was to revive cottage industries. With this goal in mind, Gandhi formed the All-India Village Industries Association (AIVIA) in 1934, explaining that "the idea behind the village industries scheme is that we should look to the villages for the supply of our daily needs and that, when we find that some needs are not so supplied, we should see whether with a little trouble and organization they cannot be profitably supplied by the villagers. In estimating the profit we should think of the villager, not of ourselves."[5] To focus on village life and cottage industry, Gandhi decided to find a suitable village for his retirement.

Gandhi looked to Wardha (now part of Maharashtra state), a town he had first visited at the invitation of the wealthy industrialist founder of the Bajaj Group, Jamnalal Bajaj, who was also a loyal supporter of Gandhi and one of the key patrons behind Sabarmati Ashram. Thomas Weber reports that Bajaj was drawn to Gandhi's spiritual asceticism and looked up to him as an adoptive father figure, and that Gandhi in turn came to view Bajaj as his "fifth son."[6] Bajaj, who was from Wardha, visited Sabarmati Ashram regularly with his wife and their five children. In an effort to draw Gandhi closer to his home, Bajaj offered some of his land in Wardha to Gandhi. In 1921, Gandhi had established a small satellite of Sabarmati Ashram in Wardha, and he sent his disciple Vinoba Bhave from Sabarmati to manage it. Bhave had arrived at Sabarmati Ashram in 1916, after reading about Gandhi in the press and deciding to quit college and join the community. Bhave had a spiritual inclination and knew Hindu classical texts. He initially helped with the education program and increasingly took on more responsibilities. Gandhi approved of Bhave's commitment to nonviolence and celibacy and enjoyed discussing the *Bhagavad Gita* with him. When Gandhi decided to establish the satellite community in Wardha, Bajaj requested Bhave be sent to manage it, if Gandhi would not do so himself. Gandhi sent Bhave.[7] Gandhi would typically make a yearly visit to Wardha before attending the annual Congress meeting, spending several weeks at the Wardha ashram visiting Bhave and the Bajaj family. In September 1933, after Gandhi was released from prison, he stayed in Wardha for six weeks before embarking upon his Harijan pilgrimage and then returned there in June 1934. Bajaj offered to house the newly formed AIVIA in Wardha, giving Gandhi his garden house and a twenty-acre orchard. Gandhi named the garden house "Maganwadi" in remembrance of his nephew Maganlal Gandhi, who had been so instrumental at Sabarmati Ashram before his death.

Gandhi studied the neighboring villages around Wardha. Seven kilometers east of Wardha was a secluded village named Segaon, with a mixed-caste population of approximately six hundred residents, a majority of whom were Dalits. Gandhi decided to live among these villagers, experiencing daily life as one of them and offering his service to them. To Henry Polak, his friend and former Phoenix Settlement coresident, Gandhi wrote after moving to Segaon, "I am trying to become a villager. The place where I am writing this has a population of about 600—no roads, no post-office, no shop."[8] Gandhi did not intentionally found his last "intentional" community at Segaon—unlike his very deliberate founding of the Phoenix Settlement, Tolstoy Farm, and Sabarmati Ashram communities—but nonetheless, the community sprang up around him as former residents of Sabarmati Ashram came to join him at this village, and as new residents who were drawn to Gandhi for a variety of reasons also arrived. Gandhi renamed Segaon, calling it Sevagram Ashram, meaning "village of service."[9]

Seva can be translated as "selfless service," and it refers to religious work that is done in Hinduism with a sense of devotion and for the benefit of others. Typical examples of *seva* include preparing ritual offerings to present to the deity during worship, preparing meals for a religious community, and cleaning the sacred space of a temple. In using the term "seva" to name this community, Gandhi sought to foreground selfless service as a way of life, emphasizing it as foundational to the pursuit of universal well-being (*sarvodaya*) and spiritual liberation (*moksha*).[10] Sevagram Ashram was Gandhi's final residential experiment with utopia, his home from 1936 until his death in 1948. Scholarship on Gandhi typically focuses on his political work during these years, particularly his leadership of the Quit India anti-colonial campaign. What is overlooked is how central Sevagram Ashram was to the continuing development of Gandhi's philosophy of universal well-being and to this political campaign. In the decade leading up to India's independence in 1947, politicians streamed in and out of Sevagram Ashram to consult with Gandhi, pulling him out of retirement and back into the anti-colonial struggle. This chapter focuses on Sevagram Ashram, examining how Gandhi's philosophy of universal well-being continued to evolve as he thought about selfless service in this village context. It argues that at Sevagram Ashram, Gandhi connected his previous emphasis on suffering and sacrifice with selfless service. Gandhi called upon his coresidents to engage in the service of his own embodied self, the villagers of Sevagram, and ultimately, the nation, increasingly emphasizing the need to be willing to sacrifice one's own life as the highest form of service.

Building Sevagram Ashram

In addition to Jamnalal Bajaj and Vinoba Bhave, the other person who played a crucial role in Gandhi's decision to settle at Segaon was Mirabehn, who was born in England as Madeleine Slade. Slade was the daughter of Sir Edmond Slade, a Royal Navy officer who served as commander in chief of the East Indies Squadron and then as director of Naval Intelligence. She learned of Gandhi from her friend Romain Rolland, the French author who wrote a biography of Gandhi in 1924 and who described Gandhi to Slade as "another Christ."[11] Slade read Rolland's biography and felt called to Gandhi, writing in her memoir, "The call was absolute, and that was all that mattered."[12] She wanted to book a ticket on an ocean liner to India at once but decided to wait one year and use the time to train herself: learning to spin, adopting a vegetarian diet, learning to sleep on the floor, and studying the Urdu language. Slade wrote to Gandhi, telling him about her desire to join him and enclosing a contribution of twenty pounds from the sale of a family brooch. Gandhi's reply invited Slade to come if she still felt compelled at the end of the year.[13] Slade gave away her possessions, said goodbye to her family, and arrived in India in late 1925. In her memoir, Slade recalls her first meeting with Gandhi at Sabarmati Ashram:

> A little garden gate led to a small enclosure where a simple building stood. We stepped up onto the veranda. I felt encumbered with the bag in my hand and hurriedly handed it to my companion. He took it and, standing a little to one side, ushered me into the room. As I entered, a slight brown figure rose up and came toward me. I was conscious of nothing but a sense of light. I fell on my knees. Hands gently raised me up, and a voice said: "You shall be my daughter."[14]

Madeleine Slade conceived of this meeting with Gandhi at Sabarmati Ashram as a religious experience—she felt called from afar to join him at this sacred space set apart from the profane world—and she fell to her knees before a vision of light during her first physical encounter with Gandhi. She felt that to be in Gandhi's presence was "to be lifted out of oneself" and to come "face to face with a Soul" that glowed with spiritual strength.[15] She quickly perceived, however, that not all residents shared this same perception and that there was a variety of approaches to Gandhi and to Sabarmati Ashram among its residents:

> I found a heterogenous collection of one or two hundred people, men, women and children of all ages and all degrees of faith, from fanatical ascetics to skeptical family women. What was more, the ascetics were few in number, and the family types were the majority. One thing that was clear was that most of the women were there not because they had themselves felt a call to join the Ashram, but because their husbands or relatives had thrown in their lot with Bapu [Gandhi]. As to the young people and children, they of course were there because of their parents. Among the men there was considerable variety in the reasons which had led them to Bapu. . . . But one and all were drawn by the magnetic power of Bapu's spirit, and had thrown up everything else to join the cause.[16]

Slade notes that she felt more akin with those drawn to Gandhi for ascetic reasons, residents who viewed their commitment to the communal observances as lifelong vows.[17]

Gandhi embraced Madeleine Slade as both a coresident and a spiritual coseeker. Gandhi wrote to Romain Rolland, thanking him for the "treasure" he had sent to him, noting that Miss Slade "shows a marvelous capacity for adaptation and we are already quite at ease with her."[18] In her first months at Sabarmati Ashram, Slade began to study the Hindi and Gujarati languages, and she joined the life of the community by taking turns on sanitation duty, learning to cook Indian meals, spinning cotton, and joining group prayer sessions.[19] Slade began to call Gandhi "Bapu," meaning "Father," as he was commonly called in the community (and increasingly, across the nation). Gandhi, in turn, renamed Madeleine Slade "Mirabehn," after the sixteenth-century Hindu poet-saint Mirabai, a name she embraced for the remainder of her life (and that I will use when discussing her from this point forward).

Mirabehn first visited Wardha in December of 1925, accompanying Gandhi on his visit there prior to attending the annual meeting of the Indian National Congress. Mirabehn reacted positively to this satellite ashram community, which more closely met her expectations for a spiritual community than Sabarmati Ashram:

> When we reached the Wardha Ashram I found quite a different type of center to Sabarmati, and I could not help being enthusiastic about it, as it was very much the kind of Ashram I had pictured to myself before reaching India. It was a small compact group of men all earnestly believing in the principles of the institution. Bapu's ideals and experiments were being carried out with great thoroughness, and onto them had been added theories and methods evolved in the austere and searching soul of Vinoba, whom the inmates looked up to as their Guru (preceptor). Quietness of atmosphere, unity of endeavor, hard work, and spiritual purposefulness were the qualities which impressed one.[20]

Mirabehn made her way back to the community at Wardha nearly a decade later through a circuitous route. She first returned to Sabarmati Ashram and spent the next year there while Gandhi was on his sabbatical (1926), and then at Gandhi's suggestion, she traveled for a few years throughout northern India, propagating spinning. When the Salt Satyagraha began, Mirabehn returned to Gandhi's side and took part in the civil disobedience movement. She accompanied Gandhi to the second Round Table Conference in London (1931), was imprisoned for civil disobedience (1932–1933), and wrote news essays and traveled to England and the United States to meet dignitaries and make the case for India's freedom (1934).[21] Mirabehn then returned to India, where she joined Gandhi in Wardha as he established the AIVIA.

The once quiet atmosphere of Wardha was now bustling. Mirabehn records that in addition to some of the former residents from Sabarmati Ashram, "a strange medley of various kinds of cranky people had collected around Bapu."[22] She began taking long, solitary walks, passing through the nearby village of Sindi. She spoke with Gandhi about the insanitary condition of Sindi, and they agreed that as a service to the villagers, Mirabehn should go there every morning, bringing with her a few volunteers, and clean up the human excrement and trash littering the lanes. Mirabehn did so but reported that the villagers were not responsive to her efforts to teach them sanitation methods. Gandhi joined the crew one day, offering the villagers advice on building earth latrines and using the waste matter as fertilizer, thereby improving their crops and reducing disease.[23] Still, the villagers were apathetic. Gandhi determined that he would go and live there alone, working for and with the villagers. But his friends and family protested out of concern for his high blood pressure. So Mirabehn offered to go and live in Sindi herself. Mirabehn recollects that as the days went by, the villagers' attitude to her gradually softened, but she was restless: "I felt we were not getting at the problems of the real villages. After all, Sindi was a suburb of Wardha, to which it was practically joined on one side."[24] She wanted a more "typical" village. Mirabehn's search led her to the village called Segaon.

Mirabehn liked that Segaon was more remote than Sindi but still within walking distance of Wardha. The villagers seemed "a little more responsive" to her. Segaon had an orchard belonging to Jamnalal Bajaj, who gave her permission to build a hut on the land.[25] Pyarelal Nayar and Sushila Nayar, a brother and sister who served as Gandhi's personal secretary and personal physician, respectively, during his Sevagram Ashram years, record that Gandhi first tried to dissuade Mirabehn from living in Segaon but ultimately yielded on one condition—that she commit to this decision, even at the expense of her life: "The village-folk had a deep mistrust of educated, city-bred people who went to 'reform' and 'elevate' them. They had had enough of the 'do-gooders,' who descended upon them like seasonal birds at harvest time and then suddenly disappeared. She must go to live and, if need be, die there."[26] Mirabehn agreed and began working with villagers to construct a hut. She instructed them to build the hut of the same local materials used to construct their own houses—wood, bamboo, mud plaster, date palm leaves, and tiles for the roof. It was located near the village well and measured seven feet by five feet, with a side alcove in one wall for storage. Before the mud plaster walls dried, Mirabehn molded them by hand to include decorative reliefs of palm trees, birds, and animals.[27]

Before long, Mirabehn's mental and physical health began to deteriorate. She was anxious about not being at Gandhi's side, particularly after she walked to Wardha one day but was denied a visit when Gandhi's blood pressure was alarmingly high. She records walking back to Segaon in a despondent state, writing Gandhi daily letters, and feeling a sense of dread about living in solitude.[28]

Nonetheless, Mirabehn carried on with her sanitation work in the village until she fell ill with malaria. Gandhi had previously told Mirabehn that she must commit to her decision to serve the villagers of Segaon, even at the cost of her own life. As she lay there on a cot under the trees in March of 1936, ill with a raging fever, she was willing to make this ultimate sacrifice. The villagers, however, carried Mirabehn to Bajaj's house in Wardha for treatment. In a letter to Mirabehn, Gandhi (then in Delhi for medical treatment) relented, telling her, "These recurring attacks of fever disturb me. If you cannot keep well in villages, you must live in Maganwadi and do what you can from there."[29]

Gandhi determined he should take Mirabehn's place in the village. Mirabehn could stay in Wardha, and if her health improved, she could move to the neighboring village of Veroda. Writing to Bajaj, Gandhi requested permission to build a new hut for himself in Segaon, located farther from the well than Mirabehn's hut to avoid mosquitos and malaria. Gandhi set forth several specific details in the letter: that the hut would be for him and potentially his wife, Kasturba, "if Ba [Kasturba] desires then with her, otherwise I would live alone in a hut"; that "as little expense as possible should be incurred in building the hut and in no case should it exceed Rs. 100"; that a separate hut might be erected for a few people involved in the AIVIA work; and that "unless there is some special reason, people from outside should not come to see me at Segaon. They may see me only at Maganwadi on the days fixed for my going there." Living in Segaon village, Gandhi wrote, would enable him to gain momentum in the work of village industries, and "whatever defects there may be in my way of thinking will come to the surface on my living in a village."[30] Venugopal Maddipati has argued that this illuminates how Gandhi, at this stage of life, believed that he and his colleagues involved in AIVIA work would find the terms of village improvement only by residing among the villagers to better understand their way of living and thinking.[31]

Gandhi's close friends, however, were unified in their opposition to Gandhi living in Segaon. B. R. Nanda, in his biography of Jamnalal Bajaj, records the storm of opposition that erupted from Gandhi's coresidents, family, and closest political allies: "Jawaharlal Nehru and Vallabhai Patel thought it a preposterous suggestion. The Mahatma's doctors shook their heads. His colleagues in the ashram failed to see what would be gained by moving from Maganwadi, which was a sort of village, to another village a few miles away."[32] In spite of this resistance, Gandhi walked to Segaon on April 30, 1936, gathered the villagers together, and gave a short speech introducing himself and his intentions. Gandhi explained that he was taking Mirabehn's place and that he was there to serve all villagers equally, without concern for caste. He elaborated:

> You must have known from Mirabehn that I have cast out all untouchability from myself, that I hold all classes of people—Brahmin,

> Kshatriya, Vaishya and Shudra, Rajput, Mahar, Chamar—all alike, and I regard these distinctions based on birth as immoral. We have suffered because of these distinctions, and this sense of high and low has vitiated our lives. But I may tell you that I should not think of imposing these convictions on you. I should try to serve you by cleaning your roads and your surroundings, by trying to render such help as I can if there is illness in the village, by teaching you self-help by way of helping you to revive your handicrafts. If you will co-operate with me I shall be happy, if you will not I shall be content to be absorbed among you as one among the few hundreds that live here.[33]

The village headman welcomed Gandhi, offering his cooperation in everything "except in the matter of mixing with Harijans."[34] Gandhi welcomed the challenge.

On that same visit, Gandhi inspected the site Mirabehn had selected for his hut, which was on high ground on the north side of the village. Gandhi and Mirabehn measured out the foundation, marking off a spot on the ground twenty-nine feet long by fourteen feet wide, and additional space for a veranda. As Gandhi left for another medical appointment, he assigned Mirabehn to supervise the building of his hut, with the help of two volunteers from Wardha (Balwant Singh, a former farmer, and Munnalal Shah, a former lawyer).[35] On June 18, 1936, Gandhi returned and began living in his newly constructed hut, which came to be known as "Adi Niwas" ("First Cottage," Gandhi's first residence at Sevagram Ashram). Gandhi intended to live in this cottage alone, or perhaps with his wife. No one else from Wardha was to reside with him at Segaon. He explained to Mirabehn, "I must make new friends and co-workers in Segaon. You can settle in any other neighbouring village if you like, so as to be near me."[36] Gandhi's goal, as he described it in the first annual AIVIA meeting held on May 7, 1936, was to work with the villagers to carry out a constructive program that would transform Segaon into a model village. This program was threefold, focusing on (1) improving the sanitation of the village, (2) improving the diet and nutrition of the villagers, and (3) cultivating cottage industry to supplement the villagers' economic subsistence.[37]

Although Gandhi longed to live alone in his hut, from the beginning, he had multiple roommates. Balwant Singh and Munnalal Shah, who helped build the hut, asked that they be allowed to stay to aid in Gandhi's work and cook for him. A wandering renouncer named Tukdoji Maharaj came through the village and then took up residence in the hut. Gandhi reserved one corner of the hut for Kasturba, who came from Wardha the following month, bringing with her two visitors, their young grandniece Manu Gandhi and the Muslim politician Abdul Gaffar Khan. Writing to Mirabehn, Gandhi described his hut as "a confused household instead of a hermitage it was expected to be."[38]

Mirabehn moved to the neighboring village of Veroda, where she built a new hut for herself. Gandhi greatly admired this hut and routinely took visitors to see it, remarking that it had the "villager's mentality about everything in it," including its use of stone for the commode, its bamboo mantlepiece, and the palms and peacocks set in relief in the mud plaster walls. He admired the use of local materials at minimal cost and yet with a beautiful sense of artistry, commenting, "any villager can do this, but never does it."[39] Venugopal Maddipati highlights that Gandhi viewed Mirabehn's hut as the apotheosis of "real-ruralmindedness" because she was able to think of architecture in terms of the villager's limitations.[40] When Mirabehn again fell ill with malaria, Gandhi brought her to Segaon to recuperate, and thereafter, she too took up residency in Segaon. Ever the prolific builder, Mirabehn built another hut for herself near Gandhi's now crowded hut, adding a small room attached to the main room to teach spinning to the villagers. Eventually, Mirabehn converted this hut into "a proper cottage" for Gandhi so that he could find some quiet for his writing and correspondence; this hut came to be known as "Bapu Kuti" ("Father's/Gandhi's Cottage").[41]

The village of Segaon was formally renamed Sevagram in 1940. Gandhi's community there, Sevagram Ashram, continued to grow as more people arrived to live and work alongside Gandhi, drawn there for a variety of reasons. B. R. Nanda describes it as a "motley crowd" that included the following noteworthy members:

> K. G. Mashruwala, the ideologist of Gandhian philosophy, who had succeeded Jamnalal [Bajaj] as president of the Gandhi Seva Sangh; Rajkumari Amrit Kaur, ever eager to serve the Mahatma as secretary; E. W. Aryanayakam, the Cambridge-trained educationist and his talented wife, Ashadevi; Maurice Friedman, a Polish engineer, who had become a convert to the Gandhian concept of a handicraft civilization based on non-violence; Parchure Shastri, a Sanskrit scholar suffering from leprosy, who was housed next to the Mahatma so that he could personally tend him; the eccentric Professor Bhansali, who used to roam the forests naked and with sealed lips, subsisting on neem leaves; and finally a Japanese monk, who worked like a horse and lived like a hermit, merrily beating his drum.[42]

Small huts were added for Kasturba, Bajaj, Parchure Shastri, and a few other residents. A guest house was built for visitors, along with a dormitory and a common kitchen. New buildings were added for the focus on providing a basic education throughout India's villages that incorporated craft. (Making homespun cloth, animal husbandry, making brown sugar from date palms, and other cottage industries were pursued.)[43] A dispensary and a small dairy were built, along with a *khadi* museum. From one lone hut in a small village, an entire community sprang up in just a couple of years. As Thomas Weber notes, in spite of Gandhi's intention to become a villager, the growing ashram community and the original villagers did not fuse together seamlessly: "What was to be Gandhi's hut in a village that would slowly become his model village, became a separate ashram at the side of Segaon, eventually having little connection with it."[44]

Daily Life at Sevagram Ashram

On June 25, 1934, while Gandhi was on his Harijan pilgrimage to promote the abolition of untouchability, a would-be assassin threw an explosive at him as he was preparing to deliver a speech. Several bystanders were hospitalized with injuries, but Gandhi was unscathed and grateful that no one had died. That week, he printed a "Statement on the Bomb Incident" in *Harijan*, criticizing the "insane act" perpetrated by the anonymous orthodox Hindu who threw the explosive and reflecting upon this attempt on his life:

> It is easy to see that causes prosper by the martyrdom of those who stand for them. I am not aching for martyrdom, but if it comes in my way in the prosecution of what I consider to be the supreme duty in defense of the faith I hold in common with millions of Hindus, I shall have well-earned it, and it will be possible for the historian of the future to say that the vow I had taken before Harijans that I would, if need be, die in the attempt to remove untouchability was literally fulfilled.[45]

In interviews to the press, Gandhi reiterated this sentiment that he was willing to die in the effort to abolish untouchability, stating, "No reform worth the name has ever been accomplished without the reformer holding his life as a stake for his or her cause."[46]

Gandhi emphasized to those who joined him at Sevagram Ashram that they too must be willing to encounter resistance working among villagers, to experience discomfort, and possibly to die in service to the villagers. He was not seeking to found an intentional community; thus, he was not focused on articulating a constitution as he had at Sabarmati Ashram (though residents later adopted the eleven observances of the Sabarmati Ashram community).[47] Rather, Gandhi emphasized selfless service. To live at Sevagram meant to serve the villagers with patience and perseverance:

> The only way is to sit down in their midst and work away in steadfast faith, as their scavengers, their nurses, their servants, not as their patrons, and to forget all our prejudices and prepossessions. Let us for a moment forget even swaraj [political self-rule], and certainly forget the "haves" whose presence oppresses us at every step. They are there. There are many who are dealing with these big problems. Let us tackle the humbler work of the village which is necessary now and would be even after we have reached our goal.[48]

In chapter 3, we saw how Gandhi experimented with caste reform at Sabarmati Ashram by bringing in one Dalit family (Dudabhai and Danibehn Dafda, and their daughter, Lakshmi) in an effort to live as equals in a multicaste community. Now Gandhi decided that rather than make such an arguably token attempt at caste integration, he would instead go to Dalits directly by living in a village with a Dalit majority and working on their behalf. Such selfless service to villagers, Gandhi now believed, was the best way to eliminate caste divisions and promote universal well-being. With the AIVIA organization and *Harijan* publication, he hoped to build an army of nonviolent volunteer-servants who would fan out throughout India's thousands of villages, transforming the country one village at a time into a nation of ideal villages.

In response to a question from one volunteer-servant, Gandhi described what such an ideal Indian village would be like:

> An ideal Indian village will be so constructed as to lend itself to perfect sanitation. It will have cottages with sufficient light and ventilation built of a material obtainable within a radius of five miles. The cottages will have courtyards enabling householders to plant vegetables for domestic use and to house their cattle. The village lanes and streets will be free of all avoidable dust. It will have wells according to its needs and accessible to all. It will have houses of worship for all; also a common meeting place, a village common for grazing its cattle, a cooperative dairy, primary and secondary schools in which industrial education will be the central fact, and it will have panchayats [village councils] for settling disputes. It will produce its own grains, vegetables and fruit, and its own khadi.[49]

Gandhi's goal in moving to Segaon, renamed Sevagram, was to transform it into the first ideal village. But those who joined Sevagram Ashram faced an array of difficulties in trying to accomplish this transformation. One difficulty was the villagers' resistance to caste reform. Mirabehn recounts that a majority of villagers were Dalits of the Mahar subcaste, with a few other Dalit households of another subcaste whom the Mahars considered lower in rank to them, and there was a sizeable minority of upper-caste households. Each group had its own well. On her first day in the village, she accepted water from a man of the lowest caste, and so neither the Mahars nor the upper-caste villagers would permit her near their wells. But the water in the well of the lowest caste group turned out not to be potable, so she had to take her bucket to another well and ask the owners to give her water. Although Mirabehn sought to demonstrate that she regarded everyone as equal regardless of caste, the villagers were only too willing to add her into their caste stratification. "I was now getting direct experience of what it was like to be an untouchable," Mirabehn wrote.[50] The village headman allowed Mirabehn, Gandhi, and others to daily clean the human excrement from the lanes—work typically done by those at the bottom of the caste hierarchy—but he was resistant to their notions of caste reform.

Gandhi advised volunteer-servants that tackling sanitation was the first priority in the threefold constructive program (of sanitation, nutrition, and cottage industry). He encouraged volunteers to become a "voluntary Bhangi," referring to a Dalit subcaste that was traditionally charged with sanitation work, writing in *Harijan* in January of 1937:

> The very first problem the villager worker will solve is its sanitation. It is the most neglected of all the problems that baffle workers and that undermine physical well-being and breed disease. If the worker became a voluntary Bhangi, he would begin by collecting night-soil and turning it into manure and sweeping village streets. He will tell people how and where they should perform daily functions and speak to them on the value of sanitation and the great injury caused by neglect. The worker will continue to do the work whether the villagers listen to him or not.[51]

Gandhi had earlier elaborated on the need for such volunteer-servants in his essay "The Ideal Bhangi," published in *Harijan* in November of 1936, after Gandhi had been living in the village for five months. Gandhi wrote that the ideal Bhangi would not only have a thorough knowledge of the principles of sanitation but would also regard their sanitation work for society as "a sacred duty." The problem, as Gandhi saw it, was twofold: Dalits didn't live up to this ideal, resulting in villages becoming "seats of dirt and insanitation"; and upper castes discriminated against Dalits rather than treating "the Bhangi as equal to that of a Brahmin as in fact and justice he deserves." Gandhi's proposed solution was to send a cadre of volunteer-servants throughout the villages. He wrote, "To clothe the Bhangi with the dignity and respect due to him is the especial task and privilege of the educated class. Some members of the class would first themselves master the science of sanitation to educate the Bhangi round them in the same. . . . Surely this is work enough to satisfy the highest ambition of one who has the spirit of service in him."[52]

Dalit lawyer and activist Dr. Babasaheb Ambedkar excoriated Gandhi for such sentiments, arguing in his essay "A Reply to the Mahatma" that it was ridiculous in the modern era to cling to the idea that everyone must follow their ancestral calling, that society should not be organized around caste because it is inherently hierarchical, and that society should instead be reorganized around the principles of liberty, equality, and fraternity.[53] Ambedkar visited Gandhi in Segaon on May 1, 1936, the day after Gandhi had first arrived there to speak with the villagers.[54] They sat together under a shade tree and talked, but the archive hasn't preserved their conversation. They surely would have discussed their differing approaches to dealing with caste discrimination. They likely discussed Ambedkar's recent pronouncement that he intended to convert from Hinduism to another religion that did not incorporate caste into its worldview. Gandhi presumably would have shared with Ambedkar his plan to live in Segaon, possibly showing him the nearby spot where his hut would be built. What we do know with certainty is that Ambedkar had no interest in joining Sevagram Ashram as a volunteer-servant. By the mid-1940s, Ambedkar expressed his frustration with Gandhi's approach in his book *What Congress and Gandhi Have Done to the Untouchables*, writing that "under Gandhism the untouchables are to be eternal scavengers," and characterizing this as "nothing short of cruelty."[55]

Ambedkar and other Dalits did not join Sevagram Ashram. The volunteer-servants who came and embraced the task of temporarily living like a Bhangi were predominantly upper-caste, well-educated Indians, though several additional white Europeans also arrived, such as Saralabehn (born Catherine Mary Heilman), who left her home in England and made her way to Sevagram Ashram in 1936, where she lived for eight years, and then remained in India engaged in reform work for the rest of her lifetime.[56] These volunteer-servants frequently fell ill. Within the first year, the residents of Sevagram Ashram dealt with outbreaks of cholera, malaria, dysentery, and typhoid. They took turns nursing one another, using nature-cure remedies. Pyarelal and Sushila Nayar (Sushila was a trained medical physician) recollect that Sevagram was "notoriously unhealthy," and they describe the residents nursing one another using "enemas, sponge baths, steam inhalations, wet-sheet packs and mud-packs."[57] When infections were life-threatening, residents had to be taken to the nearest hospital in Wardha for treatment. Though only seven kilometers away, getting to and from Wardha with an ill patient was not easy. There was a footpath but no road until 1940. Jamnalal Bajaj improvised a vehicle that he nicknamed the "Oxford," which was an old Ford motorcar drawn by a pair of oxen, that was used in fair weather; when the path was too muddy, an ordinary bullock cart was used.[58]

Snakebite was another difficulty for residents. Gandhi insisted (as he had in South Africa) that snakes not be killed, in keeping with the observance of nonviolence. Residents learned to distinguish venomous (cobras, vipers, kraits) from nonvenomous snakes. They devised a long set of tongs for grabbing venomous snakes and deposited captured snakes into a portable snake container to release them at a distance. Gandhi believed, in keeping with the *Yoga Sutra* of Patanjali, that when a person's commitment to nonviolence is fully manifested, they can no longer be harmed by wild animals. On more than one occasion, Gandhi sought to demonstrate his total commitment to nonviolence by placing snakes on his lap or letting them loose in his hut.[59]

To join Sevagram Ashram, then, one had to be willing to shovel feces and build latrines, and to live with such life-threatening dangers as venomous snakes, insect-borne diseases, and contaminated water. Gandhi reminded his team of volunteer-servants that this was part of the precarity of everyday life for millions of villagers throughout India, many of whom also faced dangers like malnutrition and famine. In *Harijan*, Gandhi emphasized his commitment to living—and possibly dying—like a Dalit villager, writing, "being saturated with the Harijan mentality, I can only think in terms of the millions of villagers and can only make my happiness dependent upon that of the poorest amongst them, and want to live only if they can live."[60]

The villagers of Segaon were initially skeptical of Mirabehn, Gandhi, and the increasing number of volunteer-servants who arrived offering to teach them how to clean their village. Mark Thomson reports that the villagers resisted the sanitation effort out of resentment over the ashram members' failure to observe caste rules: "Ashram workers swept the village lanes and urged people to use the common latrines set up earlier by Mira[behn]. The villagers refused to co-operate in carting manure, however, which meant they would not hire out their carts for this purpose. They also remained apathetic to the task of keeping the village clean. The ashramites worked and the villagers watched."[61] The villagers were also skeptical about the value of spinning as a cottage industry, but their attitude began to soften when Gandhi hired some villagers to work in the *khadi* museum. Gandhi hired additional Dalit villagers to work in the kitchen at Sevagram Ashram. Eventually, the village headman became a regular visitor to Gandhi's cottage, consuming meals there that had been prepared by Dalit villagers.[62] Once the village headman had consented to such practices that contravened traditional caste rules, the villagers became more accepting of the ashram residents, though they did not become complete converts. Mahadev Desai, one of Gandhi's secretaries, wrote of Sevagram Ashram in 1940, "There is a hiatus between the villagers and us. . . . Maybe we have, with the best wishes in the world, not succeeded in coming down to their level and becoming one with them."[63]

Nonetheless, as the villagers' resistance began to decrease, the residents of Sevagram Ashram began to make modest headway in their constructive work. Sushila and Gandhi trained villagers in cholera-prevention methods, and they worked together to reduce mosquito breeding grounds. Dr. G. L. Batra analyzed the villagers' diet and prescribed simple remedies for dealing with keratomalacia (an eye disorder resulting from vitamin A deficiency), including planting a wider variety of vegetables for consumption. They also began to focus on cash crops to supplement the villagers' income, and had success producing palm sugar and starting a dairy farm.[64] As spinning slowly caught on, Balwant Singh trained some villagers to become spinning teachers so that they could teach spinning in other villages. After Singh's first Dalit pupil used his earnings to build his own hut, other villagers signed on, and the Khadi Training School was established in 1941.[65]

By 1940, Gandhi recognized that in spite of his original intention to live on his own in a remote village, a community had grown around him. In changing the name of Segaon village to Sevagram Ashram, he emphasized the concept of selfless service (*seva*). For Gandhi, service encompassed social, political, and religious goals. Socially, he wanted to improve the well-being of the villagers, and he hoped to transform Segaon into a model Indian village, one that was sanitary, self-sufficient, and free of caste discrimination. The volunteer-servants who joined Sevagram Ashram were expected to adopt the ideal of selfless service as they undertook work in the village, placing this ideal above their own lives. The next sections of this chapter explore the religious and political implications of service in the context of daily life at Sevagram Ashram.

Service, Celibacy, and Salvation

Gandhi took a vow of celibacy (*brahmacharya*) in 1906 while living at Phoenix Settlement, his first intentional community in South Africa. For Gandhi, this vow had both religious and social significance. It was connected with the pursuit of spiritual liberation (*moksha*), for celibacy is a traditional means undertaken by Hindu renouncers to lessen attachments to householder life while striving toward spiritual liberation. It was also connected with the pursuit of social equality at Gandhi's first intentional community, for Gandhi sought to treat every coresident as an equal, without privileging his own wife or children.[66] In the Sevagram Ashram years, Gandhi remained committed to celibacy for both religious and social goals, and he now connected it with the ideal of selfless service. He believed that one could only become a selfless servant, working simultaneously to better society and pursue spiritual liberation, if one had completely eliminated ego-based desires from their body and mind. However, as Gandhi aged, he became deeply concerned that he had not yet mastered celibacy. At Sevagram Ashram, Gandhi undertook additional—and controversial—experiments with celibacy in his pursuit of universal well-being and spiritual liberation.

In February of 1936, when Gandhi was sixty-six years old, he published an essay in *Harijan* confessing that he had suffered a "lapse" in his practice of celibacy. He does not go into detail but states that he defines *brahmacharya* as "purity not merely of body but of speech and thought also." He writes that with this lapse, he feels "disgusted" with himself, adding that the lapse had shown him his "limitations and imperfections."[67] Gandhi provided more details in private correspondence with several current and former coresidents. A former coresident from Sabarmati Ashram, Premabehn (Prema Kantak), wrote to Gandhi with questions after reading his *Harijan* confession. Gandhi replied, explaining that he was in Bombay undergoing medical treatment when the incident happened, and he described to her what happened and how he felt:

> The experience which tormented me in Bombay was a strange and painful one. All my discharges so far had occurred in dreams and they never troubled me. I could forget them. But the experience in Bombay occurred while I was fully awake and had a sudden desire for intercourse. I felt of course no urge to gratify the craving, there was no self-forgetfulness whatever. I was completely master of my body. But despite my best efforts the organ remained aroused. This was an altogether strange and shameful experience. . . . Despite my imperfection, one thing has always come easily to me, viz., that thousands of women have remained safe in my company.[68]

Here, Gandhi expresses his concern to Premabehn that his erection while he was awake meant that he had not yet mastered celibacy; but he simultaneously seeks to reassure her that he had not improperly touched any woman.

Shortly after this incident, Gandhi returned to Wardha and then, in the next few months, moved to Segaon to become a villager. Part of his desire to live alone in his hut in the village was to continue to purify himself in body, speech, and thought. But as Sevagram Ashram grew around Gandhi, he experienced what he called another "lapse" in his practice of celibacy on April 14, 1938. In private conversations and correspondence with several current and former coresidents, Gandhi again confessed his lapse. He wrote about his inner turmoil to Amritlal Nanavati, a young male follower whom he had been advising about celibacy:

> I was in such a wretched and pitiable condition that in spite of my utmost efforts I could not stop the discharge though I was fully awake. I feel now that the despondency that I had been feeling deep down in me only foreshadowed this occurrence. After the event, restlessness has become acute beyond words. Where am I, where is my place, and how can a person subject to passion represent non-violence and truth? This turmoil goes on in my heart. I keep asking myself: am I worthy of you all who follow me, am I fit to lead you all?[69]

Gandhi articulates his belief that one cannot master nonviolence and truth without first mastering celibacy; and if he cannot master these things, he is not fit to lead his community. To Amrit Kaur, who had joined Gandhi in Wardha in 1934, Gandhi confessed that the experience was due to his weakness, writing that "the sexual sense" was the hardest to overcome and may be his final struggle.[70] Gandhi also confessed his lapse to Mirabehn, and their correspondence stands out to me, for a careful examination of the archive reveals that Mirabehn raised concerns about the way Gandhi had begun testing his commitment to celibacy. Mirabehn's letters to Gandhi on this topic were destroyed, and she does not address this topic in her memoir.[71] But in Gandhi's letter to Mirabehn dated May 3, 1938, he responds to her letter, thanking her for her "transparent love" and writing that she is "quite right in describing my experiment as new." Gandhi connects this new experiment in celibacy with his practice of nonviolence, writing that "the two hang together," and asks Mirabehn for advice:

> In your next letter you must tell me in concrete terms what definite changes I should make so as to fit in with your idea. Should I deny myself the service rendered by Sushila? Should I refuse to have *malish* [massage] by Lilavati or Amtul Salaam for instance? Or do you want to say that I should never lean on girls' shoulders? Needless to say you won't pain me at all by telling me frankly whatever you think I should do to get out of the terrible despondency. Just now I am most in need of support from those who surround me with service and affection, undeserved as it seems to me, for the time being.[72]

Gandhi closes the letter by asking Mirabehn, whom he often referred to as one of his adopted daughters, for support in this time of personal crisis, stating that while the "degrading, dirty, torturing experience of 14th April shook me to bits," he nonetheless "shall feel pride in my being a parent to so many children, if any of them will give a lifting hand and pull me out of the well of despair." He also reminds Mirabehn of her commitment to selfless service, saying that if she will continue to serve him, then his "faith in myself and my experiment will revive and will burn all the brighter."[73]

What precisely was this new experiment in celibacy that Gandhi undertook at Sevagram Ashram? Another letter to Mirabehn, dated May 12, 1938, gives more detail:

> I must change my manners. There will be considerable response to your suggestions. I have been daily taxing myself about my course of action. I am not yet certain what shape the change will take. About Lilavati I can't recall anything of what you say. But once I felt that I had put my arm around her neck. I asked her in the morning. She said she had no knowledge of any touch. Nevertheless from that day I asked her to sleep at a proper distance. Give me more detail about the incident you relate. You will continue to make whatever suggestions may occur to you. I must not interrupt the experiment, but there is room for revision. My problem is: Had the awful experience of the 14th April anything to do with the contacts or has it any other meaning?[74]

To test his commitment to celibacy, Gandhi had begun to invite young female coresidents—here, Lilavati Asar is named—to sleep next to him in bed at night. Gandhi seemingly hoped to prove that he no longer had any sexual cravings, neither while he was awake nor while sleeping. But his ejaculation on April 14, 1938, threw Gandhi into a crisis.

I do not know what suggestions Mirabehn gave Gandhi in her letters. But Gandhi shared three letters from Mirabehn with his coresidents Pyarelal Nayar, Sushila Nayar, and Amrit Kaur, instructing them to read the letters, and then, he writes, "You will destroy them. Robbed of Mira's hysteria, they are sound. I am contemplating some changes. I have not yet decided upon anything. You will make what suggestions you may like. The despondency is there but the inner peace is coming."[75] I do not know what suggestions these three coresidents gave Gandhi either, but as Gandhi consulted with more coresidents, Gandhi was repeatedly told that he should stop his new experiment of bringing young women into his bed at night.

On June 2, 1938, Gandhi issued a confidential circular to the residents of Sevagram Ashram. The previous day, in a group meeting of the residents, some objected to Gandhi about his behavior and asked why—if Gandhi believed it was righteous behavior (*dharmic*)—they could not all likewise bring members of the opposite sex to sleep next to them in their cots at night as an aid to their practice of celibacy. In the confidential circular, Gandhi apologized and promised to cease this experiment, writing:

> Yesterday it became clear to me as day that it had been wrong on my part to forbid my co-workers to avail themselves, during my lifetime, of the freedom I had given myself. . . . I feel my action was impelled by vanity and jealousy. If my experiment was dangerous, I should not have undertaken it. And if it was worth trying, I should have encouraged my co-workers to undertake it on my conditions. My experiment was a violation of the established norms of *brahmacharya*.[76]

Coresidents had begun raising concerns with Gandhi about his behavior toward young women as early as 1935. In response, Gandhi published an essay titled "A Renunciation," sharing that his habit of walking with his hands on the shoulders of young women was criticized by two coworkers in Wardha. Gandhi writes that he did not agree that it could set a bad example, for his act "was that of a parent," and celibacy does not require "a wall of protection against the touch of the opposite sex." Nonetheless, after he learned that a male resident had been "taking all sorts of liberties in private with a girl," Gandhi agreed to stop walking with his arms around women, writing, "The discovery quoted by me has, therefore, prompted me to renounce the practice, however pure it may have been in itself. Every act of mine is scrutinized by thousands of men and women, as I am conducting an experiment requiring ceaseless vigilance."[77] Thus, in 1935, Gandhi vowed to refrain from physically touching female coresidents.

In 1938, Gandhi again vowed to refrain from physical contact with female coresidents. He declared that he would give up his experiment of testing his celibacy by having physical contact with women and replace it with a new experiment where he would have absolutely no physical contact with women and thereby "discover whether it was physical contact with women that was obstructing my progress or whether there was some other cause."[78] But in the days following the June 1 meeting of the Sevagram Ashram community, Gandhi began to backpedal, insisting upon some exceptions to the new rule of no physical contact with women. Gandhi argued that his wife, Kasturba, must be an exception. Sushila Nayar, as a medical practitioner, must also be an exception.[79] Then he added Prabhavati Devi and Lilavati Asar as exceptions, arguing that all of these women had taken a vow of celibacy, and thus, "innocent contact" with them, such as massages and bathing, should be permissible: "Sushila has been present in the bathroom while I have bathed in the nude and in her absence Ba [Kasturba] or Prabhavati or Lilavati have attended on me. I see nothing wrong in it."[80] The next month, Gandhi added Shardabehn Shukla and Amtul Salaam to his list of exceptions, as he disclosed in a letter to Amrit Kaur: "Sharda is my constant companion. Amtul Salaam sleeps by my side, fans me and covers me when I need covering. She feeds me." Gandhi reassured Amrit Kaur that she shall have her usual place in his hut when she returns, adding, "My faith in my original conception is not shattered. Only I must learn how to realize it. Bad dreams must be avoided. There must be no repetition of 14th April."[81] Here, Gandhi expresses that he still has faith in his experiment of testing his celibacy by having physical contact with women (the "original conception" versus the later experiment of not touching women), and that as he goes about this experiment, he must be vigilant not to repeat his former "lapse" by ejaculating, whether awake or asleep.

Gandhi was away from Sevagram Ashram while he was imprisoned for the Quit India civil disobedience campaign (discussed below) from 1942 to 1944. After his return to Sevagram Ashram, he resumed the practice of sleeping next to women. In March of 1945, his coresidents again voiced concerns, asking Gandhi to stop this practice. Gandhi was then observing a vow of silence on certain days as an exercise in spiritual discipline; thus, some of Gandhi's responses to coresidents took place through written notes, several of which have been preserved. In one note to a resident named Krishnachandra Agarwal, Gandhi refused his request to stop the practice, writing that to do so would be to admit that there was something wrong with it, whereas, to the contrary, he sees this practice helping him become a perfect celibate.[82] He justified the need to try this experiment with women other than his wife, writing, "I did have experiments with Ba [Kasturba], but that was not enough. If emission took place then, it would have been less regrettable morally than any emission occurring now. Emission was a possibility then. I feel it is not a possibility now."[83] In the same note, Gandhi also defended the practice by saying that since he undertook it with an attitude of nonviolence, no harm would come to anyone.

Another coresident who raised concerns was Munnalal Shah, whom Gandhi was coaching in the practice of observing marital celibacy.[84] Munnalal pressed Gandhi about exactly how many young women had been involved in his experiment, to which Gandhi replied that it was really only four women, because many women don't count as partners: all the women who kept their clothes on, rather than sleeping naked next to him, don't count; of those who were naked, Lilavati Asar, Amtul Salaam, Amrit Kaur, and Prabhavati Devi don't count, as they are not currently in residence at Sevagram Ashram; three other young women don't count because of the short duration of their participation. Gandhi explained this latter disqualification further: "I don't consider Abha, Kanchan, and Vina as part of the experiment. . . . Abha slept with me for hardly three nights. Kanchan slept one night only. Vina's sleeping with me might be called an accident. All that can be said is that she slept close to me."[85] Munnalal was particularly concerned about the role of his own wife, Kanchan Shah, in this experiment. Gandhi explained in another note to Munnalal that he stopped sleeping next to Kanchan and Abha Gandhi when he realized that their husbands were upset about the practice (Kanchan was married to Munnalal, and Abha was married to Kanu Gandhi). Gandhi tells Munnalal to discuss the matter with the other coresidents, promising that he will address any questions they have and that he will postpone the experiment, "leaving aside Manu."[86] Gandhi does not name the four women who do count, aside from this mention of Manu. Gandhi's grandniece Manu Gandhi had moved to Sevagram in May of 1942 at the age of fifteen, having been brought there by her father a few years after his wife (Manu's mother) passed away. On March 7, 1945, Gandhi declared an end to the discussion, noting that he had now answered the community's questions, and added, "Anybody who wishes to leave is free to do so."[87] Gandhi would rather that his objectors leave Sevagram Ashram than that he be forced to stop his practice of sleeping next to young women.

Scholars have written about Gandhi's commitment to celibacy, but very few have written about his experiments with celibate sexuality. The few who have discussed this topic have focused on the final years of Gandhi's life, when, in 1947, it became more publicly known that Gandhi (then seventy-seven years old) was testing his celibacy by sleeping next to his grandniece Manu (then twenty years old). At this time, several of Gandhi's associates confronted him, arguing that this practice was wrong.[88] Gandhi responded that the traditional understanding of celibacy that required male renouncers to put up a wall between themselves and women was inadequate. Instead, as Veena Howard has highlighted, Gandhi believed that "celibacy did not mean the gradual waning of sensory desire by avoidance of enticing situations; rather, it acquired potency only when tested by exposure." Furthermore, Gandhi believed that such testing of his commitment to celibacy through exposure to young women was crucial not only to his perfection of celibacy but also of the virtues of nonviolence and truth.[89] In a letter to Amrit

Kaur from March 18, 1947, Gandhi expressed his frustration to her about those who were questioning his interpretation of celibacy and clarified his definition:

> With one solitary exception I have never looked upon a woman with a lustful eye. I have touched perhaps thousands upon thousands. I have lain with some naked, never with the intention of having any lustful satisfaction. My touch has been for our mutual uplift. I would like for those who have felt otherwise, if there are any, truly to testify against me. . . . My meaning of *brahmacharya* is this: One who never has any lustful intention, who by constant attendance upon God has become proof against conscious or unconscious emissions, who is capable of lying naked with naked women, however beautiful they may be, without being in any manner whatsoever sexually excited. Such a person should be incapable of lying, incapable of intending or doing harm to a single man or woman in the whole world, is free from anger and malice and detached in the sense of the *Bhagavad Gita*. Such a person is a full *brahmachari* [celibate renouncer].[90]

Thus, in 1947, Gandhi doubled down, arguing that sleeping naked next to Manu or other young women without experiencing any lustful desire was proof of his commitment to celibacy, nonviolence, and truth.

Vinay Lal argues that it is surprising that Gandhi's practice of celibacy has received so little scholarly analysis, given the monumental record of his life and the scrutiny to which it has been subjected. Lal points out that in the late 1940s, Gandhi practiced celibacy not only with his grandniece Manu but with two other women, writing, "In the last few years before his assassination in 1948, but most certainly no earlier than the death of his wife in 1944, Gandhi took to the practice of taking naked young women to bed with him at night. Gandhi, who never wore many clothes to begin with, would himself be naked on such occasions. Three women—his grandnieces Abha and Manu and his personal physician of sorts, Sushila Nayar, were involved in this 'experiment' in brahmacharya."[91] Tridip Suhrud, who is editing and translating Manu Gandhi's diaries, contends that Gandhi began sleeping naked next to Manu while they were staying in Noakhali in 1946 and 1947. Suhrud has importantly highlighted that Gandhi described this practice at this stage not as an "experiment" (which could have positive or negative results and should be stopped if the results are negative) but as a "*yajna*"—a sacrifice—and he saw Manu as his partner in the sacrifice. Suhrud writes, "In this short-lived yajna he [Gandhi] felt that his strivings had reached their culmination and that finally he had the glimpse of the pure state."[92]

My research on Sevagram Ashram shows that Gandhi's experiments with celibate sexuality were not limited to the final few years of his life, during the period between the death of Kasturba in 1944 and his own death in 1948, nor were they limited to only three women (Manu Gandhi, Abha Gandhi, and Sushila Nayar). To the contrary, I argue that these experiments were part of daily life at Sevagram Ashram from at least April 1938. At Sevagram Ashram, Gandhi trained an inner circle of young female coresidents to perform intimate, physical acts for him as part of their expected selfless service—they took turns massaging him, bathing him, feeding him, and sleeping next to him at night. Manu Gandhi joined this inner circle at some point after her arrival at the ashram in 1942 but was certainly part of it by March of 1945, when Gandhi penned the note to Munnalal Shah (cited above), wherein he agreed to temporarily suspend his experiment in celibacy, "leaving aside Manu."

My research on Sevagram Ashram also shows that Gandhi's experiments with celibate sexuality were not simply about the renunciation or repression of sex. Benjamin Kahan, who has theorized celibacy as a sexual identity in the context of American modernism, notes that celibacy has different valences for different historical actors. Kahan challenges us to understand celibacy as an identity with its own desires and pleasures, rather than as a failure, renunciation, or ascesis of pleasure.[93] In Gandhi's case, I argue that he practiced a form of celibate sexuality that was social, involving communal partners and pleasures. As discussed in chapter 2, one of Gandhi's earliest partners in celibate sexuality in South Africa (aside from his wife, Kasturba) was Hermann Kallenbach. Together at Tolstoy Farm, Gandhi and Kallenbach committed to sexual renunciation and experimented with restricting foods from their diet that they believed were antithetical to practicing celibacy. They took pleasure in what they perceived they gained in character as well as physical and mental vitality through renouncing sex. By the time Gandhi lived at Sevagram Ashram, his practice of celibate sexuality involved multiple female partners and new physical practices, including sleeping next to one another, at times without clothes, to test their mutual commitment to celibacy. Gandhi took pleasure on the many occasions when he did this without experiencing lust, believing this was proof that he was approaching closer to liberation. Gandhi also felt great distress on the occasions when he could not fully conquer his sexual desire.

While Hermann Kallenbach was a willing partner at Tolstoy Farm and wrote about the pleasure he experienced from joining Gandhi's experiment in celibate sexuality there, assessing how Gandhi's female partners at Sevagram Ashram felt about joining Gandhi's experiments in celibate sexuality is difficult in the absence of their writings. Perhaps some of Gandhi's female partners were drawn to Sevagram Ashram because they sought an alternative to the expectation of heteronormative life (marriage, motherhood). Perhaps some of these women took pleasure in being selected to be in Gandhi's inner circle of partners in his experiments in celibate sexuality. It is also possible that some of these young women felt compelled to participate in these experiments with the senior leader of their residential community, which would raise very serious ethical questions about consent and nonviolence. What I can say with certainty is that these experiments caused no small amount of strife within the community, as can be seen from the apology Gandhi issued in the confidential circular of 1938 after coresidents confronted him, and from the conversations that took place again in 1945. Additional glimpses of strife at Sevagram Ashram are preserved in the archive—and I suspect are related to Gandhi's practice of celibate sexuality—such as when Lilavati Asar left the ashram for a time after Gandhi lost his temper with her in September 1937; when Pyarelal Nayar got angry and left in November 1937; when Mahadev Desai threatened to quit and leave the ashram in March 1938; Mirabehn's estrangement from Gandhi from mid-1942 forward; and Kanchan Shah's departure from the ashram in 1945.[94]

In spite of such objections to his behavior and the strife it caused, Gandhi persisted, believing that the practice of celibate sexuality was crucial to his pursuit of spiritual liberation and his ability to lead the community. The commitment to selfless service therefore entailed different types of labor at Sevagram Ashram. All of the volunteers who joined Sevagram Ashram were encouraged to adopt the model of selfless service for universal well-being and to undertake work in the village, such as shoveling excrement, growing vegetables, and spinning. But for a subset of residents who were young and female, their selfless service also entailed service to Gandhi's body.

Service and Self-Rule

Although Gandhi declared that he was retiring from politics when he moved to a village in 1934, politicians came frequently to Sevagram Ashram to consult with him, and ultimately, Gandhi was pulled out of his so-called retirement and back into politics. Sevagram Ashram served as an unofficial headquarters of the Indian National Congress, with meetings of the Congress Working Committee and the All India Congress Committee frequently held there. Prominent political visitors included Jawaharlal Nehru, Subhas Chandra Bose, Maulana Abul Kalam Azad, Sarojini Naidu, Rajendra Prasad, and Abdul Gaffar Khan. These politicians were used to urban India, and many grumbled at having to travel into the remote hinterland and stay in rustic accommodations. Gandhi tried to entice his political protégé, Jawaharlal Nehru, to join Sevagram Ashram, but Nehru remained immune to the lure of village life, writing to Gandhi, "I do not understand why a village should necessarily embody truth and non-violence. A village, normally speaking, is backward intellectually and culturally and no progress can be made from a backward environment. Narrow-minded people are much more likely to be untruthful and violent."[95]

Gandhi invited politicians to Sevagram Ashram because he believed that if he could transform Segaon into his ideal village and model it before these politicians, then it would provide a road map for creating an ideal community on a national scale.[96] Gandhi explained this in a conversation with Pyarelal Nayar and Mahadev Desai in 1940:

> Sevagram is to me a laboratory for ahimsa [nonviolence]. If my experiment here were successful and I could find a solution for the little problems that confront me, I am sure the same formula would provide a solution for the bigger issues that today face us in the country. That is why I am so reluctant to leave Sevagram. It is my laboratory for satyagraha [nonviolent civil disobedience]. It is there that I expect to discover the key to India's independence, not in Simla or New Delhi.[97]

In an essay titled "Village Swaraj" published on July 26, 1942, Gandhi laid out his vision for the future of India, focusing on self-rule at the village level. Gandhi described to his *Harijan* readers what such an ideal village would be like, with its emphasis on self-sufficiency in its variety of crops and dairy cattle, a clean water supply, and a public school. Its people would embrace nonviolence and caste equality, and would work together on a cooperative basis. Describing the village as a complete republic, Gandhi also envisioned its governance: "The government of the village will be conducted by a Panchayat [village council] of five persons annually elected by the adult villagers, male and female, possessing minimum prescribed qualifications. . . . Here there is perfect democracy based upon individual freedom. The individual is the architect of his own government. The law of non-violence rules him and his government." Gandhi then transitioned immediately from nonviolence to self-sacrifice in the interest of universal well-being, writing of this ideal village citizen, "He and his village are able to defy the might of a world. For the law governing every villager is that he will suffer death in the defence of his and his village's honour."[98] Gandhi closes the essay by saying that this is the work he has been striving to do at Sevagram Ashram, and although he has not yet created the perfect village, he can "see dim traces of success." With this essay, Gandhi called upon readers to embrace his model of selfless service and to transform themselves into the ideal individual who is willing to suffer death while nonviolently serving and defending their village.

When Gandhi wrote this essay, Indian politicians had descended once again upon Sevagram Ashram in the summer of 1942. World War II was raging on, and the British now sought India's support in the war effort. In exchange, the British offered India the promise of dominion status within the British Empire once the war was over. The Congress Working Committee met at Sevagram Ashram to deliberate and decided to reject this offer, arguing that complete independence was imperative immediately. According to Mirabehn's recollection of this period, the committee met for morning and afternoon sessions over multiple days, with members debating one another intensely, until at last they had drafted a three-page resolution.[99] This resolution, adopted by the Congress Working Committee on July 14, 1942, demanded complete independence from the British and authorized Gandhi to lead a new civil disobedience campaign if the British did not agree to an immediate withdrawal from India. This resolution telling the British to "Quit India" was next passed by a vote of the All India Congress Committee at a meeting in Bombay on August 8, 1942.[100] That day, in a long speech before members of the All India Congress Committee and many news reporters, Gandhi stated that they must now await the British viceroy's response, but in the meantime, Indians should regard themselves as free and prepare for nonviolent disobedience by making this pledge:

> Here is a mantra, a short one, that I give you. You may imprint it on your hearts and let every breath of yours give expression to it. The mantra is: "Do or Die." We shall either free India or die in the attempt; we shall not live to see the perpetuation of our slavery. Every true Congressman or woman will join the struggle with an inflexible determination not to remain alive to see the country in bondage and slavery. Let that be your pledge.[101]

Gandhi asked his fellow Congress members to embrace the mantra "Do or Die" as the highest form of service to the nation. Gandhi had already asked his Sevagram Ashram coresidents to make this pledge, and he would ask the entire nation of India to make it the following morning.

Gandhi was arrested the next morning, along with most of the Congress leadership and most of Gandhi's coresidents from Sevagram Ashram who had traveled to Bombay with him. Before his arrest, he released a brief message to the nation: "Everyone is free to go the fullest length under ahimsa [nonviolence]. Complete deadlock by strikes and other non-violent means. Satyagrahis must go out to die, not to live. They must seek and face death. It is only when individuals go out to die that the nation will survive. *Karenge ya marenge* [Do or die]."[102] Scholarship on the Quit India campaign has emphasized the substantive internal debates that happened at this time over significant issues, such as the degree of commitment to nonviolence and whether and under what conditions violence should be authorized; the challenge of national unity versus communal fracturing between Hindus and religious minorities; whether India should remain whole or be divided into two countries; whether an independent India would be a secular republic or not; and what effect Britain's delaying and eventual divestment has had upon South Asia.[103] My contribution to this scholarly conversation is to demonstrate the significant role of Sevagram Ashram as both an organizing space and a community of activists to the Quit India campaign, and how the concept of selfless service, which was central to daily life at Sevagram Ashram, was applied to the Quit India campaign in the quest for independence.

In the summer of 1942, Gandhi coordinated with members of Sevagram Ashram and members of the Congress Working Committee to organize the Quit India campaign, laying plans for massive civil disobedience. They prepared a lengthy set of instructions for the public, which was to be released after they had the viceroy's response to the Quit India resolution. These instructions called upon all Indians to peacefully protest British rule by observing a twenty-four-hour general strike, closing down all schools, places of business, and transportation in a show of solidarity. After the first twenty-four hours, all Indians should boycott all forms of British governance until independence was achieved: resigning from positions in the colonial administration, leaving British-run colleges and other educational institutions, and refusing to pay taxes.[104] Gandhi dispatched a handful of his closest coresidents to different parts of India to train people for the struggle. Mirabehn, for instance, was sent to the state of Orissa, where she worked with local Congress members to travel throughout the region, informing residents of the planned strike and emphasizing the importance of nonviolence.[105] When Gandhi left for the Congress meeting in Bombay at the start of August, he assumed he would be arrested. Many of his coresidents came with him to Bombay, prepared to also be arrested. The instructions Gandhi gave to Mirabehn and Vinoba Bhave at this time provide insight into his "Do or Die" mentality.

Gandhi recalled Mirabehn from Orissa and then sent her to Delhi, instructing her to meet with the viceroy or his personal secretary to inform them of their campaign. Gandhi preferred to be transparent with his opponent in any *satyagraha* campaign, informing them of the perceived injustice and the rectification he was seeking and offering his opponent a chance to negotiate. In sending Mirabehn as his personal representative, Gandhi strategically selected someone who was his loyal follower and also a white British citizen.[106] In Mirabehn's report, she writes that the viceroy, Lord Linlithgow, refused to see her, and while she did speak with his secretary, Gilbert Laithwaite, he was not inclined to negotiate, for his mind "was attuned to a die-hard outlook." She tried to tell Laithwaite about Gandhi's attitude of selfless service and his willingness to die, saying, "You are faced with two alternatives; one to declare India's Independence, and the other to kill Gandhiji, and once you kill him you kill forever all hope of friendship between India and England. What are you going to do about it?"[107] From Delhi, Mirabehn next traveled to Bombay to join Gandhi for the All India Congress Committee meeting.

To Vinoba Bhave and other Indian coresidents, Gandhi spoke with them at Sevagram Ashram at the end of July, laying out his expectation that they would be arrested, and giving them specific instructions. Although Gandhi would publicly declare his "do or die" mantra before he was arrested and ask Indian citizens to embrace it, he made specific plans for enacting this mantra with his coresidents. Gandhi likened himself to a general in a nonviolent war, and his coresidents to soldiers, thereby differentiating them from the citizens of India. Gandhi told his coresidents that they must "put their faith in their general and plunge into the fire." If they are jailed, they must fast, unto the death if need be, in obedience to their general: "Breaking all the laws of the Government includes fasting also. If they put us in jail we will give up food and water and immolate ourselves." Gandhi stated that he would be the first to fast and sacrifice his life, and they should follow his lead: "The work won't make any progress without my sacrifice. I want your cooperation. There is no cause for anyone to get alarmed or feel unhappy. It is only a matter of doing one's duty. After all the body has to perish one day. It is therefore better to let it perish in a noble cause."[108] In his memoir, Vinoba recollects that some residents were alarmed at the idea of fasting unto death, protesting that there can be no "army of fasters," no such thing as "chain-fasting" following a leader. Vinoba was the first to pledge to carry out Gandhi's orders.[109] Following Vinoba, the other residents also pledged to carry out this plan.

When Gandhi was arrested, he was imprisoned in the Aga Khan Palace, along with Kasturba, Mirabehn, Sushila Nayar, Pyarelal Nayar, Mahadev Desai, and Sarojini Naidu.[110] Separated from Gandhi, Vinoba Bhave began his fast in Yeravda Central Prison. Gandhi, however, decided to postpone the fasting strategy while negotiating with the British from within prison. Gandhi eventually got a letter to Vinoba, informing him that it was not yet time to fast. Vinoba, who received a five-year prison sentence, records in his memoir how he remained ever ready to fulfill his pledge to fast unto death if Gandhi sent him the order, writing, "I would have done it not from knowledge (like Bapu) but from faith. I have no doubt at all that an individual can make such a sacrifice, with the fullest reverence and love, in obedience to an order accepted in faith."[111] Vinoba was prepared to sacrifice his life in selfless service to Gandhi.

Vinoba did not die during the Quit India campaign, though he was prepared to, and he lived a long and productive life after completing his prison sentence; he founded an ashram for women and led a movement to give land back to the impoverished masses. Many other coresidents from Sevagram Ashram were also willing to sacrifice their lives in selfless service. Amrit Kaur was sent to organize nonviolent Quit India protests in northern India and was beaten at one protest in Simla by the colonial police and then arrested in Kalka. She was discharged from prison after two months due to the severity of her weight loss and placed under house arrest in Simla for the remainder of her three-year sentence.[112] Like Vinoba, Amrit Kaur went on to live a long and productive life after completing her prison sentence—at India's independence, she was elected to the Constituent Assembly to work on the draft constitution, and she became India's first health minister. Mirabehn, who was imprisoned at the Aga Khan Palace along with Gandhi, fell severely ill with malaria a year into her prison sentence. Gandhi appealed after colonial officials denied her request for medical treatment, and the British eventually relented and permitted Mirabehn to receive quinine injections in prison, enabling her recovery.[113] Mirabehn also went on to live a long and productive life after completing her prison sentence—she remained in India until 1959, continuing constructive work in the villages, and then spent her final years living a simple life in Austria.

Vinoba Bhave, Amrit Kaur, and Mirabehn took the mantra "Do or Die" to heart and nearly lost their lives in the Quit India freedom struggle. Other coresidents from Sevagram Ashram did make the ultimate sacrifice. One week after being imprisoned at the Aga Khan Palace, Mahadev Desai suffered a heart attack and died in prison on August 15, 1942. As the months of imprisonment stretched on, Kasturba's mental and physical health steadily declined. Mirabehn records that Kasturba grew depressed, developed a worrisome cough, and began suffering heart palpitations.[114] Kasturba died in prison on February 22, 1944, after suffering a heart attack complicated by pneumonia. The cremated remains of both Kasturba Gandhi and Mahadev Desai were interred in the garden of the palace turned prison. When Gandhi's own health started to fail in May of 1944, the British released him from prison, fearing that if he too died while imprisoned under their watch, it would further galvanize the Indian public into action.

Do or Die

In the summer of 1945, the British summoned Gandhi and other Indian political leaders to meet and work toward the formation of an interim government leading toward independence. The Indian Independence Act was passed in the British Parliament in early 1947, which provided for the partitioning of colonial British India into two newly independent nations along communal lines, India (predominantly Hindu) and Pakistan (predominantly Muslim). When independence arrived on August 15, 1947, it was simultaneously a time of jubilant celebration for the end of colonial rule, and deep anguish over the unprecedented chaos, strife, and loss of life caused by partition. Millions of people suddenly found themselves displaced as Hindus and Sikhs left their homes in newly declared Pakistan to migrate into India, and as Muslims left their homes in India to migrate into Pakistan. Sectarian violence ran amok as refugees flowed into each country.

Gandhi traveled to hot spots and undertook fasts to restore peace, swearing not to eat until the violence ended. From Noakhali to Bihar to Calcutta, Gandhi next reached New Delhi, where he proclaimed, "I must apply the old formula 'Do or Die' to the capital of India."[115] As the violence continued, Gandhi began holding ecumenical prayer meetings in the early evenings, pleading with the crowd to be willing to die for their fellow citizens, not kill them, as in this excerpt from his prayer speech on January 11, 1948:

> It is of no consequence by what name we call God in our homes. In the work of the nation, all Indians of all faiths are one. If Hindus say that they will kill Muslims or will not permit them to live in India they will be committing suicide and the Muslims will be spared the trouble of killing the Hindus. We cannot commit suicide. We are Indians and we must lay down our lives in protecting Hindus, Muslims, Parsis, Sikhs and all others.[116]

Gandhi began another fast on January 13, declaring in his prayer speech that he had undertaken this fast "in the cause of the Muslims" and that he would end it only when peace had returned and Muslims could walk freely without fear of bloodshed from Hindus and Sikhs.[117] Gandhi's efforts galvanized many leaders in Delhi to formulate a plan to deal with the refugee crisis in the city and to begin to restore everyday life. Gandhi's public efforts also angered Hindu nationalists who felt that India should be a Hindu country.

On January 30, 1948, Gandhi walked out of the guest quarters in Birla House, where he was staying in Delhi, with one arm around Abha Gandhi and the other around Manu Gandhi. The three of them walked toward the garden, where a crowd awaited Gandhi's daily prayer session. Suddenly, a young man stepped forward and fired three shots from a gun. Gandhi died moments later. The assassin was Nathuram Godse. During his trial, Godse read aloud a lengthy confession, expressing his commitment to Hindu nationalist ideology and describing his action as a duty to the nation, stating, "Gandhi-ji failed in his duty as the Father of the Nation. He has proved to be the Father of Pakistan. It was for this reason that I as a dutiful son of Mother India thought it my duty to put an end to the life of the so-called Father of the Nation who had played a very prominent part in bringing about the vivisection of the country—our Motherland."[118] Godse and an accomplice, Narayan Apte, were tried, found guilty of Gandhi's murder, and executed by hanging. Six other coconspirators were sentenced to life in prison.

Just ten days prior to Gandhi's assassination, a previous assassination attempt took place at Gandhi's evening prayer session, when a homemade bomb exploded. Gandhi survived that attempt but recognized that another attempt might be successful. He stated in a prayer meeting the following evening that he hoped to die with a smile on his face and God's name on his lips.[119] If he was able to die in this manner, it would be God's blessing of his way of life: "If I have been sincere in my pursuit of truth, nonviolence, non-stealing, brahmacharya [celibacy] and so on and if I have done all this with God as my witness, I shall certainly be granted the kind of death that I seek."[120] Gandhi was willing to die, and he wanted Manu Gandhi at his side, prepared for the possibility that she might also die. Gandhi wrote to Jaisukhlal Gandhi, Manu's father, telling him that Manu was sitting beside him when the bomb exploded and reminding Jaisukhlal that "in this *yajna* [sacrifice] we have to do or die."[121] In a separate letter to Manu, Gandhi expressed gratitude for her purity and her selfless service and wondered whether they would die together or she would watch him die, writing, "The service you have rendered in this great *yajna* [sacrifice] is of inestimable value to me. . . . Who knows but that there may be another bomb explosion and with Ramanama [God's name] on my lips I may be taken away from you?"[122] Neither Manu nor Abha was shot when Gandhi was assassinated, but surely both women knew the risk they took in simply walking by his side as part of their ongoing selfless service to him.

In chapter 3, we saw that during the Sabarmati Ashram years, Gandhi escalated both the rhetoric and the expectation of suffering and self-sacrifice for universal well-being and communal flourishing. At Sevagram Ashram, Gandhi's final intentional community, his understanding of universal well-being continued to evolve. Layered onto suffering and self-sacrifice, he now asked his coresidents to cultivate an attitude of selfless service. Such service was to be directed toward the villagers of India; toward the nation at large during the Quit India campaign; and, for a subset of the residents who were young and female, toward Gandhi himself. To live at Sevagram Ashram, one had to being willing to die in selfless service to Gandhi, village, and nation.

Interlude 4

Sevagram Ashram after Gandhi

When I first visited Sevagram Ashram (in 2017), it was not part of any standard tourist circuit in India, so it was not easy to get there. I took a flight from Mumbai (formerly Bombay) to Nagpur, then rented a car from Nagpur to Wardha, and then had to procure hostel accommodations in a remote place that was not accustomed to hosting international visitors. At last I set foot on the grounds of Sevagram Ashram and immediately perceived how different this space was from Gandhi's other intentional community in India, Sabarmati Ashram. Sabarmati Ashram has been enfolded within the city of Ahmedabad over decades of urban growth and encroachment, and it receives an average of three thousand visitors each day, including both domestic and international tourists who come on day trips to walk through its educational museum. Sevagram Ashram, by contrast, is far more rural and receives far fewer visitors. Looking around, I observed just a handful of other visitors at Sevagram Ashram on that day. In addition to these few visitors, I also observed with interest a handful of residents going about their daily business. One elderly woman, clad in a white, homespun cotton sari, observed me as I began to walk around the grounds, joined by my mother and my young son. The resident approached us, welcomed us to walk around, and kindly offered to answer any questions we had after we had explored. She then returned to her work sweeping the veranda of one of the small houses. Sevagram Ashram is unique as the only intentional community founded by Gandhi that continues to operate as an intentional residential community—and as, simultaneously, a heritage site. It is also unique in that its nonresident visitors treat Sevagram Ashram as a spiritual place of pilgrimage, not simply as a secular heritage site.

The first sign that is seen upon entering Sevagram Ashram gestures to its dual nature as both a private residential community and a public heritage site, and as a secular historical site that is simultaneously sacred ground. Placed next to a large shade tree, the sign is titled "Welcome to Mahatma Gandhi Bapuji's Ashram in Sevagram" and states, "Bapu arrived in Sevagram on 30th April 1936. He led the Indian freedom struggle from here. Our ashram is a holy place offering all who come here valuable time for introspection and self-resolve. We hope you will make the best use of your time."[1] The sign then reminds visitors to help maintain the peace and sanctity of the space, to be quiet while exploring the grounds, and to be tidy.

Unlike Sabarmati Ashram, which Gandhi decided to close and disband in 1933, Gandhi wanted Sevagram Ashram to endure. In the final years of his life, Gandhi was increasingly drawn away from his last intentional community to engage in political matters in pursuit of Indian independence. His last stay at Sevagram Ashram took place in August of 1946, when he hosted the Congress Working Committee meeting there. He emphasized to the visiting committee members, in a speech given to commence the daily evening prayer session, how important it was that they not overlook the villages as they worked toward independence. Gandhi shared with them his vision for an independent India that would be composed of thousands of self-sufficient villages akin to the Sevagram Ashram community. In that speech, Gandhi also articulated his plans for the future, stating that when he was able to again step back from politics, he planned to spend the remainder of his days living for six months of the year at Sevagram Ashram, engaged in constructive work in the surrounding villages, and the other six months of the year at the nature cure center in the village of Uruli Kanchan that Gandhi had recently established under the management of his disciple Manibhai Desai.[2] Indeed, in a letter written on January 29, 1948, Gandhi was trying to figure out if he would be able to return to Sevagram the next week to resume his constructive work program.[3] Tragically, he was assassinated the next day.

In the months and years immediately following Gandhi's assassination, his disciple Vinoba Bhave managed the day-to-day affairs of Sevagram Ashram, traveling between the Sevagram community and the nearby community that he had founded in Paunar, just six kilometers away. Bhave's impact in the area around Sevagram Ashram is still felt to this day. In the 1950s, Bhave walked throughout central India on a Bhoodan Yajna, or Land Gift Pilgrimage, seeking to persuade landowners to give small plots of farmable land to landless villagers so that they could live rent-free and engage in subsistence farming. He met with some successes. In 1959, Bhave gave the Paunar ashram to a small group of women who had joined him in walking on his Land Gift movement and who wanted to form their own spiritual community; Bhave, in turn, went on to establish several additional ashrams before his death in 1982. The Paunar ashram, which the female founders called the Brahma Vidya Mandir, is still operational down the road from Sevagram Ashram, and its residents view farming, spinning, and producing *khadi* (homespun cotton) as central to their daily spiritual practice and their commitment to *sarvodaya* (universal well-being). They continue to spread the teachings of Gandhi and Bhave to their neighbors, including other agricultural communes and intentional communities in central India.[4]

Sevagram Ashram is now administered under the auspices of a trust called the Sevagram Ashram Pratishthan. The Sevagram Ashram Pratishthan trust seeks to preserve the ashram as both a residential community and a heritage site. They describe the community in this way on their website:

> The life at the ashram is peaceful, dignified and silent. The inmates of the Ashram follow a simple lifestyle in tune with ideals set forth by Mahatma. It imparts the experience of a simple life that starts with early Morning Prayer and voluntary manual labour such as farming, sanitation, and other works related to the management of the Ashram. This environment provides a unique and unforgettable opportunity for an individual to develop a new vision of harmonious life based on self-discipline, respect for labour, self-reliance and altruism.[5]

In my conversations with residents at Sevagram Ashram during my visits, I learned that approximately two dozen permanent residents remain there today, and they continue to practice many elements of the daily routine that were emphasized in Gandhi's time there, including farming, spinning, communal cooking and dining, and collective prayer.

Walking from building to building during my first visit, I found the atmosphere quiet and calm. I took my time wandering about the site, walking through Adi Niwas (Gandhi's first residence at Sevagram Ashram), Bapu Kuti (the cottage Mirabehn built for herself but which became Gandhi's primary cottage), Ba Kuti (the cottage of Gandhi's wife, Kasturba), and other sites, including the premises of Nai Talim (the Basic Education school buildings), where primary education that integrates intellectual and physical work to emphasize holistic development is still offered today for local residents through the tenth grade.[6]

A couple of residents checked in now and then to see if I had questions, and they were generous in answering my questions but otherwise let me be to take in the experience of the ashram at my own pace.

Walking about, one encounters numerous signs that highlight not only the national and historic significance of Sevagram Ashram but also the sanctity of the space. An example can be seen in the large sign about Bapu Kuti, Gandhi's Cottage. It provides information (in English and Hindi) about the initial building of this cottage by Gandhi's disciple, Mirabehn. It next describes how Gandhi would meet important political guests from India and around the world in this cottage, noting that the cottage has "witnessed the beginnings of many great historical events in

Figure 10. Bapu Kuti, Gandhi's cottage at Sevagram Ashram. Photo by Karline McLain.

India." This sign also includes a list of the "Seven Social Sins" to remind visitors to be morally grounded. These sins include, "politics without principles, pleasure without conscience, wealth without work, science without humanity, commerce without morality, worship without sacrifice, and education without character."[7]

Another example can be found in the large sign titled "The Mad Rush" that is posted outside of the Akhiri Niwas building, Gandhi's final cottage at Sevagram Ashram. This sign paraphrases a passage from a speech Gandhi gave in Colombo, Sri Lanka, in 1927, which was then printed in his publication *Young India*, and it offers a message encouraging visitors to slow down and contemplate their priorities:

> The people who are in the mad rush today, increasing their wants senselessly suppose that they are enhancing their importance and real knowledge. A day will come when they will exclaim, "What have we been doing?" One after another many civilizations have risen, flourished, declined and disappeared and in spite of their big boast of human progress, I am inclined to ask, "To what end all this? What's the purpose?" Darwin's contemporary Wallace has said that despite the various discoveries and inventions during the past fifty years, the moral height of man hasn't increased even an inch. Tolstoy has said the same thing. Jesus, Buddha, Prophet Mohammed all have said the same thing.[8]

Figure 11. Visitors at Akhiri Niwas, Gandhi's final cottage at Sevagram Ashram. Photo by Karline McLain.

History has remembered Gandhi as a politician, an anti-colonial activist, and as one of the key makers of modern India. Through signs such as this one, paired with the meditative environment and the multifaith communal prayer that takes place each morning and evening on the designated prayer ground, visitors to Sevagram Ashram are encouraged not simply to reflect upon Gandhi's political contributions or dismiss him as a mere politician but also to reflect upon his religious life as a "Mahatma" (an epithet meaning "Great Soul"), as well as upon their own purpose in life and their own moral choices. Many visitors who have come and stayed at Sevagram Ashram in the decades since Gandhi's passing report that they have taken inspiration from this site—and particularly from Gandhi's Cottage—to effect change in their own lives and to seek to effect change in the world.

At Sabarmati Ashram, by contrast, the primary attraction for most visitors is the Gandhi Memorial Museum, which was built in 1963 and focuses on Gandhi's political leadership in the anti-colonial struggle during the years he was in residence at that community. At Sevagram Ashram, however, the primary focus is Bapu Kuti, Gandhi's Cottage. This focus on Gandhi's residence allows for a more intimate window into Gandhi's daily life. Inside Bapu Kuti, one can see Gandhi's narrow wooden bed frame and his massage table, the small enclosure where he took his daily bath, and on display in one glass case are his walking stick and

Figure 12. Interior wall of Bapu Kuti, Gandhi's cottage at Sevagram Ashram. Note the palm trees and om symbol that were molded by hand into the wall by Gandhi's disciple Mirabehn when the cottage was built. Photo by Karline McLain.

sandals, while another glass case encloses his final few possessions. I observed visitors walk through the space with an air of reverence, taking off their shoes out of respect at the entrance to the hut, speaking in whispers, if at all, and gently caressing the decorative images of palm trees and the om symbol that were molded by hand in relief on the mud plaster walls by Mirabehn when the hut was first built. Outside of Akhiri Niwas, some visitors bow briefly before the Tulsi plant (Holy Basil, a plant that is sacred in Hinduism) that was planted there by Gandhi in homage to two residents who died in the Aga Khan Palace prison: his wife, Kasturba, and his secretary, Mahadev Desai.

Day visitors can elect to conclude their visit by joining residents on the prayer ground to take part in the multifaith prayer session at sunset, a ritual that has remained a part of the daily routine since Gandhi's time in residence. On my first visit, I joined the residents for this prayer session, sitting cross-legged on the sandy ground and listening quietly as they chanted together short verses from Hindu, Buddhist, Christian, Islamic, and, finally, Sikh scriptures. Later that evening, while entering field notes into my journal back in my hostel room, I found myself marveling at how impactful this experience was—I had read about the significance of the prayer ground as a space for uniting the residents through such daily ecumenical group prayer sessions during Gandhi's time living in this community, but taking part in such a ritual made me feel a sense of continuity with and connection to daily life at Sevagram Ashram that I had not anticipated feeling.

Since Gandhi's assassination in 1948, a number of visitors to Sevagram Ashram have come to this remote site seeking some connection to Gandhi or some inspiration from the final space he called home. Such visitors treat Sevagram Ashram as a sacred place of pilgrimage, and they report being transformed through their journey to and experience at this destination, describing how this transformation has impacted them in lasting ways as they reaggregated back into society.[9] For instance, the American modernist architect Joseph Allen Stein (1912–2001) visited Sevagram Ashram in the 1950s, and during his visit to Bapu Kuti, he experienced what he called "a revealing intensity of beauty and rightness" there that impacted how he thought about the ideal of voluntary simplicity in his future architectural work in India and the United States.[10] Over the decades, other architects have also been inspired by Gandhi's Cottage to think about the nexus between simplicity, self-sufficiency, sustainability, beauty, and community in housing design. The Indian architect Vinoo Kaley (1946–1998), commonly known as "the bamboo man," was inspired by his visit to Bapu Kuti in 1987 to urge policymakers to look to local, sustainable, and cost-effective building material—like bamboo in India—rather than industrial design.[11] The American architect Mark DeKay visited Bapu Kuti in 2000 and wrote of the impact Bapu Kuti had on him personally and on his design thinking:

> It's hard to describe what a place like this does to a person. It must be felt; it's like being immersed in a vibrant world where wholeness and integration, the profound sense of aliveness, are so palpable that one can no longer go on in the normal sleep-walking state. No one can say this of contemporary American neighborhoods, which are neither beautiful, nor do they feed our souls. Neighborhoods today are not great communities with a shared civic life. Neighborhoods today are not in sync with ecological processes.[12]

Other pilgrim-visitors to Sevagram Ashram in its post-Gandhian years have come from a wide range of national and professional backgrounds. The Austrian philosopher Ivan Illich (1926–2002) visited Sevagram Ashram in January 1978 and spent significant time sitting in Gandhi's Cottage to imbibe its message. Illich then gave a lecture about the meaning of Bapu Kuti, wherein he appreciated its "simplicity, beauty, and neatness" and admired that it "proclaims the principle of love and equality for everybody," commenting:

> Man should realize that for the good of the individual as well as of the society, it is best that people keep for themselves only as much as is sufficient for their immediate needs. We have to find a method by which this thinking finds expression in changing the values of today's world. This change cannot be brought about by the pressure of the governments or through centralized institutions. A climate of public opinion has to be created to make people understand that which constitutes the basic society.[13]

After leaving Sevagram Ashram, Illich continued to think, write, and give talks about self-sufficiency, urging people around the world to think about the relationship between economics, labor, and sustainability. Similarly, many other figures from a variety of disciplinary backgrounds—from social workers to scientists to organic farmers—have also felt transformed through their time at Gandhi's Cottage.[14] Such visitors have typically not arrived at Sevagram Ashram as casual tourists on a day trip; rather, they have come with some foreknowledge of Gandhi and his life, traveling often from a great distance in order to seek personal inspiration on their own life journeys.

Since my first visit to Sevagram Ashram, the Maharashtra state government has been working to develop the area around Sevagram Ashram with the goal of increasing tourism. The initial development plan in 2015 included a proposed convention center, heritage walk, tourist accommodations, and a "Gandhi for Tomorrow" theme park. The theme park idea was ultimately set aside, but the government did expand the roads in Wardha district in 2020 to accommodate more traffic, and in 2022, they began building the Nagpur-Mumbai Expressway to enable faster travel to and from the Mumbai metropolis. Across the street from Sevagram Ashram, a tourist accommodation area (called "Yatri Niwas") was added, featuring overnight accommodations, from simple dorm-style hostel arrangements to individual cottages with private bathrooms and parking, as well as an organic café and a book and gift shop. In 2018, on Gandhi's 150th birth anniversary, the state government celebrated by unveiling a giant spinning wheel, or *charkha*, outside Sevagram Ashram. In his remarks at the unveiling, the minister of finance and planning in Maharashtra, Sudhir Mungantiwar, proudly stated that this spinning wheel, which was created by students at J. J. School of Art in Mumbai, was the largest in the world at 18.6 feet high and thirty-one feet long, surpassing even the giant spinning wheel in New Delhi's international airport. In 2022, further plans were approved by the government to build an interactive exhibition center at Sevagram Ashram with 3D imaging and multimedia technology, and to add a library and resource center. The Maharashtra Directorate of Tourism published a new brochure, adding Sevagram Ashram and Wardha to its preexisting brochures for tourist destinations in and around Mumbai and Pune, and the chief minister of Maharashtra, Uddhav Thackeray, promised to try to seek the status of a World Heritage Site for Sevagram Ashram.[15]

All of this recent effort to develop the area around Sevagram Ashram has not gone without criticism. Some have pointed out the multiple ironies of this development that is seemingly incongruous with the mission of Sevagram Ashram, given that the development is being done for capitalist purposes and not for the primary goal of helping the local villagers and farmers; that the development does not entail the use of local and sustainable resources in the creation of new buildings and has instead entailed felling trees and reducing green areas; and that the development is being driven by self-avowed Hindu nationalist political parties, which once celebrated the assassination of Gandhi.[16] Time will tell whether Sevagram Ashram is able to retain its unique identity as the only intentional community founded by Gandhi that is still a living residential community, and whether it will continue to be treated as a spiritual place of pilgrimage by its nonresidential visitors, or whether it will instead be fully transformed into a day-trip tourist destination.

Conclusion

Experiments in Utopia

This ashram has buildings, which are its body, so to speak. They will be destroyed one day; but the ashram's soul, which is its ideals, will never perish.

— Gandhi, speaking at a multifaith communal prayer session at Sabarmati Ashram in 1926[1]

Gandhi experimented with utopia throughout his lifetime, establishing two major intentional communities in South Africa and two more in India in his ongoing pursuit of universal well-being (*sarvodaya*). This book has explored everyday life at each of these communities, asking who lived and labored at each community alongside Gandhi, what experiments they collectively undertook, and what connections they forged between daily life at these communities and larger sociopolitical issues and movements. By focusing on everyday life at these four communities, this book sheds new light on Gandhi, allowing us to see that these communities were not formed in response to his political vision; on the contrary, the collective quest for a more utopic life at these communities was foundational to the development of Gandhi's political vision and action. This book has demonstrated how the community members and their shared communal values were central to the anti-colonial activism that Gandhi became so famous for, such as the protest of the Asiatic Registration Act in South Africa, and the Salt March and Quit India campaigns in India. This book has also allowed us to see how Gandhi increasingly amplified the rhetoric and expectation of self-sacrifice and voluntary suffering for the collective good. Gandhi's coresidents were asked to sacrifice more and more over time in their shared pursuit of universal well-being, from offering up their labor and time at Gandhi's first community, to voluntarily living like prisoners at Gandhi's second community, to being willing to sacrifice their lives in the pursuit of village improvement and political self-rule at Gandhi's final communities.

Studying Gandhi's communities illustrates the productive ambiguity of the concept of utopia, how, in its ideal conceptualization, it functions as both a critique of the present and a vision for an idyllic future, and how, in practice, it is a never-ending process of striving to create a better place for all that is ultimately impossible to attain. On the one hand, Gandhi's communities were admirable experiments with utopia in many important and compelling ways: they were places where residents made a moral commitment to thinking and acting for the good of the collective in pursuit of universal well-being (*sarvodaya*); where residents agreed to work toward equality across differences of race, religion, caste, and gender; and where residents embraced a shared lifestyle of collective labor as an alternative to the colonialist and capitalist status quo. But on the other hand, Gandhi's intentional communities were also places where the reality did not always live up to the ideal: in spite of the espoused commitment to equality, some members acted in elevated leadership roles, with Gandhi positioned at the apex; Black South Africans were not invited into the South African communities; those at the bottom of the Indian caste hierarchy were not always treated as equals by all upper-caste residents; men and women did not always perform the same labor, and some young female residents were expected to perform additional selfless service (*seva*) to Gandhi in his experiments with celibate sexuality; and the increasing expectation of self-sacrifice put individual lives at risk on multiple occasions.

When considering the pros as well of the cons of living with Gandhi in hindsight, one might be tempted to ask why anyone—and, perhaps, especially Dalits and young women—would decide to join one of Gandhi's communities. Scholars within the discipline of religious studies who focus on new religious movements, and in particular on high-control religious groups (sometimes called "cults" in popular culture), have pointed out that people join such groups because they are drawn to the community's members and their shared values, not because they are weak-minded or dependent or insecure (as members of high-control groups are often depicted in the media). To quote Deborah Layton, a former member of Peoples Temple and a survivor of the mass murder-suicide ritual that resulted in the deaths of more than nine hundred people in Jonestown, Guyana, on November 18, 1978, "Nobody joins a cult. Nobody joins something that they think's gonna hurt them. You join a religious organization, you join a political movement, and you join with people that you really like."[2] Rebecca Moore has highlighted how focusing only on the scandal and outrage of Peoples Temple obscures the idealism behind this new religious movement, and she emphasizes that its members were drawn to it for its efforts to create a just and egalitarian society, first in California and then in Jonestown, to create a workable communitarian experiment and to open space for the participation of women at the highest levels of leadership.[3]

Anthony Pinn, who studies Peoples Temple through the lens of Black religious studies, underscores that a majority of the members of Peoples Temple were African American, and he argues that their participation in this movement was not a matter of socioeconomic weakness or psychological flaws; rather, they participated because the movement spoke to their full humanity by offering them a recognition of their complex subjectivity as people of color and as equals within the community.[4] These scholars help to remind us that the people who joined Peoples Temple, including those who moved to Jonestown to build an intentional community there under the leadership of Jim Jones, did so because they believed they could together make a positive impact in the world. So too of the people who joined Gandhi's communities; Gandhi's coresidents, whether white or Indian, high caste or low, male or female, were all drawn to the experiments in utopia that they collectively undertook. They joined these communities in South Africa and India because they believed in the ideals espoused by Gandhi and his coresidents, not because they wanted to endure extreme hardships such as caste or gender discrimination, undue suffering, or loss of life.

Gandhi thought long and deep about the connections between how we live our daily lives and larger social, religious, and political issues, and he came to the conclusion that self-limits and discipline were essential for the greater welfare of all. In his final community, as Gandhi lived among villagers in a handmade hut and spent his time building latrines, growing vegetables, and spinning cotton, he was responding to the poverty, deprivation, and discrimination that he witnessed all around him. He called upon people everywhere to join him in limiting their individual ego-based desire to consume more and more (more money and possessions, larger houses, richer foods, etc.) and engaging instead in selfless service to try to enhance the quality of life for all. Better than the modern, industrial urban life and an ego-based consumer mindset, Gandhi argued, was the revivification of India's villages and a service- and sacrifice-based mindset, so that all Indians could have their basic needs met and the country could begin to flourish. Gandhi also argued that such a service- and sacrifice-based mindset would help to build mutual affection for one another and thereby tackle race, religion, caste, and gender discrimination. He hoped that India might thereby become a shining light for the world. Writing to his political protégé Jawaharlal Nehru in 1945, Gandhi said, "In this village of my dreams the villager will not be dull—he will be all awareness. He will not live like an animal in filth and darkness. Men and women will live in freedom, prepared to face the whole world."[5]

What lessons should we draw from Gandhi's experiments in utopia? The challenge, I think, is not to try to live like Gandhi and view his intentional communities as a precise model to follow but rather to learn from these communities lessons about the importance of thinking deeply about what it means to live well in community with one another, the larger social and political impact of the decisions we make about how we live, and the value of engaging in experiments in our own everyday lives.[6] Informed by scholarship on new religious movements and high-control groups, I want to use this conclusion to open up this study of Gandhi's communities to larger questions with ongoing real-world relevance about what it means to live well (or not) in community with one another, including: When does an intentional community become a high-control group? How can you balance the concern with universal well-being and individual self-care? And what is the difference between a utopian experiment and a dystopian one?

Susannah Crockford argues that Peoples Temple has become the archetypal "cult" in popular culture through three symbolic strands: charisma, isolation, and poison:

> *Charisma* stands for the influence of the leader, Jim Jones (1931–1978), seemingly possessed with the power to control the will of his followers. *Isolation* stands for disconnection from society, the group's disappearance into the jungle far away from family and friends looking for the Promised Land. *Poison* stands for alleged mind control, a corruption of the individual will to survive in favor of the collective; a process given real, tangible form in the story of Jonestown through the problematic phrase "drinking the Kool-Aid."[7]

It is worth comparing Gandhi's intentional communities with Jonestown as the archetypal high-control group to ask whether Gandhi's communities entailed charisma, isolation, and poison to such an extent that one could consider membership in them as membership in a high-control group. Beginning with charisma, Gandhi was certainly a charismatic leader.[8] In the context of his communities, we have seen that residents were repeatedly drawn to the communities because of their belief in Gandhi's leadership and their desire to live and work alongside him. This was true, for instance, of Albert West, who was one of the earliest members to join Phoenix Settlement, Gandhi's first intentional community in South Africa, and who wrote, "I was certainly in love with the idea, and my love for Gandhi was sufficient to make me want to succeed in this venture."[9] It was also true of Mirabehn (Madeleine Slade), who felt called to Gandhi after reading a biography of him and therefore left Britain and moved to Sabarmati Ashram in India, Gandhi's third intentional community. In her memoir, Mirabehn writes, "The call was absolute, and that was all that mattered."[10] We have also seen that even as Gandhi emphasized equality among all members of his intentional communities and sought to enact collective decision-making processes, he simultaneously served as the de facto leader of his communities (even proposing the position of "chief controller" when the constitution for Sabarmati Ashram was being drafted).

Gandhi's intentional communities also entailed isolation. Each community was located in the rural countryside in South Africa or India, outside of major cities, where residents built their own modest housing and grew their own food. Gandhi's last community, Sevagram Ashram, was his most remote one—a village in central India that was only accessible on foot when he first began to live there, with no roads, no post office, and no shops. Gandhi rejected cities as part of the "disease" of modern industrial civilization, and he emphasized that people must learn to live "in villages, not in towns, in huts, not in palaces," for he insisted that only in the simplicity of village life could they realize truth and nonviolence.[11] Some residents flourished in such rural and rustic environments, but others did not. For instance, Millie Graham Polak, who had joined Phoenix Settlement along with her husband, Henry, decided to leave after just two months in residence and return to Johannesburg. She wrote of the experience that although she tried to make a home there, "the impossibility of getting suitable food, the knowledge and fear of the snakes, spiders and other poisonous or unpleasant creatures, the disappointment to me, a town-bred girl, of the whole place" simply proved too much.[12] While the residents who joined Gandhi's communities were geographically removed from family and friends living in more urban locations, they could chose to stay or go (unlike the residents at Jonestown, who found themselves under armed guard), and the intentional communities were not completely closed off from society. Political leaders often visited Gandhi at his communities to consult with him, and as we have seen, Gandhi's communities became organizing centers for important anti-colonial movements in both South Africa and India.

What about poison in the context of Gandhi's communities? Crockford discusses poison in the Peoples Temple movement both literally and figuratively—to refer to the literal poison in the form of the deadly punch that many members consumed (or were forced to consume) in Jonestown, which resulted in their deaths, as well as to refer to the "poisonous" mindset of being psychologically influenced and damaged by their leader, Jim Jones. In high-control groups, the influence wielded over people may be gradually increased over time, such that the control escalates and may take multiple forms, including behavior, information, thought, and emotional control.[13] Gandhi, who was committed to nonviolence, did not literally poison members of his intentional communities. But Gandhi did exert increasing levels of control over daily life at his communities: residents dressed alike in white homespun cotton; they ate the same restricted vegetarian diet (sometimes without salt, spices, sweets, or dairy based on Gandhi's ongoing dietary experiments); they practiced celibacy and were encouraged to confess any lapses in thought or deed to Gandhi (and some young women at Gandhi's last intentional community engaged in additional experiments with Gandhi and celibate sexuality); and their daily schedule was highly regulated (prayer time, spinning time, farming time, cooking time, etc.). Gandhi gave significant thought to all of these elements of daily life (dress, diet, sexuality, routine) and encouraged his coresidents to implement the experiments that he found worthwhile for their mutual moral and spiritual growth. While perhaps not intentional, these methods of control limited individual autonomy and promoted conformity.

The most significant form of control employed by Gandhi was his emphasis on voluntary service, suffering, and self-sacrifice for the greater good, which escalated with each iteration of his ideal community. As early as 1904, the year Gandhi founded his first intentional community, he published an essay titled "Self-Sacrifice" in his newspaper *Indian Opinion*, which he opened with the following lines: "Sacrifice is the law of life. It runs through and governs every walk of life. We can do nothing or get nothing without paying a price for it, as it would be said in commercial parlance or, in other words, without sacrifice."[14] In this essay, he upholds as exemplars Jesus, who died on the cross, and Joan of Arc, who burned at the stake. At his first two intentional communities in South Africa, Gandhi called upon his coresidents to voluntarily make sacrifices for their community and for the nonviolent movement for Indians' civil rights: to donate their finances and labor to the collective, to be willing to face arrest and serve time in jail, and to be willing to endure physical violence at the hands of colonial officers. At a speech in London in 1914, as Gandhi was leaving South Africa to return (via Britain) to India, he stated that he and his wife, Kasturba, stood before their audience "almost as barbarians" having lived "isolated on a little farm, cut off from the cities" of South Africa. He then attributed the successes they had achieved in the movement for Indians' civil rights in South Africa to the sacrifices made by his coresidents, and he praised, in particular, several male and female residents of Tolstoy Farm who died in the movement.[15] At his later intentional communities in India, Gandhi increasingly emphasized the virtue of selfless service in everyday life, connecting such service with sacrifice and suffering, and praising martyrdom gradually more frequently. At the start of the Quit India anti-colonial campaign in 1942, Gandhi gave the residents of Sevagram Ashram a "do or die" mantra, saying, "Satyagrahis [nonviolent civil resisters] must go out to die, not to live. They must seek and face death. It is only when individuals go out to die that the nation will survive."[16] Some members of Sevagram Ashram did die in prison, including Gandhi's wife, Kasturba, and his secretary, Mahadev Desai. In 1948, after Gandhi again applied his "do or die" mantra, declaring that Indians must unite together or die trying in the face of the communal violence that erupted during India's independence, Gandhi died when a Hindu assassin shot him.

Gandhi is often praised for his laudable commitment to nonviolence, yet such praise usually overlooks the requisite sacrifice and suffering that was central to Gandhi's philosophy of universal well-being (*sarvodaya*) and to his method of nonviolent resistance (*satyagraha*), as well as the burden this placed on his coresidents, who were asked to make and to model greater and greater sacrifices for the collective good. For Gandhi, universal well-being took precedence over the individual self. Gandhi saw this as a virtue, linking it not only with his sociopolitical goals but also with his spiritual goal to obtain liberation by reducing his ego-based desires and attachments. Thus, in his autobiography, Gandhi wrote, "I must reduce myself to zero. So long as man does not of his own free will put himself last among his fellow creatures, there is no salvation for him."[17] Gandhi wanted to reduce himself to zero, and he encouraged his coresidents to similarly embrace this goal by valuing universal well-being over the individual self, even at the cost of their own lives.

Thinking about our obligation to the greater good and the need for self-discipline and limits is crucial as we consider how we inhabit our daily lives and how we will confront the many problems and inequities facing our world today and in future generations. Our challenge is to consider how far we can enhance life for the greater good before it becomes detrimental to ourselves and/or to others, before it endangers rather than enhances life. To return to Peoples Temple and Jonestown, for Jim Jones also, the collective good took precedence over the individual self. Jones taught the residents at Jonestown to value their community above all else, and they were encouraged to express their willingness to sacrifice their own lives for the survival of Jonestown—their "Promised Land"—through oral pledges and suicide drills (called "White Nights"). Tragically, in Jonestown's final days, this resulted in the ultimate sacrifice of perceived enemies and traitors, and then the community itself in the form of the mass murder-suicide.[18] Mahatma Gandhi and Jim Jones were very different people with very different philosophies about violence and nonviolence. However, both figures endorsed extreme self-sacrifice for the collective good. Taken together, these two examples help to illustrate why it is important to think critically about any charismatic leader's control over a group and their call for extreme self-sacrifice; to ask ourselves, "How much suffering and sacrifice is too much in the pursuit of the collective good?"; and to arrive at our own conclusions about the appropriate balance to strike between concern for the greater good of the group (whether that group is an intentional community, a religious group, a family, a village, a nation, or the world) and individual self-care.

The concept of utopia is paradoxical because the quest for an ideal society is always a goal to strive for, never a reality. Derived from the Greek words *outopia*, meaning "no-place," and *eutopia*, meaning "good-place," the word *utopia* literally refers to a place that is simultaneously good and nonexistent.[19] For over four decades, Gandhi tried to bring his vision for an ideal society into reality with his intentional communities, but toward the end of his life, he believed he had ultimately failed. As he wrote to Jawaharlal Nehru in 1945 from his final intentional community, "My ideal village still exists only in my imagination." Even Sevagram Ashram did not fully live up to Gandhi's utopic vision, which would entail a community of free, equal, and educated villagers, as well as "no plague, no cholera, and no smallpox. Nobody will be allowed to be idle or to wallow in luxury. Everyone will have to do body labor."[20] A processual understanding of utopia, however, allows us to expand our focus beyond the outcome (i.e., the question of the success or failure of a utopic community) and embrace the process, recognizing the ambiguous and paradoxical nature of utopia. As Anne Beutter and E. Sasu Kwami Sewordor write, rather than viewing the absence of the achieved utopic ideal as a failure, utopia "needs to be thought of as both vision and a process. It needs to be understood as a continuous re-orientation towards and production of the *ought* as an imaginative horizon ever-retreating into the future as collectives move through time."[21] Gandhi's communities illustrate how his utopic vision of universal well-being (*sarvodaya*) evolved through the iterative process of striving to bring the ideal into reality while he worked in collaboration with his coresidents at these four communities. I suggest there is value in the process as well as the vision. Even if it is impossible by definition to make utopia a reality, and even if Gandhi's communities today have failed as living residential communities, in that they are now predominantly heritage museums, they are nonetheless worthy examples of the effort not only to envision but also to enact a better world—to try to create a multiracial, multireligious, and multicaste society whose members could live and labor side by side with mutual respect and affection.

The obverse side of the utopia is the dystopia. Many of Gandhi's close friends and allies could not be persuaded to join his intentional communities, such as Jawaharlal Nehru, who visited Gandhi at his Indian ashrams on numerous occasions but never wanted to live there, preferring instead a modern urban environment. Some residents who did join Gandhi's communities chose not to stay in the end, finding the experiments in utopia too remote, too rustic, too rife with hardship, or in other ways too disappointing. For a handful of residents, the communities felt more dystopic than utopic, such as Gandhi's eldest son, Harilal, who left Tolstoy Farm because he no longer wanted to volunteer to live like a prisoner and wanted to pursue other educational and career opportunities. Thus, by exploring Gandhi's intentional communities, we also learn that no single vision of an ideal community will work for all people, for one person's utopia is another person's dystopia.[22] Our task, then, is to reflect upon Gandhi's experiments with utopia to better help each of us give thought to our own core values and how they relate to where and how and with whom we live, to articulate for ourselves what it means to live well in community with one another, and to consider the larger social and political impact of the decisions we make about our everyday lifestyles. Once we have reflected in this way, perhaps we may be bold enough to try our own experiments in utopia, risking the possibility of failure and learning from it as we strive to create the ever elusive "good-place."

Notes

Notes to the Introduction

[1] M. K. Gandhi, *Collected Works of Mahatma Gandhi*, 100 vols. (Publications Division, Government of India, electronic edition, 2015), 85:33.

[2] Gandhi, *Collected Works of Mahatma Gandhi*, 63:122.

[3] Gandhi, *Collected Works of Mahatma Gandhi*, 85:33.

[4] Examples of scholarship on Gandhi's political philosophy and legacy, including his method of nonviolent civil disobedience (*satyagraha*), include Dennis Dalton, *Mahatma Gandhi: Nonviolent Power in Action* (Columbia University Press, 2012); Ramachandra Guha, *Gandhi: The Years That Changed the World, 1914–1948* (Vintage Books, 2018); David Hardiman, *Noncooperation in India: Nonviolent Strategy and Protest, 1920–22* (Oxford University Press, 2021); Mark Juergensmeyer, *Gandhi's Way: A Handbook of Conflict Resolution* (University of California Press, 2005); Ajay Skaria, *Unconditional Equality: Gandhi's Religion of Resistance* (University of Minnesota Press, 2016); and Thomas Weber, *On the Salt March: The Historiography of Gandhi's March to Dandi* (HarperCollins India, 1997).

[5] Joseph Alter, for instance, argued in *Gandhi's Body: Sex, Diet, and the Politics of Nationalism* (University of Pennsylvania Press, 2000) that the standard account of Gandhi and Gandhi's place in India's national history needs to be rewritten from the vantage point of his body, thereby enabling the reader to better understand Gandhi in particular, and important facets of Indian nationalism more broadly. Nico Slate has turned to Gandhi's diet in *Gandhi's Search for the Perfect Diet: Eating with the World in Mind* (University of Washington Press, 2019), arguing that what Gandhi chose to eat was intimately tied to his ethics and his politics. Thomas Weber examined the topic of Gandhi's friendships in *Gandhi as Disciple and Mentor* (Cambridge University Press, 2004), arguing that Gandhi not only influenced his followers but was himself influenced by his own network of friends.

[6] There is very limited prior scholarship on Gandhi's intentional communities or his evolving concept of universal well-being (*sarvodaya*). On the intentional communities, see Mark Thomson, *Gandhi and His Ashrams* (Popular Prakashan, 1993). This work considers Gandhi's nonviolent methodology (*satyagraha*) in action in the context of his intentional communities in the effort to "rediscover the non-violent alternative" (2). It is particularly

useful as a scholarly resource for its inclusion of several personal accounts of life at Gandhi's communities in India that Thomson recorded with former residents during his fieldwork in India from 1978 to 1982. For a preliminary essay on *sarvodaya* (universal well-being) in the context of Gandhi's intentional communities, see Karline McLain, "Gandhi's Ashrams: Residential Experiments for Universal Welfare in South Africa and India," *Journal of Utopian Studies* 30, no. 3 (2019): 462–485.

[7] See, for instance, Gregory Claeys and Lyman Tower Sargent, eds., *The Utopia Reader* (New York University Press, 1999); Lawrence Foster, *Women, Family, and Utopia: Communal Experiments of the Shakers, the Oneida Community, and the Mormons* (Syracuse University Press, 1991); Richard Francis, *Transcendental Utopias: Individual and Community at Brook Farm, Fruitlands, and Walden* (Cornell University Press, 1997); Roland Schaer, Gregory Claeys, and Lyman Tower Sargent, eds., *Utopia: The Search for the Ideal Society in the Western World* (Oxford University Press, 2000); and Stephen Stein, *Communities of Dissent: A History of Alternative Religions in America* (Oxford University Press, 2003).

[8] For recent efforts to broaden and decolonize utopian studies in conversation with religious studies, see Karina Kosicki Bellotti, "Decolonizing Utopias," *Religion* 54, no. 3 (2024): 580–586; Anne Beutter and E. Sasu Kwame Sewordor, "A Processual Perspective on Utopia as a Lived Social Project: The Case of a Ghanaian 'Christian Town,'" *Religion* 54, no. 3 (2024): 514–537; Anja Kirsch and Andrea Rota, "Religion and Utopia: A Critical Overview of the Field," *Religion* 54, no. 3 (2024): 396–411; and Amanda J. Lucia, *White Utopias: The Religious Exoticism of Transformational Festivals* (University of California Press, 2020).

[9] M. K. Gandhi, *Autobiography: The Story of My Experiments with Truth* (Beacon Press, 1993), 55.

[10] Gandhi, *Collected Works of Mahatma Gandhi*, 10:70.

[11] Gandhi, *Collected Works of Mahatma Gandhi*, 76:308–309.

[12] M. K. Gandhi with Anthony Parel, *Hind Swaraj and Other Writings* (Cambridge University Press, 1997), 150. Jawaharlal Nehru was never persuaded about the ideal of village living, and though he visited Gandhi at both of his intentional communities in India on multiple occasions, he never joined the communal life. To the contrary, in his reply to Gandhi on October 9, 1945, Nehru agreed to the ideal of a truthful and nonviolent society but disagreed that the village was the way to attain it.

Notes to Chapter 1

[1] M. K. Gandhi, *Autobiography: The Story of My Experiments with Truth* (Beacon Press, 1993), 131.

[2] Isabel Hofmeyr, *Gandhi's Printing Press: Experiments in Slow Reading* (Harvard University Press, 2013), 46–53. On the first decade of *Indian Opinion*, see also Uma Shashikant Mesthrie, "From Advocacy to Mobilization: *Indian Opinion*, 1903–1914" in Les Switzer, ed., *South Africa's Alternative Press: Voices of Protest and Resistance, 1880s–1960s* (Cambridge University Press, 1997), 99–126.

[3] Gandhi, *Autobiography*, 286.

[4] Hofmeyr, *Gandhi's Printing Press*, 72.

[5] On the correspondence between Nazar and Gandhi, see Surendra Bhana and James D. Hunt, eds., *Gandhi's Editor: The Letters of M. H. Nazar* (Promilla Publications, 1989).

[6] Gandhi, *Autobiography*, 299. See also Ramachandra Guha, *Gandhi Before India* (Alfred A. Knopf, 2013), 174–177.

[7] Gandhi, *Autobiography*, 300.

[8] Albert West, "In the Early Days with Gandhi," *Illustrated Weekly of India*, October 3, 1965, 33.

[9] Gandhi, *Autobiography*, 300–301; West, "In the Early Days with Gandhi," 33.

[10] Thomas Weber, *Gandhi as Disciple and Mentor* (Cambridge University Press, 2004), 58.

[11] Prabhudas Gandhi, *My Childhood with Gandhiji* (Navajivan Publishing House, 1957), 36.

[12] Gandhi, *Autobiography*, 301.

[13] West, "In the Early Days with Gandhi," 33.

[14] West, "In the Early Days with Gandhi," 33.

[15] M. K. Gandhi, *Collected Works of Mahatma Gandhi* (Publications Division, Government of India, 2015 electronic edition in 100 volumes), 4:319–321. Gandhi reprinted the essay "Ourselves" again in *Indian Opinion* one week later, on December 31, 1904.

[16] Gandhi, *Collected Works of Mahatma Gandhi*, 4:320.

[17] Gandhi, *Collected Works of Mahatma Gandhi*, 4:320.

[18] Gandhi, *Collected Works of Mahatma Gandhi*, 4:320–321.

[19] Hofmeyr, *Gandhi's Printing Press*, 62.

[20] Gandhi, *Autobiography*, 304.

[21] Gandhi referred to Chhaganlal Gandhi as his nephew, though they were technically cousins once removed; Chhaganlal Gandhi was the son of Gandhi's cousin Kushalbhai Gandhi.

[22] Gandhi, *Autobiography*, 300.

[23] Sam Govindswamy moved to Phoenix Settlement and lived there but continued to retain his original salary, as opposed to accepting the £3 per month scheme that Albert West, Chhaganlal Gandhi, and the other settlers agreed to. See Hofmeyr, *Gandhi's Printing Press*, 61.

[24] Gandhi, *Autobiography*, 300.

[25] Hofmeyr, *Gandhi's Printing Press*, 54.

[26] M. H. Nazar, *Gandhi's Editor: The Letters of M. H. Nazar, 1902–1903*, edited by Surendra Bhana and James D. Hunt (Promilla & Co., 1989), 5.

[27] Uma Dhupelia Mesthrie notes who some of these day laborers were in *Gandhi's Prisoner? The Life of Gandhi's Son Manilal* (Permanent Black, 2004), 69–70.

[28] Gandhi, *Autobiography*, 301.

[29] Gandhi, *Autobiography*, 304–305.

[30] Hofmeyr, *Gandhi's Printing Press*, 60; P. Gandhi, *My Childhood with Gandhiji*, 35–36.

[31] Henry S. L. Polak, "My Ten Years' Service," in *Golden Jubilee, 1904–1954: Phoenix Settlement* (International Printing Press, 1954), n.p.

[32] Henry S. L. Polak, "Some South African Reminiscences," in *Incidents of Gandhiji's Life*, ed. by Chandrashanker Shukla (M. K. Vora & Co. Publishers Ltd., 1949), 238–239.

[33] Gandhi, *Autobiography*, 305.

[34] H. Polak, "My Ten Years' Service," n.p.

[35] Gandhi, *Collected Works of Mahatma Gandhi*, 5:217; Gandhi, *Autobiography*, 305.

[36] Mesthrie, *Gandhi's Prisoner?*, 70; Gandhi, *Collected Works of Mahatma Gandhi*, 9:138–139, 200, 208, 213, 363, 412, 10:132. On Gandhi's interest in nature cure, see Joseph Alter, *Gandhi's Body: Sex, Diet, and the Politics of Nationalism* (University of Pennsylvania Press, 2000); and Nico Slate, *Gandhi's Search for the Perfect Diet: Eating with the World in Mind* (University of Washington Press, 2019), 100–118.

[37] Joseph J. Doke, *M. K. Gandhi: Indian Patriot in South Africa* (Indian Chronicle, 1909).

[38] Preserved correspondence shows that Kitchin had multiple disagreements with the other settlers and resigned the editorship and left the settlement. See Gandhi, *Collected Works of Mahatma Gandhi*, 5:77, 87, 125–126, 199; and H. Polak, "My Ten Years' Service," n.p.

[39] For more on Gandhi's relationship with theosophy and esotericism, see Michael Bergunder, "Experiments with Theosophical Truth: Gandhi, Esotericism, and Global Religious History," *Journal of the American Academy of Religion* 82, no. 2 (2014): 398–426; and J. T. F. Jordens, *Gandhi's Religion: A Homespun Shawl* (St. Martin's Press, 1998).

[40] Gandhi, *Autobiography*, 313–314.

[41] Gandhi, *Autobiography*, 306–309; Millie Graham Polak, *Mr. Gandhi: The Man* (George Allen & Unwin Ltd., 1931), 47–51.

[42] M. Polak, *Mr. Gandhi: The Man*, 48.

[43] M. Polak, *Mr. Gandhi: The Man*, 49–50.

[44] M. Polak, *Mr. Gandhi: The Man*, 49.

[45] Mesthrie, *Gandhi's Prisoner?*, 70–71.

[46] Gandhi, *Autobiography*, 309.

[47] Gandhi, *Autobiography*, 309.

[48] Gandhi, *Autobiography*, 309.

[49] Heather Hughes, "'The Coolies Will Elbow Us Out of the Country': African Reactions to Indian Immigration in the Colony of Natal, South Africa," *Labour History Review* 72, no. 2 (2007): 155–168.

[50] Heather Hughes, *First President: A Life of John L. Dube, Founding President of the ANC* (Jacana Media, 2011), 110.

[51] Hughes, *First President*, 111. Hughes discusses in detail the 1905 meeting between Dube and Gandhi on pages 111–113.

[52] P. Gandhi, *My Childhood with Gandhiji*, 39.

[53] For instance, see Gandhi, *Collected Works of Mahatma Gandhi*, 5:216–217, for a discussion of proposed additions to one house at Phoenix Settlement, including a sketch of the proposed alterations.

[54] James D. Hunt, "Experiments in Forming a Community of Service: The Evolution of Gandhi's First Ashrams, Phoenix and Tolstoy Farm," in *World Problems and Human Responsibility: Gandhian Perspectives*, ed. K. L. Seshagiri Rao and Henry O. Thompson (Unification Theological Seminary, 1988), 182.

[55] On the farming challenges at Phoenix Settlement, see M. Polak, *Mr. Gandhi: The Man*, 55–61, and P. Gandhi, *My Childhood with Gandhiji*, 37–39.

[56] P. Gandhi, *My Childhood with Gandhiji*, 39.

[57] M. Polak, *Mr. Gandhi: The Man*, 50–51.

[58] M. Polak, *Mr. Gandhi: The Man*, 51.

[59] M. Polak, *Mr. Gandhi: The Man*, 68–69.

[60] Gandhi, *Collected Works of Mahatma Gandhi*, 12:67–69 and 73–75. Gandhi would continue his experiments in nature cure at his later intentional communities, and he eventually wrote numerous articles and then a book on this topic. See M. K. Gandhi, *A Guide to Health* (S. Ganesan, 1921).

[61] Gandhi, *Collected Works of Mahatma Gandhi*, 10:81.

[62] P. Gandhi, *My Childhood with Gandhiji*, 59.

[63] P. Gandhi, *My Childhood with Gandhiji*, 60.

[64] P. Gandhi, *My Childhood with Gandhiji*, 59–61.

[65] Gandhi, *Autobiography*, 206.

[66] As Veena Howard notes, because Kasturba Gandhi never expressed her feelings about Gandhi's vow, we cannot know her direct thoughts on *brahmacharya*. Howard concludes that from Gandhi's writings, it seems that the vow of celibacy did not create marital strain but instead "served to inject joy and deeper meaning into his marriage and united husband and wife in the common goal of service." Veena R. Howard, *Gandhi's Ascetic Activism: Renunciation and Social Action* (State University of New York Press, 2013), 150. I discuss Gandhi's commitment to celibacy, and his controversial experiments with celibate sexuality and their impact on his coresidents, in chapter 4.

[67] M. K. Gandhi, *Ashram Observances in Action* (Navajivan Publishing House, 1955), v.

[68] Gandhi, *Autobiography*, 208. On the relationship between Gandhi's celibacy and his activism, see Howard, *Gandhi's Ascetic Activism*.

[69] Gandhi, *Collected Works of Mahatma Gandhi*, 68:204.

[70] For an introduction to *satyagraha* as a method of conflict resolution, see Mark Juergensmeyer, *Gandhi's Way: A Handbook of Conflict Resolution* (University of California Press, 2005).

[71] M. K. Gandhi, *Satyagraha in South Africa* (Navajivan Publishing House, rev. ed., 2008), 92.

[72] Gandhi, *Satyagraha in South Africa*, 91.

[73] Gandhi, *Collected Works of Mahatma Gandhi*, 5:421.

[74] Gandhi, *Collected Works of Mahatma Gandhi*, 5:422.

[75] Gandhi, *Collected Works of Mahatma Gandhi*, 5:422–423. See also Gandhi, *Satyagraha in South Africa*, 95–102.

[76] Gandhi, *Satyagraha in South Africa*, 131–132.

[77] Hofmeyr, *Gandhi's Printing Press*, 128–131. For a broader discussion of differences between Gandhi's writings in Gujarati and his writings in English, see Ajay Skaria, *Unconditional Equality: Gandhi's Religion of Resistance* (University of Minnesota Press, 2016).

[78] Gandhi, *Collected Works of Mahatma Gandhi*, 7:186–187. See also Hofmeyr, *Gandhi's Printing Press*, 128–129.

[79] Hofmeyr, *Gandhi's Printing Press*, 132–133.

[80] Gandhi, *Collected Works of Mahatma Gandhi*, 7:212.

[81] Gandhi, *Satyagraha in South Africa*, 134. Hofmeyr also points out that the English edition of *Indian Opinion* was read by journalists working for other papers; see Hofmeyr, *Gandhi's Printing Press*, 110.

[82] Gandhi, *Collected Works of Mahatma Gandhi*, 7:67. On Gandhi's thoughts about the limitations of the term "passive resistance" and other English phrases, see Dennis Dalton, *Mahatma Gandhi: Nonviolent Power in Action* (Columbia University Press, 2012), 14–15. Skaria notes the connection between *satyagraha* and self-sacrifice, writing that long before Gandhi came up with the term "satyagraha," the related terms he used from Gujarati and Sanskrit languages were all interchangeable with "self-sacrifice." See Skaria, *Unconditional Equality*, 91.

[83] Gandhi, *Satyagraha in South Africa*, 102.

[84] Gandhi asked the magistrate for a heavier penalty, noting that many of his fellow resisters were sentenced to three months' imprisonment with hard labor and a fine of £500. The magistrate denied this request, stating that two months' simple imprisonment was a fair sentence in his case. Gandhi, *Collected Works of Mahatma Gandhi*, 8:37–38; Gandhi, *Satyagraha in South Africa*, 137–138.

[85] Gandhi, *Collected Works of Mahatma Gandhi*, 8:32.

[86] Gandhi, *Collected Works of Mahatma Gandhi*, 8:44.

[87] When Gandhi went to submit his registration on February 10, he was physically attacked by an acquaintance, Mir Alam, along with several other Indians. Gandhi, *Collected Works of Mahatma Gandhi*, 8:61; and Gandhi, *Satyagraha in South Africa*, 153–157.

[88] Gandhi, *Collected Works of Mahatma Gandhi*, 8:86. Significantly, this dialogue between the reader and the editor is a format that Gandhi later employed in his most famous political treatise, *Indian Home Rule* (*Hind Swaraj*).

[89] Gandhi, *Collected Works of Mahatma Gandhi*, 8:134.

[90] Gandhi, *Collected Works of Mahatma Gandhi*, 8:135.

[91] See Gandhi, *Collected Works of Mahatma Gandhi*, 8:39–40, for the petition. For an excellent analysis of Gandhi's evolving attitude toward mealie pap in particular, and on race more generally, see Slate, *Gandhi's Search for the Perfect Diet*, 24–45.

[92] Gandhi, *Collected Works of Mahatma Gandhi*, 8:155.

[93] Hofmeyr, *Gandhi's Printing Press*, 64.

[94] Gandhi, *Collected Works of Mahatma Gandhi*, 8:241. See also M. K. Gandhi, *Ruskin: Unto This Last: A Paraphrase* (Navajivan Publishing House, 1956).

[95] Gandhi, *Collected Works of Mahatma Gandhi*, 8:239–240.

[96] Gandhi, *Collected Works of Mahatma Gandhi*, 8:258.

[97] Gandhi, *Collected Works of Mahatma Gandhi*, 8:270.

[98] Gandhi, *Collected Works of Mahatma Gandhi*, 8:282.

[99] Gandhi, *Collected Works of Mahatma Gandhi*, 8:282–283.

[100] Gandhi, *Collected Works of Mahatma Gandhi*, 8:289.

[101] Gandhi, *Collected Works of Mahatma Gandhi*, 8:325.

[102] Gandhi, *Collected Works of Mahatma Gandhi*, 8:339.

[103] Gandhi, *Collected Works of Mahatma Gandhi*, 8:371.

[104] Gandhi, *Collected Works of Mahatma Gandhi*, 8:374.

[105] Gandhi, *Collected Works of Mahatma Gandhi*, 8:373.

[106] Gandhi, *Collected Works of Mahatma Gandhi*, 8:266–269.

[107] Gandhi, *Collected Works of Mahatma Gandhi*, 8:432–433; see also 8:442.

[108] Gandhi, *Collected Works of Mahatma Gandhi*, 8:457.

[109] On the life of Harilal Gandhi, see Chandulal Bhagubhai Dalal with Tridip Suhrud, *Harilal Gandhi: A Life* (Orient Longman Pvt. Ltd., 2007).

[110] Gandhi, *Collected Works of Mahatma Gandhi*, 9:182–183.

[111] Gandhi, *Collected Works of Mahatma Gandhi*, 9:502.

[112] Gandhi, *Collected Works of Mahatma Gandhi*, 9:447.

[113] Gandhi, *Collected Works of Mahatma Gandhi*, 9:464.

[114] Gandhi, *Collected Works of Mahatma Gandhi*, 9:480.

[115] M. K. Gandhi with Anthony J. Parel, *Hind Swaraj and Other Writings* (Cambridge University Press, 1997), 73.

[116] Gandhi with Parel, *Hind Swaraj and Other Writings*, 73.

[117] On the significance of Gandhi's refusal to copyright *Hind Swaraj* so that readers could copy and distribute it, see Hofmeyr, *Gandhi's Printing Press*, 155–158.

Notes to Interlude 1

[1] M. K. Gandhi, *Collected Works of Mahatma Gandhi* (Publications Division, Government of India, 2015 electronic edition in 100 volumes): 11:320–325. For a discussion of the drafting and evolution of these rules, see also James D. Hunt, "Experiments in Forming a Community of Service: The Evolution of Gandhi's First Ashrams, Phoenix and Tolstoy Farm," in *World Problems and Human Responsibility: Gandhian Perspectives*, eds. K. L. Seshagiri Rao and Henry O. Thompson (Unification Theological Seminary, 1988), 177–203.

[2] On the life of Manilal Gandhi, see Uma Dhupelia-Mesthrie, *Gandhi's Prisoner? The Life of Gandhi's Son Manilal* (Permanent Black, 2004). On the life of Sushila Gandhi, see Uma Shashikant Mesthrie, "Sushila Gandhi (1907–1988), Guardian of Gandhian Traditions in South Africa: Obituary," *Natalia* 6, no. 4 (1989): 55–63; and Uma Dhupelia Mesthrie, "The Letters of Sushila Gandhi: From Press Worker to Managing Trustee of Phoenix Settlement in South Africa, 1927 to 1977," *Indian Journal of Gender Studies* 30, no. 1 (2023): 11–32.

[3] Mesthrie, "The Letters of Sushila Gandhi," 23.

[4] Mesthrie, "The Letters of Sushila Gandhi," 26.

[5] Mesthrie, "The Letters of Sushila Gandhi," 27.

[6] On the life of Ela Gandhi and her role in South African politics, see Charles Villa-Vicencio, "Ela Gandhi," in *The Spirit of Freedom: South African Leaders on Religion and Politics* (University of California Press, 1996), 91–101.

[7] Mesthrie, "The Letters of Sushila Gandhi," 28–29; Uma Dhupelia Mesthrie, *Gandhi's African Legacy: Phoenix Settlement 1904 to 2024, A History through Letters* (UWC Press, 2024), 565–578.

[8] Amy Waldman, "Phoenix Site in South Africa Still Sits in Ashes," *Christian Science Monitor*, April 6, 1994, https://www.csmonitor.com/1994/0406/06171.html; Heather Hughes, "Violence in Inanda, August 1985," *Journal of Southern African Studies* 13, no. 3 (1987): 331–354; Mesthrie, *Gandhi's African Legacy*, 578–590.

[9] On my initial visits to Phoenix Settlement in 2015, taxi drivers frequently had no idea where to find it but could locate the nearby Phoenix Hospital, suggesting that the number of tourists visiting Phoenix Settlement were small; I also did not meet other tourists at the site on these visits. On a later return visit in 2023, I noticed that taxi drivers were now more familiar with this site. On efforts to promote the Inanda Heritage Trail, see Sabine Marschall, "Sustainable Heritage Tourism: The Inanda Heritage Route and the 2010 FIFA World Cup," *Journal of Sustainable Tourism* 20, no. 5 (2012): 721–736; and Sabine Marschall, "Woza eNanda: Perceptions of and Attitudes Towards Heritage and Tourism in a South African Township," *Transformation: Critical Perspectives on South Africa* 83, no. 1 (2013): 32–55; on heritage tourism in South Africa more broadly, see Olga Bialostocka, "Using the Past to Build the Future: A Critical Review of the Liberation Heritage Route (LHR) Project of South Africa," *Africa Insight* 44, no. 2 (2014): 94–107.

[10] Wall text, Phoenix Settlement Museum, Durban, Kwazulu-Natal, South Africa.

[11] Wall text, Phoenix Settlement Museum, Durban, Kwazulu-Natal, South Africa.

[12] Wall text, Phoenix Settlement Museum, Durban, Kwazulu-Natal, South Africa.

[13] Plaque no. 3, Phoenix Settlement Museum, Durban, Kwazulu-Natal, South Africa.

[14] Ashwin Desai and Goolam H. Vahed, *The South African Gandhi: Stretcher-Bearer of Empire* (Stanford University Press, 2015), 304–305. See also Arundhati Roy, "The Doctor and the Saint," *Caravan Magazine*, February 28, 2014, https://caravanmagazine.in/essay/doctor-and-saint.

[15] Ajay Skaria, "Thinking with Gandhi on Racism and Violence: A Letter to a Friend," *ABC*, July 6, 2020, https://www.abc.net.au/religion/thinking-with-gandhi-on-racism-and-violence/12424422. For additional scholarship that discusses Gandhi's evolving attitude toward race in general, and Black South Africans in particular, see Nico Slate, *Gandhi's Search for the Perfect Diet: Eating with the World in Mind* (University of Washington Press, 2019), 24–45; and Vinay Lal, "Was Mohandas Gandhi a Racist?" *Lal Salaam* blog, June 25, 2020, https://vinaylal.wordpress.com/2020/06/25/was-mohandas-gandhi-a-racist/.

Notes to Chapter 2

[1] M. K. Gandhi, *Collected Works of Mahatma Gandhi* (Publications Division, Government of India, 2015 electronic edition in 100 volumes), 10:255.

[2] M. K. Gandhi, *Satyagraha in South Africa* (Navajivan Publishing House, rev. ed., 2008), 213.

[3] Gandhi, *Satyagraha in South Africa*, 213–214.

[4] Gandhi, *Satyagraha in South Africa*, 214.

[5] Gandhi, *Collected Works of Mahatma Gandhi*, 10:262, note 1

[6] Gandhi, *Collected Works of Mahatma Gandhi*, 10:262.

[7] Gandhi, *Collected Works of Mahatma Gandhi*, 10:269.

[8] Gandhi, *Collected Works of Mahatma Gandhi*, 10:271–272.

[9] M. K. Gandhi, *Autobiography: The Story of My Experiments with Truth* (Beacon Press, 1993), 328.

[10] James Hunt and Surendra Bhana note that Kallenbach's letters were likely destroyed at his own request. James D. Hunt and Surendra Bhana, "Spiritual Rope-Walkers: Gandhi, Kallenbach, and the Tolstoy Farm, 1910–13," *South African Historical Journal* 58 (2007): 175. This has led to some speculation about the nature of the relationship between Gandhi and Kallenbach, who did share a close bond. Joseph Lleyveld concludes that it was a platonic and possibly homoerotic attraction between Gandhi and Kallenbach but unlikely a homosexual one. See Joseph Lleyveld, *Great Soul: Mahatma Gandhi and His Struggle with India* (Alfred A. Knopf, 2011). From my read of the archive, I note that the two men bonded especially over their shared attempt to practice celibacy and forego intimate relations with women, as well as over other attempts at ascetic discipline, such as dietary restrictions. On the correspondence from Gandhi to Kallenbach, see Gillian Berning, ed.,

Gandhi Letters: From Upper House to Lower House, 1906–1914 (Local History Museum, 1994). Gandhi's practice of celibate sexuality is discussed further in chapter 4.

[11] Shimon Lev, *Soulmates: The Story of Mahatma Gandhi and Hermann Kallenbach* (Orient BlackSwan Pvt. Ltd., 2012), xxix–xxxi; Thomas Weber, *Gandhi as Disciple and Mentor* (Cambridge University Press, 2004), 70; Isa Sarid and Christian Bartolf, *Hermann Kallenbach: Mahatma Gandhi's Friend in South Africa* (Gandhi Informations Zentrum, 1997), 10–13.

[12] Gandhi, *Satyagraha in South Africa*, 163.

[13] Gandhi, *Autobiography*, 329.

[14] Gandhi, *Autobiography*, 321.

[15] Gandhi, *Collected Works of Mahatma Gandhi*, 9:161; 10:152; 10:209.

[16] Gandhi, *Collected Works of Mahatma Gandhi*, 9:566–569.

[17] Weber, *Gandhi as Disciple and Mentor*, 71.

[18] Sarid and Bartolf, *Hermann Kallenbach*, 14–15. See also Weber, *Gandhi as Disciple and Mentor*, 71.

[19] Gandhi, *Collected Works of Mahatma Gandhi*, 10:272.

[20] Gandhi, *Autobiography*, 90 and 137.

[21] Sarid and Bartolf, *Hermann Kallenbach*, 22.

[22] Gandhi, *Collected Works of Mahatma Gandhi*, 9:243; also see 9:213 and 274.

[23] Interestingly, in this letter, Gandhi also requests that Tolstoy remove his criticism of reincarnation from the final paragraph of the letter, noting that while he is not attempting to convince him of the truth of this doctrine, it is a solace to many passive resisters imprisoned in South Africa. Tolstoy permitted Gandhi to remove mention of reincarnation. Gandhi, *Collected Works of Mahatma Gandhi*, 9:444–446.

[24] Gandhi, *Collected Works of Mahatma Gandhi*, 9:369.

[25] As quoted in Hunt and Bhana, "Spiritual Rope-Walkers," 178.

[26] Hunt and Bhana, "Spiritual Rope-Walkers," 180.

[27] Gandhi, *Satyagraha in South Africa*, 215.

[28] Hunt and Bhana, "Spiritual Rope-Walkers," 176.

[29] Sarid and Bartolf, *Hermann Kallenbach*, 16.

[30] On Gandhi's experiments with celibacy, see Veena R. Howard, *Gandhi's Ascetic Activism: Renunciation and Social Action* (State University of New York Press, 2013) and Joseph Alter, *Gandhi's Body: Sex, Diet, and the Politics of Nationalism* (University of Pennsylvania Press, 2000).

[31] Gandhi, *Collected Works of Mahatma Gandhi*, 10:273.

[32] Gandhi, *Satyagraha in South Africa*, 215.

[33] Gandhi, *Satyagraha in South Africa*, 215.

[34] Sarid and Bartolf, *Hermann Kallenbach*, 23.

[35] Gandhi, *Collected Works of Mahatma Gandhi*, 10:307–308.

[36] Gandhi, *Collected Works of Mahatma Gandhi*, 10:375.

[37] Gandhi, *Collected Works of Mahatma Gandhi*, 10:266.

[38] Gandhi, *Satyagraha in South Africa*, 235. On Gandhi's ever evolving dietary experiments, see Nico Slate, *Gandhi's Search for the Perfect Diet: Eating with the World in Mind* (University of Washington Press, 2019).

[39] Gandhi, *Satyagraha in South Africa*, 216.

[40] Gandhi, *Collected Works of Mahatma Gandhi*, 10:281.

[41] Gandhi, *Satyagraha in South Africa*, 219.

[42] Gandhi, *Satyagraha in South Africa*, 219.

[43] Gandhi, *Satyagraha in South Africa*, 218–219.

[44] Gandhi, *Satyagraha in South Africa*, 226. On Gandhi's experiments with nature cure and alternative medicine, see also Alter, *Gandhi's Body*.

[45] Gandhi, *Satyagraha in South Africa*, 232–234.

[46] Gandhi, *Satyagraha in South Africa*, 234.

[47] Gandhi, *Collected Works of Mahatma Gandhi*, 11:155.

[48] Gandhi, *Collected Works of Mahatma Gandhi*, 11:130.

[49] Gandhi, *Satyagraha in South Africa*, 221–222.

[50] Gandhi, *Satyagraha in South Africa*, 221.

[51] Gandhi, *Collected Works of Mahatma Gandhi*, 10:101.

[52] Gandhi, *Collected Works of Mahatma Gandhi*, 10:70.

[53] Gandhi, *Satyagraha in South Africa*, 231.

[54] Gandhi, *Satyagraha in South Africa*, 224.

[55] Slate, *Gandhi's Search for the Perfect Diet*, 31–32.

[56] Photographs in *Indian Opinion*, August 5, 1911, and May 11, 1912.

[57] On Gandhi and Kallenbach's relationship, see Weber, *Gandhi as Disciple and Mentor*, 69–83.

[58] Gandhi, *Collected Works of Mahatma Gandhi*, 11:78. Harilal was particularly upset because Gandhi had received a donation from his friend and benefactor Dr. Pranjivan Mehta to send his eldest sons to school in London, but Gandhi instead first sent his nephew Chhaganlal Gandhi, and then a Parsi resident named Sorabji Shapurji Adajania who was a strong student and whom Gandhi hoped would eventually take his place as a lawyer working on behalf of the Indian community in South Africa once Gandhi returned to India. See Gandhi, *Autobiography*, 310–312, 346; and Chandulal Bhagubhai Dalal with Tridip Suhrud, *Harilal Gandhi: A Life* (Orient Longman Pvt. Ltd., 2007), 21–32.

[59] Dalal with Suhrud, *Harilal Gandhi*, 26.

[60] Gandhi, *Collected Works of Mahatma Gandhi*, 11:165–166.

[61] On the life of Harilal Gandhi, see Dalal with Suhrud, *Harilal Gandhi.*

[62] Gandhi, *Satyagraha in South Africa*, 236.

[63] Gandhi, *Collected Works of Mahatma Gandhi*, 10:344–345.

[64] Gandhi, *Collected Works of Mahatma Gandhi*, 11:219.

[65] See, for instance, Gandhi, *Collected Works of Mahatma Gandhi*, 11:286–287.

[66] Gandhi, *Satyagraha in South Africa*, 226–228.

[67] Gandhi, *Satyagraha in South Africa*, 244–245.

[68] Gandhi, *Collected Works of Mahatma Gandhi*, 11:460–461.

[69] Gandhi, *Collected Works of Mahatma Gandhi*, 11:497.

[70] Gandhi, *Satyagraha in South Africa*, 251–252. See also Gandhi, *Collected Works of Mahatma Gandhi*, 11:504–505 and 12:178–179.

[71] On indentured labor in South Africa, see Goolam Vahed, "The Protector, Plantocracy, and Indentured Labour in Natal, 1860–1911," *Pacific Historical Review* 87, no. 1 (2018): 101–127. For a brief discussion of Gandhi's efforts toward ending indentured labor, see Karline McLain, "Food and Anticolonialism at Gandhi's Intentional Communities in South Africa and India" in *The Provisions of War: Expanding the Boundaries of Food and Conflict, 1840–1990*, ed. Justin Nordstrom (The University of Arkansas Press, 2021), 57–73.

[72] Gandhi, *Collected Works of Mahatma Gandhi*, 12:106–107.

[73] Gandhi, *Collected Works of Mahatma Gandhi*, 12:108.

[74] Gandhi, *Collected Works of Mahatma Gandhi*, 12:113.

[75] Gandhi, *Satyagraha in South Africa*, 252–253.

[76] Gandhi, *Satyagraha in South Africa*, 252–255.

[77] See, for instance, Gandhi's letters to the private secretary to the minister of the interior and the secretary for the interior, as well as his reports on these exchanges in *Indian Opinion* in Gandhi, *Collected Works of Mahatma Gandhi*, 12:120–122, 122–125, 173–175, 180, 182–183, and 183–186.

[78] Gandhi, *Collected Works of Mahatma Gandhi*, 12:187–188.

[79] Gandhi, *Collected Works of Mahatma Gandhi*, 12:196–198.

[80] Gandhi, *Satyagraha in South Africa*, 257–260.

[81] Gandhi, *Satyagraha in South Africa*, 264.

[82] Gandhi, *Satyagraha in South Africa*, 267–270.

[83] Gandhi, *Satyagraha in South Africa*, 271–272.

[84] Gandhi, *Satyagraha in South Africa*, 273.

[85] Gandhi granted interviews to Reuters and *The Natal Mercury*, and he also published an update in *Indian Opinion*. See Gandhi, *Collected Works of Mahatma Gandhi*, 12:257, 258, and 259–260.

[86] Gandhi, *Collected Works of Mahatma Gandhi*, 12:260.

[87] Gandhi, *Satyagraha in South Africa*, 281.

[88] Sarid and Bartolf, *Hermann Kallenbach*, 56.

[89] Sarid and Bartolf, *Hermann Kallenbach*, 57.

[90] Sarid and Bartolf, *Hermann Kallenbach*, 58–61.

[91] Gandhi, *Satyagraha in South Africa*, 283.

[92] Gandhi, *Satyagraha in South Africa*, 286.

[93] For these cases, see Gandhi, *Satyagraha in South Africa*, 283; and Gandhi, *Collected Works of Mahatma Gandhi*, 12:357, 447, 486–487.

[94] Gandhi, *Satyagraha in South Africa*, 235–236.

[95] Lev, *Soulmates*, 102.

[96] Gandhi, *Collected Works of Mahatma Gandhi*, 12:502. This farewell letter was published in the *Rand Daily Mail* on July 20, 1914, and in *The Transvaal Leader* on July 24, 1914.

[97] Jan Smuts kept the sandals Gandhi had made for him and wore them for many years before returning them to Gandhi on his seventieth birthday, along with a note remarking that it was his "fate to be the antagonist of a man for whom even then I had the highest respect." See Louis Fischer, ed., *The Essential Gandhi: An Anthology of His Writings on His Life, Work, and Ideas* (Random House, 2002), 98.

Notes to Interlude 2

[1] M. K. Gandhi, *Autobiography: The Story of My Experiments with Truth* (Beacon Press, 1993), 344–361; Shimon Lev, *Soulmates: The Story of Mahatma Gandhi and Hermann Kallenbach* (Orient BlackSwan Pvt. Ltd., 2012), 105–114; Isa Sarid and Christian Bartolf, *Hermann Kallenbach: Mahatma Gandhi's Friend in South Africa* (Gandhi Informations Zentrum, 1997), 62–65.

[2] Shimon Lev writes that at this point in his life, Kallenbach "saw himself as having accomplished nothing during his two and a half years of pointless internment" and "must have felt deserted by Gandhi" and therefore decided to take some time away from Gandhi to reexamine his life. Lev, *Soulmates*, 111.

[3] Cited in Lev, *Soulmates*, 114.

[4] Hunt and Bhana note that in the 1960s, a small part of the original farm was restored as a historical site to acknowledge its significance, and annual commemorative functions honor its legacy. James Hunt and Surendra Bhana, "Spiritual Rope-Walkers: Gandhi, Kallenbach, and the Tolstoy Farm, 1910–13," *South African Historical Journal* 58 (2007): 174, footnote 3. There have also been efforts to raise funding to revive the site; see "Indian Firms to Help Revive Tolstoy Farm," *Business Standard*, May 13, 2017, http://www.business-standard.com/article/international/indian-firms-to-help-revive-tolstoy-farm-mahatma-gandhi-s-sa-ashram-117051300195_1.html. I tried to reach the community organization responsible for this site before traveling to South Africa to set up an interview and learn more about their plans for the site but did not receive a reply to my queries.

[5] Historical sign, Tolstoy Farm site, Roodepoort, Gauteng, South Africa.

[6] Commemorative plaques, Tolstoy Farm site, Roodepoort, Gauteng, South Africa.

[7] "Indian-Origin Activist Lauded for Efforts in Restoration of Gandhi's Erstwhile Commune in South Africa." *The Week*, January 31, 2025, https://www.theweek.in/wire-updates/international/2025/01/31/fes25-safrica-indian-activist.html; "Johannesburg Farm Started by Mahatma Gandhi Unveils his Life-Size Statue." *India Today*, October 10, 2023, https://www.indiatoday.in/world/story/johannesburg-farm-started-by-mahatma-gandhi-unveils-his-life-size-statue-2446959-2023-10-10; "Man Who Restored Gandhi's Tolstoy Farm Seeks World Heritage Status For It." *Indian Express*, January 23, 2023, https://indianexpress.com/article/cities/mumbai/mohan-hira-tolstoy-farm-mahatma-gandhi-unesco-world-heritage-8394893/.

[8] Thomas Blom Hansen, *Melancholia of Freedom: Social Life in an Indian Township in South Africa* (Princeton University Press, 2012), 201.

Notes to Chapter 3

[1] Gandhi referred to Maganlal Gandhi as his nephew, though they were technically first cousins once removed; Maganlal was the son of Gandhi's cousin Kushalbhai Gandhi. When he left South Africa, Gandhi was concerned to leave Phoenix Settlement operational. Albert West remained at Phoenix Settlement and continued serving as editor of *Indian Opinion*. In 1917, Gandhi's son Manilal returned to Phoenix Settlement, eventually taking over as the editor of *Indian Opinion* and making South Africa his permanent home. On the life of Manilal Gandhi, see Uma Dhupelia Mesthrie, *Gandhi's Prisoner? The Life of Gandhi's Son Manilal* (Permanent Black, 2004).

[2] M. K. Gandhi, *Autobiography: The Story of My Experiments with Truth* (Beacon Press, 1993), 383.

[3] Gandhi, *Autobiography*, 376.

[4] Gandhi, *Autobiography*, 396.

[5] M. K. Gandhi, *Ashram Observances in Action* (Navajivan Publishing House, 1955), 65.

[6] Gandhi, *Ashram Observances in Action*, 65–69.

[7] The draft editions of the constitution can be seen in M. K. Gandhi, *Collected Works of Mahatma Gandhi* (Publications Division, Government of India, 2015 electronic edition in 100 volumes), 13:90–98.

[8] Gandhi, *Ashram Observances in Action*, ix.

[9] Gandhi, *Collected Works of Mahatma Gandhi*, 13:91–96.

[10] Gandhi, *Autobiography*, 429.

[11] Gandhi, *Autobiography*, 429.

[12] Gandhi, *Autobiography*, 429.

[13] Thomas Weber, *Gandhi as Disciple and Mentor* (Cambridge University Press, 2004), 89.

[14] Vinoba Bhave and Mirabehn are discussed further in chapter 4.

[15] Gandhi, *Ashram Observances in Action*, 67–68.

[16] Gandhi, *Autobiography*, 489–494.

[17] On the spinning wheel and *khadi*, see Rebecca M. Brown, *Gandhi's Spinning Wheel and the Making of India* (Routledge, 2010); Nikhil Menon, "Gandhi's Spinning Wheel: The Charkha and Its Regenerative Effects," *Journal of the History of Ideas*, vol. 81, no. 4 (2020): 643–62; Emma Tarlo, *Clothing Matters: Dress and Identity in India* (University of Chicago Press, 1996), 62–128; and Lisa Trivedi, *Clothing Gandhi's Nation: Homespun and Modern India* (Bloomington: Indiana University Press, 2007).

[18] Gandhi, *Autobiography*, 471–474. Originally, *Young India* was published in Bombay but moved to Ahmedabad after Gandhi became editor. As in South Africa, in India, Gandhi wanted to publish in English but in an Indian vernacular in an effort to reach a broader audience. For a broader discussion of differences between Gandhi's writings in Gujarati and English, see Ajay Skaria, *Unconditional Equality: Gandhi's Religion of Resistance* (University of Minnesota Press, 2016).

[19] Gandhi, *Collected Works of Mahatma Gandhi*, 16:92–93.

[20] Gandhi, *Collected Works of Mahatma Gandhi*, 13:332–334 and 446–448; Gandhi, *Ashram Observances in Action*, 71–73.

[21] Gandhi, *Collected Works of Mahatma Gandhi*, 18:466. For information on Gandhi's approach to education, see Pallavi Varma Patil and Sujit Sinha, "Nai Talim Today: Gandhi's Critique of Industrialism and an Education for Swaraj," *Journal of Human Values* vol. 28, no. 1 (2022): 44–56; and Sudarshan Iyengar, "Gandhiji in Ahmedabad," *Journal of Social and Economic Development*, vol. 23, no. Suppl 1 (2021): 4–24.

[22] Weber, *Gandhi as Disciple and Mentor*, 89–90.

[23] Gandhi, *Collected Works of Mahatma Gandhi*, 15:92.

[24] Gandhi, *Collected Works of Mahatma Gandhi*, 36:261–263.

[25] Madeleine Slade (Mirabehn) and Reginald Reynolds each wrote their own memoir and discussed living at Sabarmati Ashram. See Mirabehn, *The Spirit's Pilgrimage* (Great Ocean Publishers, 1960); and Reginald Reynolds, *My Life and Crimes* (Jarrolds, 1956).

[26] Gandhi, *Collected Works of Mahatma Gandhi*, 13:93–94.

[27] Several terms are used to refer to so-called "untouchables," members at the bottom of the caste hierarchy of Indian society: *Dalit* means "broken down" and is a term embraced by Ambedkar and many other "untouchables"; *Harijan* means "children of God" and is a term coined by Gandhi but not used widely by "untouchables" to refer to themselves; *Depressed Classes* was a British colonial term used to refer to both "untouchables" as well as indigenous tribal groups.

[28] Gandhi, *Ashram Observances in Action*, 68.

[29] *The Servants of India Society* (pamphlet). (A. B. Press, 1915), 4.

[30] *The Servants of India Society*, 6.

[31] Gandhi, *Autobiography*, 397. Notably, one young Dalit boy named Naiker lived temporarily with Gandhi at this time. Naiker's father, Selvan Guruvadu, had joined the

civil disobedience movement in South Africa and was shot to death when police fired on Indian strikers on November 27, 1913. Naiker's older brother received three bullet wounds, and their mother had to nurse him back to health. The family stayed at Tolstoy Farm in South Africa after Selvan's death, and Naiker was part of the group that moved to India in 1915. Naiker rejoined his mother and brother in November of 1915. See Gandhi, *Collected Works of Mahatma Gandhi*, 13:72, 76, 183; and *Golden Jubilee, 1904–1954: Phoenix Settlement* (International Printing Press, 1954), n.p.

32 Gandhi, *Ashram Observances in Action*, 44–45 and 56–57.

33 Gandhi, *Autobiography*, 397.

34 Gandhi, *Collected Works of Mahatma Gandhi*, 13:181.

35 Gandhi, *Collected Works of Mahatma Gandhi*, 13:127–128.

36 Maganlal eventually became proficient in weaving and spinning and coauthored a how-to manual on spinning using a *takli*, a portable spinning device. See Richard B. Gregg and Maganlal K. Gandhi, *The Takli Teacher* (All India Spinners' Association, 1931).

37 Gandhi, *Ashram Observances in Action*, 44. Thomas Weber points out that Maganlal's attitude toward the Dalit family may have changed, but Santok's may not have. See Weber, *Gandhi as Disciple and Mentor*, 88.

38 Gandhi, *Collected Works of Mahatma Gandhi*, 13:94.

39 Gandhi, *Collected Works of Mahatma Gandhi*, 96:223.

40 Gandhi, *Ashram Observances in Action*, 45.

41 Gandhi, *Collected Works of Mahatma Gandhi*, 38:352; see also 13:430, and Weber, *Gandhi as Disciple and Mentor*, 88.

42 Gandhi, *Ashram Observances in Action*, 68–69.

43 Gandhi, *Autobiography*, 375.

44 Gandhi, *Autobiography*, 386. Gandhi wrote to Sastri on January 13, 1916, to withdraw his membership application. See Gandhi, *Collected Works of Mahatma Gandhi*, 13:200.

45 Methodologically, I am indebted to Saidiya Hartman's work with slavery archives, and I too attempt to "listen for the unsaid" as I recuperate Lakshmi's life: to read between the lines, extract details, piece information together, and make educated extrapolations. See Saidiya Hartman, "Venus in Two Acts," *Small Axe: A Caribbean Journal of Criticism* 26, no. 3 (2008): 1–14.

46 Gandhi, *Autobiography*, 398–399.

47 Gandhi, *Collected Works of Mahatma Gandhi*, 18:328 and 338–339.

48 Gandhi, *Collected Works of Mahatma Gandhi*, 28:410.

49 Gandhi, *Collected Works of Mahatma Gandhi*, 18:338–339.

50 Gandhi, *Collected Works of Mahatma Gandhi*, 26:521.

51 Gandhi, *Collected Works of Mahatma Gandhi*, 41:457.

52 Gandhi, *Collected Works of Mahatma Gandhi*, 53:288–289.

[53] Gandhi, *Collected Works of Mahatma Gandhi*, 46:170.

[54] Gandhi, *Collected Works of Mahatma Gandhi*, 46:268–269.

[55] See the letters to Narandas and Premabehn in Gandhi, *Collected Works of Mahatma Gandhi*, 53:325, 358, 382, and 422.

[56] Gandhi, *Collected Works of Mahatma Gandhi*, 53:382.

[57] Gandhi, *Collected Works of Mahatma Gandhi*, 54:15–16.

[58] Gandhi, *Autobiography*, 397.

[59] Gandhi, *Collected Works of Mahatma Gandhi*, 19:153–154. For another recounting of this incident, see Gandhi, *Collected Works of Mahatma Gandhi*, 26:180–181.

[60] On *tapas* in the context of classical Indian asceticism, see Patrick Olivelle, "The Early History of Renunciation," in *Hindu Practice*, ed. Gavin Flood (Oxford University Press, 2020), 101–121.

[61] Ajay Skaria discusses Gandhi's usage of the concept of *tapas* in the context of what he calls a politics of "nonviolent neighborliness." He argues that whereas liberal politics produce a neutral shared space that seeks to transcend difference, Gandhi's neighborly nationalism instead acknowledges differences between neighbors and seeks to create relations between them through *tapasya*, or suffering: "The *tapasya* of neighborliness differed depending on the kind of absolute difference being addressed: the equal was met with *mitrata* ("friendship"), the subordinate with *seva* ("service"), and the superior with *satyagraha* ("civil disobedience"). These practices of neighborliness sought to sustain a friendship with the world based on distinctive Gandhian notions of justice and equality." See *Ajay Skaria*, "Gandhi's Politics: Liberalism and the Question of the Ashram," *South Atlantic Quarterly*, vol. 101, 2002: 955–986. Following Skaria, Dudabhai's suffering would be that of *satyagraha* offered to his neighborly "superior" (the upper-caste villager at the well), as opposed to service or friendship.

[62] Gandhi, *Collected Works of Mahatma Gandhi*, 19:150–151.

[63] Gandhi, *Collected Works of Mahatma Gandhi*, 19:153.

[64] Gandhi, *Collected Works of Mahatma Gandhi*, 19:574.

[65] Harold Coward, "Gandhi, Ambedkar, and Untouchability," in *Indian Critiques of Gandhi*, ed. Harold Coward (State University of New York Press, 2003), 49.

[66] Gandhi, *Collected Works of Mahatma Gandhi*, 49:191. On Gandhi and fasting, see Nico Slate, *Gandhi's Search for the Perfect Diet: Eating with the World in Mind* (University of Washington Press, 2019), 141–161; and Veena R. Howard, *Gandhi's Ascetic Activism: Renunciation and Social Action* (State University of New York Press, 2013), especially pages 201–203.

[67] Gandhi, *Collected Works of Mahatma Gandhi*, 50:383–384.

[68] Gandhi, *Collected Works of Mahatma Gandhi*, 51:91.

[69] Gandhi, *Collected Works of Mahatma Gandhi*, 51:96.

[70] Gandhi, *Collected Works of Mahatma Gandhi*, 51:98.

[71] On Gandhi's decision to take a sabbatical in 1926, see his essay in *Young India* titled "Indulgence or Self-Denial" in *Collected Works of Mahatma Gandhi*, 29:380–382. For Gandhi's translation of and commentary on the *Bhagavad Gita*, see M. K. Gandhi, *The Bhagavad Gita According to Gandhi* (Berkeley Hills Books, 2000). For a discussion of Gandhi's efforts to enact the message of the *Bhagavad Gita* at his intentional communities, see Karline McLain, "Living the *Bhagavad Gita* at Gandhi's Ashrams," *Religions*, vol. 10, no. 11, 2019, https://www.mdpi.com/2077-1444/10/11/619/htm. On the *Bhagavad Gita* in the larger political context of the Indian nationalist movement, and Gandhi's nonviolent interpretation of its message, see Richard H. Davis, *The Bhagavad Gita: A Biography* (Princeton University Press, 2015), 115–153; and J. T. F. Jordens, "Gandhi and the *Bhagavadgita*" in *Modern Indian Interpreters of the Bhagavadgita*, ed. by Robert N. Minor (State University of New York Press, 1986), 88–109.

[72] Gandhi, *The Bhagavad Gita According to Gandhi*, 63.

[73] Gandhi, *The Bhagavad Gita According to Gandhi*, 63–64. On Gandhi's use of the classical Hindu religious terms "*tapas*" and "*yajna*" in connection with "*brahmacharya*" (celibacy) and his sociopolitical activism, see Howard, *Gandhi's Ascetic Activism*, 81–161.

[74] Jawaharlal Nehru, *The Discovery of India* (Doubleday, Anchor Edition, 1960), 237. On the relationship between Nehru and Gandhi, see Robert D. Baird, "The Convergence of Distinct Worlds: Nehru and Gandhi" in *Indian Critiques of Gandhi*, ed. by Harold Coward, 19–39.

[75] Gandhi, *Collected Works of Mahatma Gandhi*, 51:125–126.

[76] Gandhi, *Collected Works of Mahatma Gandhi*, 51:126.

[77] See, for instance, the resolution passed at the Hindu Leaders Conference in Bombay in Gandhi, *Collected Works of Mahatma Gandhi*, 51:139.

[78] Gandhi, *Collected Works of Mahatma Gandhi*, 51:143–145.

[79] B. R. Ambedkar, *Dr. Babasaheb Ambedkar: Writings and Speeches* (Education Department, Government of Maharashtra, 1979–2003), 9:259.

[80] Arundhati Roy, "The Doctor and the Saint," in B. R. Ambedkar and Arundhati Roy, *Annihilation of Caste* (Verso, 2016), 127.

[81] Mark Juergensmeyer, *Gandhi's Way: A Handbook of Conflict Resolution* (University of California Press, 2005), 28–29, 45–47, and 55.

[82] Ambedkar, *Dr. Babasaheb Ambedkar*, 5:21–22. See also Anil Kumar Patel, "Spatial Inequality and Untouchability: Ambedkar's Gaze on Caste and Space in Hindu Villages," *Journal of Social Inclusion Studies*, vol. 7, no. 2 (2021): 186–198.

[83] Roy, "The Doctor and the Saint," 43–47.

[84] The most comprehensive overview and analysis of the Salt March is Thomas Weber, *On the Salt March: The Historiography of Gandhi's March to Dandi* (HarperCollins India, 1997). See also Dennis Dalton, *Mahatma Gandhi: Nonviolent Power in Action* (Columbia University Press, 2012), 91–138. For scholarship on connections between the Salt March and other nonviolent civil disobedience movements around the world, see Peter Ackerman and Jack DuVall, *A Force More Powerful: A Century of Nonviolent Conflict*

(St. Martin's Press, 2000); Adam Roberts and Timothy Garton Ash, *Civil Resistance and Power Politics: The Experience of Non-Violent Action from Gandhi to the Present* (Oxford University Press, 2011); and Sean Scalmer, *Gandhi in the West: The Mahatma and the Rise of Radical Protest* (Cambridge University Press, 2011).

85 On Gandhi, salt, diet, and politics, see also Slate, *Gandhi's Search for the Perfect Diet*, 9–23; and Karline McLain, "Food and Anticolonialism at Gandhi's Intentional Communities in South Africa and India," in *The Provisions of War: Expanding the Boundaries of Food and Conflict, 1840–1990*, ed. Justin Nordstrom (University of Arkansas Press, 2021), 57–73.

86 Gandhi, *Collected Works of Mahatma Gandhi*, 15:16.

87 Gandhi, *Collected Works of Mahatma Gandhi*, 42:432–35.

88 Dalton, *Mahatma Gandhi: Nonviolent Power in Action*, 100.

89 Mirabehn, *The Spirit's Pilgrimage*, 109–110.

90 Gandhi, *Collected Works of Mahatma Gandhi*, 42:382–383.

91 Thomas Weber discusses the process of selecting which residents would be among the first batch of marchers in detail in *On the Salt March*, 100–124; on bringing women into the movement, see pages 370–378. On the role of women in this campaign, see Rosalind Parr, "Self-Sacrifice, Suffrage and Socialism: Gandhi and the Mobilisation of Women, 1930–31," *South Asia: Journal of South Asian Studies*, vol. 46, no. 4 (2023): 834–850.

92 Reginald Reynolds discusses this in his book *To Live in Mankind: A Quest for Gandhi* (A. Deutsch, 1951), 51–52; for Gandhi's letter to Lord Irwin, see Gandhi, *Collected Works of Mahatma Gandhi*, 43:2–8.

93 Gandhi, *Collected Works of Mahatma Gandhi*, 43:59–60.

94 Gandhi, *Collected Works of Mahatma Gandhi*, 43:146–149. See also Dalton, *Mahatma Gandhi*, 110–111.

95 Gandhi, *Collected Works of Mahatma Gandhi*, 43:72–73.

96 Gandhi, *Collected Works of Mahatma Gandhi*, 43:216–217.

97 Gandhi, *Collected Works of Mahatma Gandhi*, 43:220.

98 Dalton, *Mahatma Gandhi*, 118–119.

99 Dalton, *Mahatma Gandhi*, 131.

100 Dalton, *Mahatma Gandhi*, 103–104. A list of the names and places of origins of the seventy-eight marchers from Sabarmati Ashram who accompanied Gandhi along the Salt March was published in *Young India* on March 12, 1930; see Gandhi, *Collected Works of Mahatma Gandhi*, 43:454–455; see also Weber, *On the Salt March*, 490–496.

101 Haridas T. Muzumdar, *Gandhi Versus the Empire* (Universal Publishing Company, 1932), 68–70.

102 Gandhi, *Collected Works of Mahatma Gandhi*, 44:260.

103 Louis Fischer, ed., *The Essential Gandhi: An Anthology of His Writings on His Life, Work, and Ideas* (Random House, 2002), 233–234.

[104] Gandhi, *Collected Works of Mahatma Gandhi*, 55:288–289. Vinoba Bhave and the satellite ashram are discussed in chapter 4.

[105] Mark Thomson, *Gandhi and His Ashrams* (Popular Prakashan, 1993), 267.

[106] Gandhi, *Collected Works of Mahatma Gandhi*, 55:86–91, 113, and 126.

[107] Weber, *Gandhi as Disciple and Mentor*, 100.

[108] Gandhi, *Collected Works of Mahatma Gandhi*, 55:288.

[109] Gandhi, *Collected Works of Mahatma Gandhi*, 55:302.

[110] Gandhi, *Collected Works of Mahatma Gandhi*, 55:303.

[111] Gandhi, *Collected Works of Mahatma Gandhi*, 55:294.

[112] Gandhi, *Collected Works of Mahatma Gandhi*, 55:310.

Notes to Interlude 3

[1] Historical sign, Upasana Mandir, Sabarmati Ashram Museum, Ahmedabad, Gujarat, India. Note that "Gandhi-ji" is an honorific way of referring to Gandhi.

[2] M. K. Gandhi, *Collected Works of Mahatma Gandhi* (Publications Division, Government of India, 2015 electronic edition in 100 volumes), 56:41–43. Several terms are used to refer to so-called "untouchables," members at the bottom of the caste hierarchy of Indian society: *Dalit* means "broken down" and is a term embraced by Ambedkar and many other "untouchables." *Harijan* means "children of God" and is a term coined by Gandhi but not used widely by "untouchables" to refer to themselves. *Ex-untouchables* is sometimes used by government officials to categorize former "untouchables" after untouchability was legally abolished by the constitution of independent India.

[3] Historical sign, Hridaya Kunj, Sabarmati Ashram, Ahmedabad, Gujarat, India.

[4] Charles Correa, *A Place in the Shade: The New Landscape and Other Essays* (Hatje Cantz Verlag, 2012), 47.

[5] Gandhi Ashram at Sabarmati, "The Museum," accessed June 19, 2024, https://www.gandhiashramsabarmati.org/en/the-museum-falang.html.

[6] Wall text, Sabarmati Ashram Museum, Ahmedabad, Gujarat, India.

[7] Gandhi, *Collected Works of Mahatma Gandhi*, 54:15–16.

[8] Gandhi, *Collected Works of Mahatma Gandhi*, 49:191.

[9] B. R. Ambedkar and Arundhati Roy, *Annihilation of Caste* (Verso, 2016).

[10] Arundhati Roy, "The Doctor and the Saint," *Caravan Magazine*, February 28, 2014, https://caravanmagazine.in/essay/doctor-and-saint.

[11] Harold Coward, "Gandhi, Ambedkar, and Untouchability," in *Indian Critiques of Gandhi*, ed. Harold Coward (State University of New York Press, 2003), 62.

[12] Wall text, Sabarmati Ashram Museum, Ahmedabad, Gujarat, India.

[13] Wall text, Sabarmati Ashram Museum, Ahmedabad, Gujarat, India.

[14] Gandhi, *Collected Works of Mahatma Gandhi*, 82:162 and 326.

[15] "PM Modi Lays Foundation For Redevelopment of Sabarmati Ashram," *The Hindu*, March 12, 2024, https://www.thehindu.com/news/national/other-states/pm-modi-inaugurates-mahatma-gandhi-sabarmati-ashram-redevelopment-project-worth-1200-crore/article67941870.ece.

[16] Mahatma Gandhi Sabarmati Ashram Memorial Trust, "Gandhi Ashram Restoration and Expansion" plan and promotional video, accessed June 21, 2024, https://mahatmagandhimemorial.org/.

[17] Sarosh Anklesaria, "Architectures of Dissent: Building Memorials to Gandhi through Everyday Praxis," *The Plan Journal* 9, no. 2 (2024): 520.

[18] Maya Jasanoff, "What Modi's Plan for Gandhi's Old Home Reveals About India's Future," *The New Yorker*, June 19, 2024, https://www.newyorker.com/news/dispatch/what-modis-plan-for-gandhis-old-home-reveals-about-indias-future.

[19] "'Trivialises Sanctity': Eminent Citizens Oppose Govt's Rs 1200-Cr Plan For Sabarmati Ashram," *The Wire*, August 5, 2021, https://thewire.in/rights/sabarmati-ashram-world-class-memorial-gandhi-simplicity; and "Gujarat HC Rejects PIL By Gandhi's Great Grandson Against Sabarmati Ashram Project," *The Wire*, September 9, 2022, https://thewire.in/law/gujarat-high-court-tushar-gandhi-sabarmati-ashram.

[20] Anklesaria worked with his architecture students to envision multiple intriguing possibilities of alternative memorials, including one that envisioned Sabarmati Ashram as a model for Dalit housing. See Anklesaria, "Architectures of Dissent."

Notes to Chapter 4

[1] M. K. Gandhi, *Collected Works of Mahatma Gandhi* (Publications Division, Government of India, 2015 electronic edition in 100 volumes), 55:366. Multiple terms are used to refer to so-called "untouchables," members at the bottom of the caste hierarchy of Indian society: *Harijan* means "children of God" and is a term coined by Gandhi but not used widely by "untouchables" to refer to themselves; *Dalit* means "broken down" and is a term embraced by Ambedkar and many other "untouchables."

[2] Gandhi, *Collected Works of Mahatma Gandhi*, 55:368.

[3] Gandhi, *Collected Works of Mahatma Gandhi*, 59:3–12; see also 174–184.

[4] Gandhi, *Collected Works of Mahatma Gandhi*, 59:414.

[5] Gandhi, *Collected Works of Mahatma Gandhi*, 59:388.

[6] Thomas Weber, *Gandhi as Disciple and Mentor* (Cambridge University Press, 2004), 106–107. On the relationship between Bajaj and Gandhi, see also B. R. Nanda, *In Gandhi's Footsteps: The Life and Times of Jamnalal Bajaj* (Oxford University Press, 2002).

[7] For more on Vinoba Bhave, see Vinoba Bhave with Marjorie Sykes, *Moved by Love: The Memoirs of Vinoba Bhave, Translated by Marjorie Sykes from a Hindi Text Prepared by Kalindi* (Green Books, 1994); D. Mackenzie Brown, "Vinoba Bhave" in *The Nationalist Movement: Indian Political Thought from Ranade to Bhave* (University of California Press, 1961), 186–205; and Ramachandra Guha, "What Gandhi Was Not: Vinoba Bhave" in *An Anthropologist Among the Marxists and Other Essays* (Permanent Black, 2001), 101–105.

[8] Gandhi, *Collected Works of Mahatma Gandhi*, 63:122.

[9] Gandhi worked with the government to officially rename Segaon village as Sevagram. After Gandhi moved to Segaon, the amount of postal correspondence to and from the village increased significantly, causing confusion because there was another village called Shegaon in the province. To clarify this confusion, the government approved the name change. See Nanda, *In Gandhi's Footsteps*, 218.

[10] On Gandhi's usage of the concept of *seva* in the broader context of India's movement for independence, see R. Srivatsan, "Concept of 'Seva' and the 'Sevak' in the Freedom Movement," *Economic and Political Weekly* 41, no. 5 (2006): 427–438.

[11] Mirabehn, *The Spirit's Pilgrimage* (Great Ocean Publishers, 1960), 58.

[12] Mirabehn, *The Spirit's Pilgrimage*, 60.

[13] Mirabehn, *The Spirit's Pilgrimage*, 62–63; Gandhi, *Collected Works of Mahatma Gandhi*, 25:525.

[14] Mirabehn, *The Spirit's Pilgrimage*, 66.

[15] Mirabehn, *The Spirit's Pilgrimage*, 69–70.

[16] Mirabehn, *The Spirit's Pilgrimage*, 70–71.

[17] Mirabehn, *The Spirit's Pilgrimage*, 71.

[18] Gandhi, *Collected Works of Mahatma Gandhi*, 25:320.

[19] Mirabehn, *The Spirit's Pilgrimage*, 66–69.

[20] Mirabehn, *The Spirit's Pilgrimage*, 74.

[21] Mirabehn, *The Spirit's Pilgrimage*. On the life of Mirabehn, see also Ramachandra Guha, *Rebels Against the Raj: Western Fighters for India's Freedom* (Alfred A. Knopf, 2022) and Bidisha Mallik, *Legends in Gandhian Social Activism: Mira Behn and Sarala Behn: Addressing Environmental Issues by Dissolving Gender and Colonial Barriers* (Springer, 2022).

[22] Mirabehn, *The Spirit's Pilgrimage*, 191.

[23] Mirabehn, *The Spirit's Pilgrimage*, 194; Gandhi, *Collected Works of Mahatma Gandhi*, 60:299–300.

[24] Mirabehn, *The Spirit's Pilgrimage*, 196.

[25] Mirabehn, *The Spirit's Pilgrimage*, 196–197.

[26] Pyarelal Nayar and Sushila Nayar, *In Gandhiji's Mirror* (Oxford University Press, 2004), 35.

[27] Mirabehn, *The Spirit's Pilgrimage*, 196–197.

[28] Mirabehn, *The Spirit's Pilgrimage*, 197–199.

[29] Gandhi, *Collected Works of Mahatma Gandhi*, 62:274, see also 286.

[30] Gandhi, *Collected Works of Mahatma Gandhi*, 62:272.

[31] Venugopal Maddipati, "Building Impressions: Gandhi and Mira Behn's Hut: 1935–1936," *NMML Occasional Papers*, Nehru Memorial Museum and Library, 2014, 5–9.

32 Nanda, *In Gandhi's Footsteps*, 216.

33 Gandhi, *Collected Works of Mahatma Gandhi*, 62:331–332.

34 Nayar and Nayar, *In Gandhiji's Mirror*, 36; also Mirabehn, *The Spirit's Pilgrimage*, 203.

35 Mirabehn, *The Spirit's Pilgrimage*, 203–205.

36 Gandhi, *Collected Works of Mahatma Gandhi*, 62:189; see also 357.

37 Gandhi, *Collected Works of Mahatma Gandhi*, 62:378–380.

38 Gandhi, *Collected Works of Mahatma Gandhi*, 63:161.

39 Gandhi, *Collected Works of Mahatma Gandhi*, 63:152.

40 Maddipati, "Building Impressions," 15. On the architecture of Sevagram Ashram, see Venugopal Maddipati, *Gandhi and Architecture: A Time for Low-Cost Housing* (Routledge, 2021), 30–61.

41 Mirabehn, *The Spirit's Pilgrimage*, 208–209.

42 Nanda, *In Gandhi's Footsteps*, 221.

43 On Nai Talim (Basic Education) at Sevagram, see Pallavi Varma Patil and Sujit Sinha, "Nai Talim Today: Gandhi's Critique of Industrialism and an Education for Swaraj," *Journal of Human Values* 28, no. 1 (2022): 44–56.

44 Weber, *Gandhi as Disciple and Mentor*, 115.

45 Gandhi, *Collected Works of Mahatma Gandhi*, 58:108.

46 Statement to the Associated Press of India, *The Hindu*, and *Harijanbandhu*. Gandhi, *Collected Works of Mahatma Gandhi*, 58:110.

47 On the adoption of the observances from Sabarmati Ashram at Sevagram Ashram in 1938, see Gandhi, *Collected Works of Mahatma Gandhi*, 67:109–110, and M. K. Gandhi, *Ashram Observances in Action* (Navajivan Publishing House, 1955), 89–92.

48 Gandhi, *Collected Works of Mahatma Gandhi*, 62:379.

49 Gandhi, *Collected Works of Mahatma Gandhi*, 64:217.

50 Mirabehn, *The Spirit's Pilgrimage*, 194–195.

51 Gandhi, *Collected Works of Mahatma Gandhi*, 64:218.

52 Gandhi, *Collected Works of Mahatma Gandhi*, 64:86–88.

53 B. R. Ambedkar and Arundhati Roy, *Annihilation of Caste* (Verso, 2016), 333–356.

54 Gandhi, *Collected Works of Mahatma Gandhi*, 62:350, 360, 482.

55 B. R. Ambedkar, *Dr Babasaheb Ambedkar: Writings and Speeches* (Education Department, Government of Maharashtra, 1979–2003), 9:295.

56 On Saralabehn, see Rebecca M. Klenk, "Gandhi's Other Daughter: Sarala Devi and Lakshmi Ashram," *Himalaya* 34, no. 1 (2014): 94–104; and Mallik, *Legends in Gandhian Social Activism*.

57 Nayar and Nayar, *In Gandhiji's Mirror*, 38. See also Mirabehn, *The Spirit's Pilgrimage*, 206–207.

[58] Nanda, *In Gandhi's Footsteps*, 220.

[59] Nayar and Nayar, *In Gandhiji's Mirror*, 39. See also Mirabehn, *The Spirit's Pilgrimage*, 208.

[60] Gandhi, *Collected Works of Mahatma Gandhi*, 56:147.

[61] Mark Thomson, *Gandhi and His Ashrams* (Popular Prakashan, 1993), 218.

[62] Thomson, *Gandhi and His Ashrams*, 220–221.

[63] Thomson, *Gandhi and His Ashrams*, 219.

[64] Thomson, *Gandhi and His Ashrams*, 206–211.

[65] Thomson, *Gandhi and His Ashrams*, 212–213.

[66] On *brahmacharya* as traditionally conceived in Indian religions, and as practiced by Gandhi with spiritual and social goals, see Veena R. Howard, *Gandhi's Ascetic Activism: Renunciation and Social Action* (State University of New York Press, 2013).

[67] Gandhi, *Collected Works of Mahatma Gandhi*, 62:211–212.

[68] Gandhi, *Collected Works of Mahatma Gandhi*, 62:429; also see 62:372–373.

[69] Gandhi, *Collected Works of Mahatma Gandhi*, 67:58.

[70] Gandhi, *Collected Works of Mahatma Gandhi*, 67:69. On Amrit Kaur, see Emily Rook-Koepsel, "Constructing Women's Citizenship: The Local, National, and Global Civics Lessons of Rajkumari Amrit Kaur," *Journal of Women's History* 27, no. 3 (2015): 154–175; and Amrit Kaur, *Rajkumari Amrit Kaur: Eminent Parliamentarians Monograph Series* (Lok Sabha Secretariat, 1993).

[71] These letters from Mirabehn to Gandhi were destroyed per his request to Amrit Kaur, to whom he forwarded them. Tridip Suhrud and Thomas Weber note that Mirabehn was selective in her memoir and in her curation of letters from Gandhi to publish in order to preserve a certain version of herself for posterity, as well as of Gandhi; she does not discuss disagreements they had or periods of estrangement. See Suhrud and Weber, eds., *Beloved Bapu: The Gandhi-Mirabehn Correspondence* (Orient Blackswan, 2014), 3–4.

[72] Gandhi, *Collected Works of Mahatma Gandhi*, 67:60–61.

[73] Gandhi, *Collected Works of Mahatma Gandhi*, 67:61.

[74] Gandhi, *Collected Works of Mahatma Gandhi*, 67:79–80.

[75] Gandhi, *Collected Works of Mahatma Gandhi*, 67:84.

[76] Gandhi, *Collected Works of Mahatma Gandhi*, 67:104.

[77] Gandhi, *Collected Works of Mahatma Gandhi*, 61:437. Gandhi's statement in his "A Renunciation" essay, as well as correspondence between Gandhi and Chhaganlal Joshi, suggest that concerns were raised about Gandhi's contact with women at Sabarmati Ashram as well. See *Collected Works of Mahatma Gandhi*, 67:147–149.

[78] See letters to Munnalal Shah and Chhaganlal Joshi in Gandhi, *Collected Works of Mahatma Gandhi*, 67:106 and 132–133.

[79] For discussion of these exceptions, see Gandhi, *Collected Works of Mahatma Gandhi*, 67:112–113, 116–117, 118, and 136.

[80] Gandhi, *Collected Works of Mahatma Gandhi*, 67:117.

[81] Gandhi, *Collected Works of Mahatma Gandhi*, 67:166.

[82] Gandhi, *Collected Works of Mahatma Gandhi*, 79:221–222.

[83] Gandhi, *Collected Works of Mahatma Gandhi*, 79:192.

[84] Gandhi, *Collected Works of Mahatma Gandhi*, 79:44, 59, 72–73, and 83–84.

[85] Gandhi, *Collected Works of Mahatma Gandhi*, 79:212.

[86] Gandhi, *Collected Works of Mahatma Gandhi*, 79:216. For more on Manu Gandhi, see Manu Gandhi, *The Diary of Manu Gandhi: 1943–1944*, ed. Tridip Suhrud (Oxford University Press, 2020); and Tridip Suhrud, "The Woman Who Cradled Gandhi," *Seminar*, vol. 746, 2021: https://www.india-seminar.com/2021/746/8%20The%20woman%20who%20cradled%20Gandhi-Tridip%20Suhrud.htm.

[87] Gandhi, *Collected Works of Mahatma Gandhi*, 79:218.

[88] Nirmal Kumar Bose was with Gandhi in Noahkhali in 1947 and observed that Gandhi was sleeping next to Manu at night. Bose decided to leave. In his memoir, Bose notes that Gandhi was not only testing his own celibacy by sleeping next to Manu and others but that of his companions as well. Nirmal Kumar Bose, *My Days with Gandhi* (Orient BlackSwan, 1974), 176.

[89] Howard, *Gandhi's Ascetic Activism*, 156.

[90] Gandhi, *Collected Works of Mahatma Gandhi*, 87:108.

[91] Vinay Lal, "Nakedness, Nonviolence, and Brahmacharya: Gandhi's Experiments in Celibate Sexuality," *Journal of the History of Sexuality* 9, no. 1–2 (2000): 105. Thomson addresses Gandhi's experiments in celibate sexuality briefly in *Gandhi and His Ashrams*, 201–202, concluding that his emphasis on *brahmacharya* diverted attention unnecessarily from the main question of village uplift.

[92] Tridip Suhrud, "Introduction" to Manu Gandhi, *The Diary of Manu Gandhi: 1943–1944*, ed. Tridip Suhrud (Oxford University Press, 2020), xl. At the time of writing, the next edition of Manu Gandhi's diary, from the years when she was involved in Gandhi's practice of celibate sexuality, is not yet in publication.

[93] Benjamin Kahan, *Celibacies: American Modernism and Sexual Life* (Duke University Press, 2013), 3–4.

[94] Gandhi, *Collected Works of Mahatma Gandhi*, 66:115–116, 307, 455–457; 79:148–149, 150–151, 243, 251.

[95] Jawaharlal Nehru, *A Bunch of Old Letters: Written Mostly to Jawaharlal Nehru and Some Written by Him* (Oxford University Press, 1960), 508.

[96] Gandhi also insisted that the fiftieth annual Indian National Congress session, presided over by Jawaharlal Nehru, be held in a village for the first time, and thus it was held in Faizpur, Maharashtra, in 1936 and 1937. Gandhi, *Collected Works of Mahatma Gandhi*, 63:17.

[97] Gandhi, *Collected Works of Mahatma Gandhi*, 72:211.

[98] Gandhi, *Collected Works of Mahatma Gandhi*, 76:308–309.

[99] Mirabehn, *The Spirit's Pilgrimage*, 227–230. American journalist Louis Fischer traveled to Sevagram Ashram to interview Gandhi a month before the Congress Working Committee met, while Jawaharlal Nehru and Maulana Abul Kalam Azad were both there to begin discussing the matter with Gandhi in preparation for the upcoming meeting. He describes these conversations in detail in Louis Fischer, *A Week With Gandhi* (Duell, Sloan, and Pearce, 1942).

[100] The full text of the resolution is given in Gandhi, *Collected Works of Mahatma Gandhi*, 76:458–461. For the earlier resolution passed by the Working Committee at Sevagram Ashram, see 76:451–453; and for an earlier draft of the resolution composed by Gandhi, see 76:282–284.

[101] Gandhi, *Collected Works of Mahatma Gandhi*, 76:392.

[102] Gandhi, *Collected Works of Mahatma Gandhi*, 76:403.

[103] On the Quit India movement, see Stanley Wolpert, *Shameful Flight: The Last Years of the British Empire in India* (Oxford University Press, 2009); and Walter Reid, *Keeping the Jewel in the Crown: The British Betrayal of India* (Birlinn Limited, 2016).

[104] Gandhi, *Collected Works of Mahatma Gandhi*, 76:364–367.

[105] Mirabehn, *The Spirit's Pilgrimage*, 230–233.

[106] Gandhi used a similar strategy before launching the Salt March, when he sent Reginald Reynolds as his representative from Sabarmati Ashram. See chapter 3; also Guha, *Rebels Against the Raj*, 247–248.

[107] Mirabehn, *The Spirit's Pilgrimage*, 236–237.

[108] Gandhi, *Collected Works of Mahatma Gandhi*, 76:333–334.

[109] Bhave, *Moved by Love*, 101; Gandhi, *Collected Works of Mahatma Gandhi*, 76:335.

[110] Mirabehn, *The Spirit's Pilgrimage*, 238–242.

[111] Bhave, *Moved by Love*, 102.

[112] Kaur, *Rajkumari Amrit Kaur*, 29–30 and 61.

[113] Guha, *Rebels Against the Raj*, 251–253; and Mirabehn, *The Spirit's Pilgrimage*, 251–252.

[114] Mirabehn, *The Spirit's Pilgrimage*, 254–255. On political prisoners and the conditions of imprisonment in India's independence struggle, see Mushirul Hasan, *Roads to Freedom: Prisoners in Colonial India* (Oxford University Press, 2016).

[115] Gandhi, *Collected Works of Mahatma Gandhi*, 89:166; see also 90:35.

[116] Gandhi, *Collected Works of Mahatma Gandhi*, 90:403–404.

[117] Gandhi, *Collected Works of Mahatma Gandhi*, 90:415–417.

[118] Cited by Ashis Nandy, *At the Edge of Psychology: Essays in Politics and Culture* (Oxford University Press, 1980), 83.

[119] Gandhi, *Collected Works of Mahatma Gandhi*, 90:472–473.

[120] Gandhi, *Collected Works of Mahatma Gandhi*, 90:489.

[121] Gandhi, *Collected Works of Mahatma Gandhi*, 90:488.

[122] Gandhi, *Collected Works of Mahatma Gandhi*, 90:481–482.

Notes to Interlude 4

[1] "Welcome to Mahatma Gandhi Bapuji's Ashram in Sevagram" sign, Sevagram Ashram, Wardha, Maharashtra, India.

[2] M. K. Gandhi, *Collected Works of Mahatma Gandhi* (Publications Division, Government of India, 2015 electronic edition in 100 volumes), 85:128–130.

[3] See Gandhi's letter to Kishorelal dated January 29, 1948, in Gandhi, *Collected Works of Mahatma Gandhi*, 90:520.

[4] For more on the Brahma Vidya Mandir, see Swasti Bhattacharyya, "Khadi: A Narrative of Lived Theology," *Religions* 13, no. 5 (2022), https://doi.org/10.3390/rel13050454; and A. Whitney Sanford, "Gandhi's Agrarian Legacy: Practicing Food, Justice, and Sustainability in India," in *Religion and Sustainable Agriculture: World Spiritual Traditions and Food Ethics*, ed. Norman Wirzba, Pramod Parajuli, and Todd LeVasseur (University Press of Kentucky, 2016), 153–172. For more on the life of Vinoba Bhave, see Vinoba Bhave with Marjorie Sykes, *Moved by Love: The Memoirs of Vinoba Bhave, Translated by Marjorie Sykes from a Hindi Text Prepared by Kalindi* (Green Books, 1994).

[5] Sevagram Ashram Pratishthan, "Library and Research Center," Accessed June 4, 2025, https://sevagramashram.org.in/index.php/library-and-research-centre-2/. The politics of trustee membership are occasionally reported in the Indian press. In 2011, a national Gandhian council called the Sarva Seva Sangh announced its intention to partner with the Sevagram Ashram Pratishthan to help manage the ashram due to alleged prior mismanagement. See "Newly Formed Council to Help Manage Gandhiji's Sevagram Ashram," *Economic Times*, September 6, 2011, https://economictimes.indiatimes.com/news/politics-and-nation/newly-formed-council-to-help-manage-gandhijis-sevagram-ashram/articleshow/9881822.cms. In 2020, there were reports of a power struggle between the president of the Sarva Seva Sangh and the president of the Sevagram Ashram Pratishthan. See "Functionary's Exit Brings to Fore Power Play at Gandhi Ashram," *Mumbai Mirror*, June 5, 2020, https://mumbaimirror.indiatimes.com/mumbai/civic/functionarys-exit-brings-to-fore-power-play-at-gandhi-ashram/articleshow/76204279.cms.

[6] The Nai Talim school at Sevagram Ashram is called Anand Niketan and is managed separately by the Akhil Bharatiya Nai Talim Samiti trust. It has been recognized as a Heritage School by the National Council of Educational Research and Training in India. On Nai Talim education, see Pallavi Varma Patil and Sujit Sinha, "Nai Talim Today: Gandhi's Critique of Industrialism and an Education for Swaraj," *Journal of Human Values* 28, no. 1 (2022): 44–56.

[7] "Bapu Kuti" sign, Sevagram Ashram, Wardha, Maharashtra, India.

[8] "The Mad Rush" sign, Sevagram Ashram, Wardha, Maharashtra, India. For the original quotation, see Gandhi, *Collected Works of Mahatma Gandhi*, 35:251.

[9] The theorist of pilgrimage Victor Turner views pilgrimage as a process of beginning in a Familiar Place, going to a Far Place, and returning ideally "changed" to a Familiar Place. In the middle or liminal phase, social relationships are charged with *communitas*, bonding free of hierarchy, which Turner argues is the common and essential feature of all pilgrimages. The pilgrim's goal, then, is the sacred "center out there" which serves as a symbol of the ideal and provides a transformative experience of relief from the burdens of ordinary existence. See Victor Turner, "The Center Out There: Pilgrim's Goal," *History of Religions* 12, no. 3 (1973): 191–230. Other scholars of pilgrimage, however, have highlighted that this linear model of pilgrimage does not apply to all pilgrimage experiences. See, for instance, David Haberman, who argues for the addition of another, circular model of pilgrimage in his work *Journey through the Twelve Forests: An Encounter with Krishna* (Oxford University Press, 1994).

[10] Christine Cipriani, "Architect of Independence," *Dwell*, November 2008, 114.

[11] Vinoo Kaley, *Venu Bharati: A Comprehensive Volume on Bamboo* (Aroop Nirman, 1998). See also Rajni Bakshi, *Bapu Kuti: Journeys in Rediscovery of Gandhi* (Penguin Books, 1998), 13–17.

[12] Mark Dekay, "Teachings from Bapu Kuti," in *Migrants and Stowaways: An Anthology of Journeys*, eds. Emily Dziuban with Kristin Robertson (Knoxville Writers' Guild, 2004), 49.

[13] Ivan Illich, *In the Mirror of the Past: Lectures and Addresses, 1978–1990* (Marion Boyars, 1991), 68.

[14] Rajni Bakshi profiles a number of figures who have visited Sevagram Ashram in its post-Gandhian years. See Bakshi, *Bapu Kuti*.

[15] For news coverage of these development plans at and around Sevagram Ashram, see "World's Biggest Charkha To Be Unveiled," *Deccan Herald*, October 1, 2018, https://www.deccanherald.com/india/worlds-biggest-charkha-be-695579.html; "Maharashtra's Tribute To 'Father Of Nation': Mumbai-Nagpur Corridor To Have 'Charkha' Bridge," *Hindustan Times*, October 10, 2020, https://www.hindustantimes.com/mumbai-news/maharashtra-s-tribute-to-father-of-nation-mumbai-nagpur-corridor-to-have-charkha-bridge/story-KymgBdwuEc0I8Xwp3aRURN.html.

[16] For news coverage of protests against the development plans at and around Sevagram Ashram, see "After Letter From Mahatma Gandhi's Kin, Maharashtra Govt To Re-examine Tree Felling Near Sevagram Ashram," *Hindustan Times*, September 4, 2020, https://www.hindustantimes.com/mumbai-news/after-letter-from-gandhi-s-kin-maharashtra-govt-to-re-examine-tree-felling-near-sevagram-ashram/story-pXVlG5w6cYAKcSm6mIXctN.html; "'Trivialises Sanctity': Eminent Citizens Oppose Govt's Rs 1200-Cr Plan For Sabarmati Ashram," *The Wire*, August 5, 2021, https://thewire.in/rights/sabarmati-ashram-world-class-memorial-gandhi-simplicity; and "Gandhi-ji's Minimalist Sevagram To Give Way To A ₹266 Crore Project," *National Herald*, October 1, 2018, https://www.nationalheraldindia.com/opinion/gandhi-jis-minimalist-sevagram-to-give-way-to-a-266-crore-project.

Notes to the Conclusion

[1] M. K. Gandhi, *The Bhagavad Gita According to Gandhi* (Berkeley Hills Books, 2000), 148.

[2] Stanley Nelson, director, *Jonestown: The Life and Death of Peoples Temple* (PBS Home Video, 2006). See also Deborah Layton, *Seductive Poison: A Jonestown Survivor's Story of Life and Death in the Peoples Temple* (Anchor Books, 1999).

[3] Rebecca Moore, "The Controversies About Peoples Temple and Jonestown," in *Controversial New Religions*, eds. James R. Lewis and Jesper A. Petersen (Oxford University Press, 2015), 65.

[4] Anthony Pinn, "Peoples Temple as Black Religion: Re-imagining the Contours of Black Religious Studies," in *Peoples Temple and Black Religion in America*, ed. Rebecca Moore et al., (Indiana University Press, 2004), 1–27.

[5] M. K. Gandhi, *Collected Works of Mahatma Gandhi* (Publications Division, Government of India, 2015 electronic edition in 100 volumes), 81:320.

[6] In the epilogue to his book about Gandhi's diet, Nico Slate similarly cautions against following Gandhi's diet as a "model" to follow given that he had a constantly evolving, remarkably complex relationship with food. See Nico Slate, *Gandhi's Search for the Perfect Diet: Eating with the World in Mind* (University of Washington Press, 2019), 171.

[7] Susannah Crockford, "How Do You Know When You're in a Cult?" *Nova Religio: The Journal of Alternative and Emergent Religions* 22, no. 2 (2018): 94.

[8] For scholarly discussions of Gandhi and charisma, see Lloyd Rudolph and Susanne Rudolph, *Gandhi: The Traditional Roots of Charisma* (University of Chicago Press, 1983); and Michelle C. Bligh and Jill L. Robinson, "Was Gandhi "Charismatic"? Exploring the Rhetorical Leadership of Mahatma Gandhi," *The Leadership Quarterly* 21, no. 5 (2010): 844–855.

[9] Albert West, "In the Early Days with Gandhi," *The Illustrated Weekly of India*, October 3, 1965, 33.

[10] Mirabehn, *The Spirit's Pilgrimage* (Great Ocean Publishers, 1960), 60.

[11] M. K. Gandhi with Anthony Parel, *Hind Swaraj and Other Writings* (Cambridge University Press, 1997), 150.

[12] Millie Graham Polak, *Mr. Gandhi: The Man* (George Allen & Unwin Ltd., 1931), 68–69.

[13] On the "BITE model" of control (behavior, information, thought, and emotional control), see Steven A. Hassan, *The BITE Model of Authoritarian Control: Undue Influence, Thought Reform, Brainwashing, Mind Control, Trafficking and the Law* (Fielding Graduate University, 2020). On high control groups and the "cult mentality," see also Janja Lalich, *Bounded Choice: True Believers and Charismatic Cults* (University of California Press, 2004); and Alexandra Stein, *Terror, Love and Brainwashing: Attachment in Cults and Totalitarian Systems* (Routledge, 2021).

[14] Gandhi, *Collected Works of Mahatma Gandhi*, 4:112.

[15] Gandhi, *Collected Works of Mahatma Gandhi*, 12:523–526.

[16] Gandhi, *Collected Works of Mahatma Gandhi*, 76:403.

[17] M. K. Gandhi, *Autobiography: The Story of My Experiments with Truth* (Beacon Press, 1993), 454.

[18] On violence in Peoples Temple and the final days at Jonestown, see Catherine Wessinger, *How the Millennium Comes Violently: From Jonestown to Heaven's Gate* (Seven Bridges Press, 1999), 30–55; and Rebecca Moore, "'American as Cherry Pie': Peoples Temple and Violence in America," in *Millennialism, Persecution, and Violence: Historical Cases*, ed. Catherine Wessinger (Syracuse University Press, 2000), 121–137.

[19] Merlin Coverley, *Utopia* (Oldcastle Books, 2010), 9–10.

[20] Gandhi, *Collected Works of Mahatma Gandhi*, 81:320.

[21] Anne Beutter and E. Sasu Kwame Sewordor, "A Processual Perspective on Utopia as a Lived Social Project: The Case of a Ghanaian 'Christian Town,'" *Religion* 54, no. 3 (2024): 532.

[22] Of course, the different communities founded by Gandhi and Jim Jones are not unique in this regard; given the paradoxical nature of utopia, such utopian-dystopian dynamics are widespread patterns in utopian religious and social communities, both in South Asia and globally. For some of the scholarship on this subject, see Lewis F. Carter, *Charisma and Control in Rajneeshpuram: The Role of Shared Values in the Creation of a Community* (Cambridge University Press, 1990); Peter Heehs, "Sri Aurobindo and His Ashram, 1910–2010: An Unfinished History," *Nova Religio: The Journal of Alternative and Emergent Religions* 19, no. 1 (2015): 65–86; Lawrence Foster, *Women, Family, and Utopia: Communal Experiments of the Shakers, the Oneida Community, and the Mormons* (Syracuse University Press, 1991); Akash Kapur, *Better to Have Gone: Love, Death, and the Quest for Utopia in Auroville* (Scribner, 2021); Stephen Stein, *Communities of Dissent: A History of Alternative Religions in America* (Oxford University Press, 2003); James D. Tabor and Eugene V. Gallagher, *Why Waco?: Cults and the Battle for Religious Freedom in America* (University of California Press, 1995); and Hugh B. Urban, *Zorba the Buddha: Sex, Spirituality, and Capitalism in the Global Osho Movement* (University of California Press, 2015).

Bibliography

Ackerman, Peter and Jack DuVall. *A Force More Powerful: A Century of Nonviolent Conflict*. St. Martin's Press, 2000.

"After Letter from Mahatma Gandhi's Kin, Maharashtra Govt to Re-examine Tree Felling Near Sevagram Ashram." *Hindustan Times*, September 4, 2020, https://www.hindustantimes.com/mumbai-news/after-letter-from-gandhi-s-kin-maharashtra-govt-to-re-examine-tree-felling-near-sevagram-ashram/story-pXVlG5w6cYAKcSm6mIXctN.html.

Alter, Joseph. *Gandhi's Body: Sex, Diet, and the Politics of Nationalism*. University of Pennsylvania Press, 2000.

Ambedkar, B. R. *Dr Babasaheb Ambedkar: Writings and Speeches*. Education Department, Government of Maharashtra, 1979–2003.

Ambedkar, B. R. and Arundhati Roy. *Annihilation of Caste*. Verso, 2016.

Anklesaria, Sarosh. "Architectures of Dissent: Building Memorials to Gandhi through Everyday Praxis." *The Plan Journal* 9, no. 2 (2024): 517–539.

Baird, Robert D. "The Convergence of Distinct Worlds: Nehru and Gandhi." In *Indian Critiques of Gandhi*, ed. Harold Coward. State University of New York Press, 2003.

Bakshi, Rajni. *Bapu Kuti: Journeys in Rediscovery of Gandhi*. Penguin Books, 1998.

Bellotti, Karina Kosicki. "Decolonizing Utopias." *Religion* 54, no. 3 (2024): 580–586.

Bergunder, Michael. "Experiments with Theosophical Truth: Gandhi, Esotericism, and Global Religious History." *Journal of the American Academy of Religion* 82, no. 2 (2014): 398–426.

Berning, Gillian, ed. *Gandhi Letters: From Upper House to Lower House, 1906–1914*. Local History Museum, 1994.

Beutter, Anne and E. Sasu Kwame Sewordor. "A Processual Perspective on Utopia as a Lived Social Project: The Case of a Ghanaian 'Christian Town.'" *Religion* 54, no. 3 (2024): 514–537.

Bhana, Surendra and James D. Hunt, eds. *Gandhi's Editor: The Letters of M. H. Nazar*. Promilla Publications, 1989.

Bhattacharyya, Swasti. "Khadi: A Narrative of Lived Theology." *Religions* 13, no. 5 (2022): https://doi.org/10.3390/rel13050454.

Bhave, Vinoba with Marjorie Sykes. *Moved by Love: The Memoirs of Vinoba Bhave, Translated by Marjorie Sykes from a Hindi Text Prepared by Kalindi*. Green Books, 1994.

Bialostocka, Olga. "Using the Past to Build the Future: A Critical Review of the Liberation Heritage Route (LHR) Project of South Africa." *Africa Insight* 44, no. 2 (2014): 94–107.

Bligh, Michelle C. and Jill L. Robinson. "Was Gandhi 'Charismatic'? Exploring the Rhetorical Leadership of Mahatma Gandhi," *The Leadership Quarterly* 21, no. 5 (2010): 844–855.

Bose, Nirmal Kumar. *My Days with Gandhi*. Orient BlackSwan, 1974.

Brown, D. Mackenzie. "Vinoba Bhave." In *The Nationalist Movement: Indian Political Thought from Ranade to Bhave*. University of California Press, 1961.

Brown, Rebecca M. *Gandhi's Spinning Wheel and the Making of India*. Routledge, 2010.

Carter, Lewis F. *Charisma and Control in Rajneeshpuram: The Role of Shared Values in the Creation of a Community*. Cambridge University Press, 1990.

Cipriani, Christine. "Architect of Independence." *Dwell*, November 2008, 114–120.

Claeys, Gregory and Lyman Tower Sargent, eds. *The Utopia Reader*. New York University Press, 1999.

Correa, Charles. *A Place in the Shade: The New Landscape & Other Essays*. Hatje Cantz Verlag, 2012.

Coverley, Merlin. *Utopia*. Oldcastle Books, 2010.

Coward, Harold, ed. *Indian Critiques of Gandhi*. State University of New York Press, 2003.

Crockford, Susannah. "How Do You Know When You're in a Cult?" *Nova Religio: The Journal of Alternative and Emergent Religions* 22, no. 2 (2018): 93–114.

Dalal, Chandulal Bhagubhai with Tridip Suhrud. *Harilal Gandhi: A Life*. Orient Longman Pvt. Ltd., 2007.

Dalton, Dennis. *Mahatma Gandhi: Nonviolent Power in Action*. Columbia University Press, 2012.

Davis, Richard H. *The Bhagavad Gita: A Biography*. Princeton University Press, 2015.

Dekay, Mark. "Teachings from Bapu Kuti." In *Migrants and Stowaways: An Anthology of Journeys*, eds. Emily Dziuban with Kristin Robertson. Knoxville Writers' Guild, 2004.

Desai, Ashwin and Goolam H. Vahed. *The South African Gandhi: Stretcher-Bearer of Empire*. Stanford University Press, 2015.

Doke, Joseph J. *M. K. Gandhi: Indian Patriot in South Africa*. Indian Chronicle, 1909.

Fischer, Louis. *A Week with Gandhi*. Duell, Sloan and Pearce, 1942.

Fischer, Louis, ed. *The Essential Gandhi: An Anthology of His Writings on His Life, Work, and Ideas*. Random House, 2002.

Foster, Lawrence. *Women, Family, and Utopia: Communal Experiments of the Shakers, the Oneida Community, and the Mormons*. Syracuse University Press, 1991.

Francis, Richard. *Transcendental Utopias: Individual and Community at Brook Farm, Fruitlands, and Walden*. Cornell University Press, 1997.

"Functionary's Exit Brings to Fore Power Play at Gandhi Ashram." *Mumbai Mirror*, June 5, 2020, https://mumbaimirror.indiatimes.com/mumbai/civic/functionarys-exit-brings-to-fore-power-play-at-gandhi-ashram/articleshow/76204279.cms.

Gandhi Ashram at Sabarmati. "The Museum." https://www.gandhiashramsabarmati.org/en/the-museum-falang.html.

Gandhi, M. K. *A Guide to Health*. S. Ganesan, 1921.

Gandhi, M. K. *Ashram Observances in Action*. Navajivan Publishing House, 1955.

Gandhi, M. K. *Ruskin: Unto This Last: A Paraphrase*. Navajivan Publishing House, 1956.

Gandhi, M. K. *Autobiography: The Story of My Experiments with Truth*. Beacon Press, 1993.

Gandhi, M. K. *The Bhagavad Gita According to Gandhi*. Berkeley Hills Books, 2000.

Gandhi, M. K. *Satyagraha in South Africa*. Rev ed. Navajivan Publishing House, 2008.

Gandhi, M. K. *Collected Works of Mahatma Gandhi*, 100 volumes. Publications Division, Government of India, electronic edition, 2015.

Gandhi, M. K. with Anthony Parel. *Hind Swaraj and Other Writings*. Cambridge University Press, 1997.

Gandhi, Manu. *The Diary of Manu Gandhi: 1943–1944*. Ed. Tridip Suhrud. Oxford University Press, 2020.

Gandhi, Prabhudas. *My Childhood with Gandhiji*. Navajivan Publishing House, 1957.

"Gandhi-ji's Minimalist Sevagram to Give Way to a ₹266 Crore Project." *National Herald*, October 1, 2018: https://www.nationalheraldindia.com/opinion/gandhi-jis-minimalist-sevagram-to-give-way-to-a-266-crore-project.

Golden Jubilee, 1904–1954: Phoenix Settlement. International Printing Press, 1954.

Gregg, Richard B. and Maganlal K. Gandhi. *The Takli Teacher*. All India Spinners' Association, 1931.

Guha, Ramachandra. "What Gandhi Was Not: Vinoba Bhave." In *An Anthropologist Among the Marxists and Other Essays*. Permanent Black, 2001.

Guha, Ramachandra. *Gandhi Before India*. Alfred A. Knopf, 2013.

Guha, Ramachandra. *Gandhi: The Years That Changed the World, 1914–1948*. Vintage Books, 2018.

Guha, Ramachandra. *Rebels Against the Raj: Western Fighters for India's Freedom*. Alfred A. Knopf, 2022.

"Gujarat HC Rejects PIL By Gandhi's Great Grandson Against Sabarmati Ashram Project." *The Wire*, September 9, 2022, https://thewire.in/law/gujarat-high-court-tushar-gandhi-sabarmati-ashram.

Haberman, David. *Journey through the Twelve Forests: An Encounter with Krishna*. Oxford University Press, 1994.

Hansen, Thomas Blom. *Melancholia of Freedom: Social Life in an Indian Township in South Africa*. Princeton University Press, 2012.

Hardiman, David. *Noncooperation in India: Nonviolent Strategy and Protest, 1920–22*. Oxford University Press, 2021.

Hartman, Saidiya. "Venus in Two Acts." *Small Axe: A Caribbean Journal of Criticism* 26, no. 3 (2008): 1–14.

Hasan, Mushirul. *Roads to Freedom: Prisoners in Colonial India*. Oxford University Press, 2016.

Hassan, Steven A. *The BITE Model of Authoritarian Control: Undue Influence, Thought Reform, Brainwashing, Mind Control, Trafficking and the Law*. Fielding Graduate University, 2020.

Heehs, Peter. "Sri Aurobindo and His Ashram, 1910–2010: An Unfinished History." *Nova Religio: The Journal of Alternative and Emergent Religions* 19, no. 1 (2015): 65–86.

Hofmeyr, Isabel. *Gandhi's Printing Press: Experiments in Slow Reading*. Harvard University Press, 2013.

Howard, Veena R. *Gandhi's Ascetic Activism: Renunciation and Social Action*. State University of New York Press, 2013.

Hughes, Heather. "Violence in Inanda, August 1985." *Journal of Southern African Studies* 13, no. 3 (1987): 331–354.

Hughes, Heather. "'The Coolies Will Elbow Us Out of the Country': African Reactions to Indian Immigration in the Colony of Natal, South Africa." *Labour History Review* 72, no. 2 (2007): 155–168.

Hughes, Heather. *First President: A Life of John L. Dube, Founding President of the ANC*. Jacana Media, 2011.

Hunt, James D. "Experiments in Forming a Community of Service: The Evolution of Gandhi's First Ashrams, Phoenix and Tolstoy Farm." In *World Problems and Human Responsibility: Gandhian Perspectives*, ed. K. L. Seshagiri Rao and Henry O. Thompson. Unification Theological Seminary, 1988.

Hunt, James D. and Surendra Bhana. "Spiritual Rope-Walkers: Gandhi, Kallenbach, and the Tolstoy Farm, 1910–13." *South African Historical Journal* 58 (2007): 174–202.

Illich, Ivan. *In the Mirror of the Past: Lectures and Addresses, 1978–1990*. Marion Boyars, 1991.

"Indian Firms to Help Revive Tolstoy Farm." *Business Standard*, May 13, 2017, http://www.business-standard.com/article/international/indian-firms-to-help-revive-tolstoy-farm-mahatma-gandhi-s-sa-ashram-117051300195_1.html.

"Indian-Origin Activist Lauded for Efforts in Restoration of Gandhi's Erstwhile Commune in South Africa." *The Week*, January 31, 2025, https://www.theweek.in/wire-updates/international/2025/01/31/fes25-safrica-indian-activist.html.

Iyengar, Sudarshan. "Gandhiji in Ahmedabad." *Journal of Social and Economic Development* 23, no. Suppl 1 (2021): 4–24.

Jasanoff, Maya. "What Modi's Plan for Gandhi's Old Home Reveals About India's Future." *The New Yorker*, June 19, 2024, https://www.newyorker.com/news/dispatch/what-modis-plan-for-gandhis-old-home-reveals-about-indias-future.

"Johannesburg Farm Started by Mahatma Gandhi Unveils his Life-Size Statue." *India Today*, October 10, 2023, https://www.indiatoday.in/world/story/johannesburg-farm-started-by-mahatma-gandhi-unveils-his-life-size-statue-2446959-2023-10-10.

Jordens, J. T. F. "Gandhi and the *Bhagavadgita*." In *Modern Indian Interpreters of the Bhagavadgita*, ed. by Robert N. Minor, 88–109. State University of New York Press, 1986.

Jordens, J. T. F. *Gandhi's Religion: A Homespun Shawl*. St. Martin's Press, 1998.

Juergensmeyer, Mark. *Gandhi's Way: A Handbook of Conflict Resolution*. University of California Press, 2005.

Kahan, Benjamin. *Celibacies: American Modernism and Sexual Life*. Duke University Press, 2013.

Kaley, Vinoo. *Venu Bharati: A Comprehensive Volume on Bamboo*. Aroop Nirman, 1998.

Kapur, Akash. *Better to Have Gone: Love, Death, and the Quest for Utopia in Auroville*. Scribner, 2021.

Kaur, Amrit. *Rajkumari Amrit Kaur: Eminent Parliamentarians Monograph Series*. Lok Sabha Secretariat, 1993.

Kirsch, Anja and Andrea Rota. "Religion and Utopia: A Critical Overview of the Field." *Religion* 54, no. 3 (2024): 396–411.

Klenk, Rebecca M. "Gandhi's Other Daughter: Sarala Devi and Lakshmi Ashram." *Himalaya* 34, no. 1 (2014): 94–104.

Lal, Vinay. "Nakedness, Nonviolence, and Brahmacharya: Gandhi's Experiments in Celibate Sexuality." *Journal of the History of Sexuality* 9, no. 1–2 (2000): 105–136.

Lal, Vinay. "Was Mohandas Gandhi a Racist?" *Lal Salaam* blog, June 25, 2020, https://vinaylal.wordpress.com/2020/06/25/was-mohandas-gandhi-a-racist/.

Lalich, Janja. *Bounded Choice: True Believers and Charismatic Cults*. University of California Press, 2004.

Layton, Deborah. *Seductive Poison: A Jonestown Survivor's Story of Life and Death in the Peoples Temple*. Anchor Books, 1999.

Lev, Shimon. *Soulmates: The Story of Mahatma Gandhi and Hermann Kallenbach*. Orient BlackSwan Pvt. Ltd., 2012.

Lleyveld, Joseph. *Great Soul: Mahatma Gandhi and His Struggle with India*. Alfred A. Knopf, 2011.

Lucia, Amanda J. *White Utopias: The Religious Exoticism of Transformational Festivals*. University of California Press, 2020.

Maddipati, Venugopal. "Building Impressions: Gandhi and Mira Behn's Hut: 1935–1936." *NMML Occasional Papers*, Nehru Memorial Museum and Library (2014): 5–9.

Maddipati, Venugopal. *Gandhi and Architecture: A Time for Low-Cost Housing*. Routledge, 2021.

"Maharashtra's Tribute To 'Father of Nation': Mumbai-Nagpur Corridor to Have 'Charkha' Bridge." *Hindustan Times*, Oct. 10, 2020, https://www.hindustantimes.com/mumbai-news/maharashtra-s-tribute-to-father-of-nation-mumbai-nagpur-corridor-to-have-charkha-bridge/story-KymgBdwuEc0I8Xwp3aRURN.html.

Mahatma Gandhi Sabarmati Ashram Memorial Trust. "Gandhi Ashram Restoration and Expansion" plan and promotional video. https://mahatmagandhimemorial.org.

Mallik, Bidisha. *Legends in Gandhian Social Activism: Mira Behn and Sarala Behn: Addressing Environmental Issues by Dissolving Gender and Colonial Barriers*. Springer, 2022.

"Man Who Restored Gandhi's Tolstoy Farm Seeks World Heritage Status for It." *Indian Express*, January 23, 2023, https://indianexpress.com/article/cities/mumbai/mohan-hira-tolstoy-farm-mahatma-gandhi-unesco-world-heritage-8394893/.

Marschall, Sabine. "Sustainable Heritage Tourism: The Inanda Heritage Route and the 2010 FIFA World Cup." *Journal of Sustainable Tourism* 20, no. 5 (2012): 721–736.

Marschall, Sabine. "Woza eNanda: Perceptions of and Attitudes Towards Heritage and Tourism in a South African Township." *Transformation: Critical Perspectives on South Africa* 83, no. 1 (2013): 32–55.

McLain, Karline. "Gandhi's Ashrams: Residential Experiments for Universal Welfare in South Africa and India." *Journal of Utopian Studies* 30, no. 3 (2019): 462–485.

McLain, Karline. "Living the *Bhagavad Gita* at Gandhi's Ashrams." *Religions* 10, no. 11 (2019), https://www.mdpi.com/2077-1444/10/11/619/htm.

McLain, Karline. "Food and Anticolonialism at Gandhi's Intentional Communities in South Africa and India." In *The Provisions of War: Expanding the Boundaries of Food and Conflict, 1840–1990*, ed. Justin Nordstrom. University of Arkansas Press, 2021.

Menon, Nikhil. "Gandhi's Spinning Wheel: The Charkha and Its Regenerative Effects." *Journal of the History of Ideas* 81, no. 4 (2020): 643–662.

Mesthrie, Uma Dhupelia. *Gandhi's Prisoner? The Life of Gandhi's Son Manilal*. Permanent Black, 2004.

Mesthrie, Uma Dhupelia. "The Letters of Sushila Gandhi: From Press Worker to Managing Trustee of Phoenix Settlement in South Africa, 1927 to 1977." *Indian Journal of Gender Studies* 30, no. 1 (2023): 11–32.

Mesthrie, Uma Dhupelia. *Gandhi's African Legacy: Phoenix Settlement 1904 to 2024, A History through Letters*. UWC Press, 2024.

Mesthrie, Uma Shashikant. "Sushila Gandhi (1907–1988), Guardian of Gandhian Traditions in South Africa: Obituary." *Natalia* 6, no. 4 (1989): 55–63.

Mesthrie, Uma Shashikant. "From Advocacy to Mobilization: *Indian Opinion*, 1903–1914." In *South Africa's Alternative Press: Voices of Protest and Resistance, 1880s–1960s*, ed. Les Switzer. Cambridge University Press, 1997.

Mirabehn. *The Spirit's Pilgrimage*. Great Ocean Publishers, 1960.

Moore, Rebecca. "The Controversies About Peoples Temple and Jonestown." In *Controversial New Religions*, eds. James R. Lewis and Jesper A. Petersen. Oxford University Press, 2015.

Moore, Rebecca. "'American as Cherry Pie': Peoples Temple and Violence in America." In *Millennialism, Persecution, and Violence: Historical Cases*, ed. Catherine Wessinger. Syracuse University Press, 2000.

Muzumdar, Haridas T. *Gandhi versus the Empire*. Universal Publishing Company, 1932.

Nanda, B. R. *In Gandhi's Footsteps: The Life and Times of Jamnalal Bajaj*. Oxford University Press, 2002.

Nandy, Ashis. *At the Edge of Psychology: Essays in Politics and Culture*. Oxford University Press, 1980.

Nayar, Pyarelal and Sushila Nayar. *In Gandhiji's Mirror*. Oxford University Press, 2004.

Nazar, M. H. *Gandhi's Editor: The Letters of M. H. Nazar, 1902–1903*. Ed. Surendra Bhana and James D. Hunt. Promilla & Co., 1989.

Nehru, Jawaharlal. *A Bunch of Old Letters: Written Mostly to Jawaharlal Nehru and Some Written by Him*. Oxford University Press, 1960.

Nehru, Jawaharlal. *The Discovery of India*. Doubleday, Anchor Edition, 1960.

Nelson, Stanley, director. *Jonestown: The Life and Death of Peoples Temple*. PBS Home Video, 2006.

"Newly Formed Council to Help Manage Gandhiji's Sevagram Ashram." *The Economic Times*, September 6, 2011, https://economictimes.indiatimes.com/news/politics-and-nation/newly-formed-council-to-help-manage-gandhijis-sevagram-ashram/articleshow/9881822.cms.

Olivelle, Patrick. "The Early History of Renunciation." In *Hindu Practice*. Ed. Gavin Flood. Oxford University Press, 2020.

Parr, Rosalind. "Self-Sacrifice, Suffrage and Socialism: Gandhi and the Mobilisation of Women, 1930–31." *South Asia: Journal of South Asian Studies* 46, no. 4 (2023): 834–850.

Patel, Anil Kumar. "Spatial Inequality and Untouchability: Ambedkar's Gaze on Caste and Space in Hindu Villages." *Journal of Social Inclusion Studies* 7, no. 2 (2021): 186–198.

Patil, Pallavi Varma and Sujit Sinha. "Nai Talim Today: Gandhi's Critique of Industrialism and an Education for Swaraj." *Journal of Human Values* 28, no. 1 (2022): 44–56.

Pinn, Anthony B. "Peoples Temple as Black Religion: Re-imagining the Contours of Black Religious Studies." In *Peoples Temple and Black Religion in America*, ed. Rebecca Moore et al. Indiana University Press, 2004.

"PM Modi Lays Foundation For Redevelopment of Sabarmati Ashram." *The Hindu*, March 12, 2024, https://www.thehindu.com/news/national/other-states/pm-modi-inaugurates-mahatma-gandhi-sabarmati-ashram-redevelopment-project-worth-1200-crore/article67941870.ece.

Polak, Henry S. L. "My Ten Years' Service." In *Golden Jubilee, 1904–1954: Phoenix Settlement*. International Printing Press, 1954.

Polak, Henry S. L. "Some South African Reminiscences." In *Incidents of Gandhiji's Life*. Ed. Chandrashanker Shukla. M. K. Vora & Co. Publishers Ltd., 1949.

Polak, Millie Graham. *Mr. Gandhi: The Man*. George Allen & Unwin Ltd., 1931.

Reid, Walter. *Keeping the Jewel in the Crown: The British Betrayal of India*. Birlinn Limited, 2016.

Reynolds, Reginald. *To Live in Mankind: A Quest for Gandhi*. A. Deutsch, 1951.

Reynolds, Reginald. *My Life and Crimes*. Jarrolds, 1956.

Roberts, Adam and Timothy Garton Ash. *Civil Resistance and Power Politics: The Experience of Non-Violent Action from Gandhi to the Present*. Oxford University Press, 2011.

Rook-Koepsel, Emily. "Constructing Women's Citizenship: The Local, National, and Global Civics Lessons of Rajkumari Amrit Kaur." *Journal of Women's History* 27, no. 3 (2015): 154–175.

Roy, Arundhati. "The Doctor and the Saint." *Caravan Magazine*, February 28, 2014, https://caravanmagazine.in/essay/doctor-and-saint.

Rudolph, Lloyd and Susanne Rudolph. *Gandhi: The Traditional Roots of Charisma*. University of Chicago Press, 1983.

Sanford, A. Whitney. "Gandhi's Agrarian Legacy: Practicing Food, Justice, and Sustainability in India." In *Religion and Sustainable Agriculture: World Spiritual Traditions and Food Ethics*, ed. Norman Wirzba, Pramod Parajuli, and Todd LeVasseur. University Press of Kentucky, 2016.

Sarid, Isa and Christian Bartolf. *Hermann Kallenbach: Mahatma Gandhi's Friend in South Africa*. Gandhi Informations Zentrum, 1997.

Scalmer, Sean. *Gandhi in the West: The Mahatma and the Rise of Radical Protest*. Cambridge University Press, 2011.

Schaer, Roland, Gregory Claeys, and Lyman Tower Sargent, eds. *Utopia: The Search for the Ideal Society in the Western World*. Oxford University Press, 2000.

The Servants of India Society (pamphlet). A. B. Press, 1915.

Sevagram Ashram Pratishthan. "Library and Research Center." https://sevagramashram.org.in/index.php/library-and-research-centre-2.

Skaria, Ajay. "Gandhi's Politics: Liberalism and the Question of the Ashram." *South Atlantic Quarterly* 101 (2002): 955–986.

Skaria, Ajay. *Unconditional Equality: Gandhi's Religion of Resistance*. University of Minnesota Press, 2016.

Skaria, Ajay. "Thinking with Gandhi on Racism and Violence: A Letter to a Friend." *ABC*, July 6, 2020, https://www.abc.net.au/religion/thinking-with-gandhi-on-racism-and-violence/12424422.

Slate, Nico. *Gandhi's Search for the Perfect Diet: Eating with the World in Mind*. University of Washington Press, 2019.

Srivatsan, R. "Concept of 'Seva' and the 'Sevak' in the Freedom Movement." *Economic and Political Weekly* 41, no. 5 (2006): 427–438.

Stein, Alexandra. *Terror, Love and Brainwashing: Attachment in Cults and Totalitarian Systems*. Routledge, 2021.

Stein, Stephen. *Communities of Dissent: A History of Alternative Religions in America*. Oxford University Press, 2003.

Suhrud, Tridip. "The Woman Who Cradled Gandhi." *Seminar* 746 (2021), https://www.india-seminar.com/2021/746/8%20The%20woman%20who%20cradled%20Gandhi-Tridip%20Suhrud.htm.

Suhrud, Tridip and Thomas Weber, eds. *Beloved Bapu: The Gandhi-Mirabehn Correspondence*. Orient Blackswan, 2014.

Tabor, James D. and Eugene V. Gallagher. *Why Waco?: Cults and the Battle for Religious Freedom in America*. University of California Press, 1995.

Tarlo, Emma. *Clothing Matters: Dress and Identity in India*. University of Chicago Press, 1996.

Thomson, Mark. *Gandhi and His Ashrams*. Popular Prakashan, 1993.

Trivedi, Lisa. *Clothing Gandhi's Nation: Homespun and Modern India*. Indiana University Press, 2007.

"'Trivialises Sanctity': Eminent Citizens Oppose Govt's Rs 1200-Cr Plan for Sabarmati Ashram." *The Wire*, August 5, 2021, https://thewire.in/rights/sabarmati-ashram-world-class-memorial-gandhi-simplicity.

Turner, Victor. "The Center Out There: Pilgrim's Goal." *History of Religions* 12, no. 3 (1973): 191–230.

Urban, Hugh B. *Zorba the Buddha: Sex, Spirituality, and Capitalism in the Global Osho Movement*. University of California Press, 2015.

Vahed, Goolam. "The Protector, Plantocracy, and Indentured Labour in Natal, 1860–1911." *Pacific Historical Review* 87, no. 1 (2018): 101–127.

Villa-Vicencio, Charles. *The Spirit of Freedom: South African Leaders on Religion and Politics*. University of California Press, 1996.

Waldman, Amy. "Phoenix Site in South Africa Still Sits in Ashes." *Christian Science Monitor*, April 6, 1994, https://www.csmonitor.com/1994/0406/06171.html.

Weber, Thomas. *On the Salt March: The Historiography of Gandhi's March to Dandi*. HarperCollins India, 1997.

Weber, Thomas. *Gandhi as Disciple and Mentor*. Cambridge University Press, 2004.

Wessinger, Catherine. *How the Millennium Comes Violently: From Jonestown to Heaven's Gate*. Seven Bridges Press, 1999.

West, Albert. "In the Early Days with Gandhi." *The Illustrated Weekly of India*, October 3, 1965, 30–33.

Wolpert, Stanley. *Shameful Flight: The Last Years of the British Empire in India*. Oxford University Press, 2009.

"World's Biggest Charkha to Be Unveiled." *Deccan Herald*, October 1, 2018, https://www.deccanherald.com/india/worlds-biggest-charkha-be-695579.html.

Index

Note: page numbers in *italics* refer to figures; those followed by "n" indicate notes.

Discussion Questions

1. Gandhi gave a lot of thought to the concept of "universal well-being" (*sarvodaya*) during his lifetime. How would you personally define "universal well-being"? In what ways does your definition overlap with Gandhi's? In what ways does your definition depart from Gandhi's?
2. At his intentional communities, Gandhi and his coresidents engaged in a wide variety of experiments in their everyday lives to try to facilitate universal well-being. For instance, to promote equality and self-sufficiency, the residents tried to equally share the labor (no matter their race, religion, caste, or gender), growing and cooking their own food, building their own houses, making their own clothing, and running their own schools and microbusinesses. Which residential experiments with daily life do you find most compelling, and why? Which do you find least compelling, and why?
3. Gandhi tried to create more inclusive communities in his historical time and context and had both successes and failures in this regard. In our own historical time and context, what steps can we take to create communities that emphasize greater belonging as well as inclusion?
4. If you lived during Gandhi's time, do you think you would have been interested in joining any of his intentional communities in South Africa or India? If so, which one, and why? If none, why not?
5. Think about the community you live in. What would your community look like if it was intentionally designed for the purpose of enhancing universal well-being? How might the physical space need to change? What daily practices might need to change? What attitudes might need to change?
6. Think about your everyday lifestyle. What is the larger impact (socially, politically, environmentally, etc.) of your individual micro-level practices on the well-being of the larger macro-level community (this community could be defined as your family, school, town, nation, etc.)? Which of your practices help to enhance the greater well-being? Which of your practices might endanger the greater well-being?

7. Gandhi believed that cultivating an attitude of self-discipline was needed for universal well-being. What do you think it means to flourish as an individual while simultaneously living well in community with one another? Do you agree that there must be some individual limits placed in order to foster the enhancement of life for the greater good? If so, what sort of limits do you advocate for, and why? If not, why not?
8. Gandhi increasingly emphasized the virtues of self-sacrifice and voluntary suffering at his intentional communities, and he believed that some causes are worth dying for. Do you think there are causes worth dying for? If so, which cause(s)? Do you think Gandhi's coresidents who were willing to die were willing to do so for a cause, for the community, or for Gandhi's charisma?
9. How do you personally define "utopia"? What core values undergird your definition of utopia? What does this mean for how you might define "dystopia"?
10. How can we create communities that are flexible enough to allow for multiple and even contrasting definitions of universal well-being and utopia?

GPSR Authorized Representative: Easy Access System Europe, Mustamäe tee 50, 10621 Tallinn, Estonia, gpsr.requests@easproject.com

www.ingramcontent.com/pod-product-compliance
Ingram Content Group UK Ltd.
Pitfield, Milton Keynes, MK11 3LW, UK
UKHW012123110926
475327UK00003B/19
* 9 7 8 1 9 5 2 6 3 6 5 5 4 *